Λ

CW00482636

By the same author

I am the Sea
A Collar for Cerberus

NAFPLIO

Biography of a Greek town

Matt Stanley

Aetos Press

Copyright © Matt Stanley 2022

First published 2022 by Aetos Press
36 Moor Lane, Huddersfield, HD8 0QS, UK

All rights reserved. No part of this publication may be
reproduced, stored in a retrieval system or transmitted in any
form or by any means, electronic, mechanical, photocopying,
recording or otherwise, without the prior permission, in
writing, of the publisher.

ISBN: 978-0-9575846-3-1

A CIP catalogue record for this book is available from the
British Library

Aetos Press has no responsibility for the persistence or
accuracy of URLs for third-party internet websites referenced
in this book, and does not guarantee that any content on these
websites is, or will remain, accurate or appropriate.

www.aetospress.co.uk

For my mother, who saw Nafplio before me

There can seem nowhere in Greece that retains so much of its architecture and so little of its history. There is an elegance about even its fortifications that belies their past, that touch of unreality which is Venice's supreme gift to her former possessions.
David Crane, Lord Byron's Jackal

I had everything a man could desire, and I knew it. I knew too that I might never have it again.
Henry Miller, The Colossus of Maroussi

CONTENTS

ACKNOWLEDGEMENTS

This book wouldn't have been possible without the research of Greek historians in Nafplio and the Argolid. I'm indebted to the many articles I read on www.argolikivivliothiki.gr and www.argolikeseidhseis.gr, as well as the work of local bloggers. I'd also like to thank Allan Brooks for his gracious permission to use maps from his book, and the Städtische Galerie im Lenbachhaus, Munich, for permission to use the cover image by Carl Heideck.

If you believe any of the details in the book to be incorrect, or if you have additional interesting stories about Nafplio, please contact me via social media and I will amend future editions.

ABOUT THE AUTHOR

Matt Stanley was born in Sheffield, England, in 1971. He has lived in Greece, China, Poland and Spain, and has written twenty books under different pseudonyms.

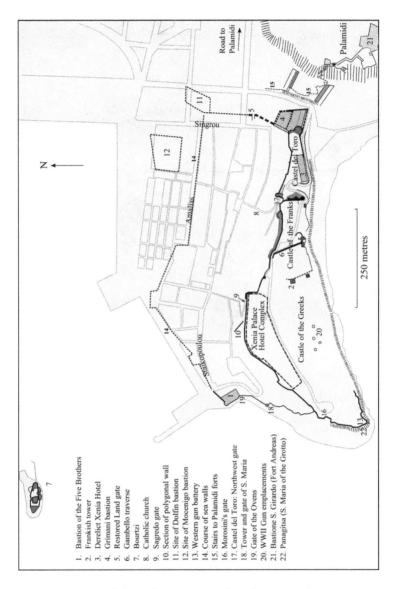

1. Bastion of the Five Brothers
2. Frankish tower
3. Derelict Xenia Hotel
4. Grimani bastion
5. Restored Land gate
6. Gambello traverse
7. Bourtzi
8. Catholic church
9. Sagredo gate
10. Section of polygonal wall
11. Site of Dolfin bastion
12. Site of Mocenigo bastion
13. Western gun battery
14. Course of sea walls
15. Stairs to Palamidi forts
16. Morosini's gate
17. Castel del Toro: Northwest gate
18. Tower and gate of S. Maria
19. Gate of the Ovens
20. WWII Gun emplacements
21. Bastione S. Girardo (Fort Andreas)
22. Panagitsa (S. Maria of the Grotto)

Modern Nafplio: The surviving fortifications showing the line of the demolished sea walls and land front.

ix

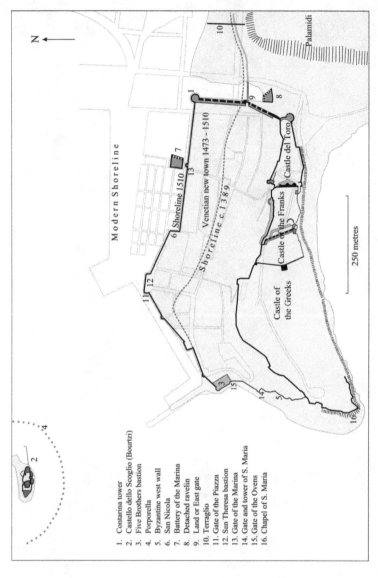

1. Contarina tower
2. Castello dello Scoglio (Bourtzi)
3. Five Brothers bastion
4. Porporella
5. Byzantine west wall
6. San Nicola
7. Battery of the Marina
8. Detached ravelin
9. Land or East gate
10. Terraglio
11. Gate of the Piazza
12. San Theresa bastion
13. Gate of the Marina
14. Gate and tower of S. Maria
15. Gate of the Ovens
16. Chapel of S. Maria

Nafplio c. 1540 superimposed on the modern street plan.

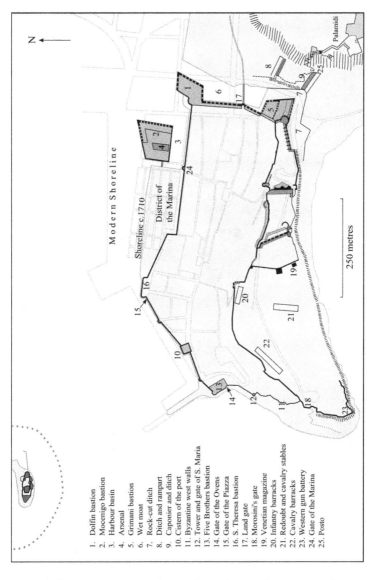

1. Dolfin bastion
2. Mocenigo bastion
3. Harbour basin
4. Arsenal
5. Grimani bastion
6. Wet moat
7. Rock-cut ditch
8. Ditch and rampart
9. Caponier and ditch
10. Cistern of the port
11. Byzantine west walls
12. Tower and gate of S. Maria
13. Five Brothers bastion
14. Gate of the Ovens
15. Gate of the Piazza
16. S. Theresa bastion
17. Land gate
18. Morosini's gate
19. Venetian magazine
20. Infantry barracks
21. Redoubt and cavalry stables
22. Cavalry barracks
23. Western gun battery
24. Gate of the Marina
25. Posto

Nafplio c. 1714 superimposed on the modern streetplan.

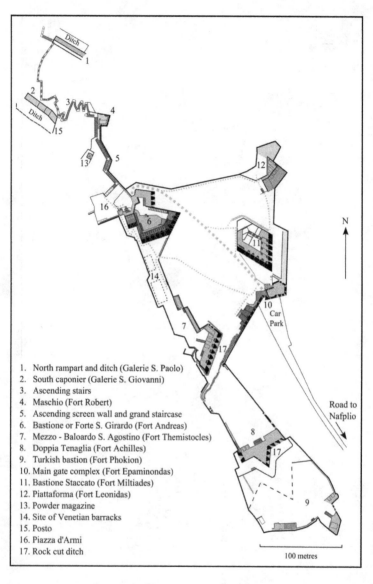

1. North rampart and ditch (Galerie S. Paolo)
2. South caponier (Galerie S. Giovanni)
3. Ascending stairs
4. Maschio (Fort Robert)
5. Ascending screen wall and grand staircase
6. Bastione or Forte S. Girardo (Fort Andreas)
7. Mezzo - Baloardo S. Agostino (Fort Themistocles)
8. Doppia Tenaglia (Fort Achilles)
9. Turkish bastion (Fort Phokion)
10. Main gate complex (Fort Epaminondas)
11. Bastione Staccato (Fort Miltiades)
12. Piattaforma (Fort Leonidas)
13. Powder magazine
14. Site of Venetian barracks
15. Posto
16. Piazza d'Armi
17. Rock cut ditch

Overview of the Palamidi fortification complex.

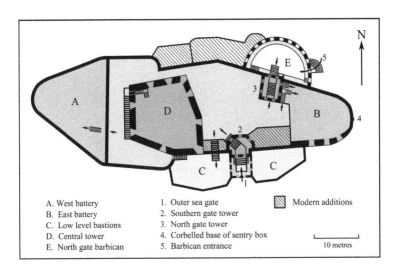

The Castle of the Rock (The Bourtzi).

ARRIVALS

It starts as it always did, unpromisingly, in the dismal, diesel-smogged shed of the KTEL bus terminal on Kifisou Avenue, Athens, where I spent so many hours drinking bad coffee from chipped Formica tables in the half-light of nicotine-yellowed fluorescent tubes or those crazed fibreglass skylights lichened with fifty odd years of accumulated carbon monoxide particulate. Other ticket offices promise arrow-shower trajectories to Ioannina, Grevena, Igoumenitsa or Zakynthos, but there is only one destination for me.

I sit by the Argolida office with my hand on the paper ticket in my pocket and listen to the low thunder of engines, the city's roiling traffic beyond. A stray three-legged dog wanders past. Pigeons swoop among the metal rafters. Airport and Omonia shuttles come and go, channelling travellers like sand out through the station's portals. Then the bus arrives – larger and more modern than the old charabanc with the stiff manual windows that I used to take – and the luggage is loaded below.

Finally, we move.

Out via the traffic-choked overpasses, the paint-spraying garages, crane accessory emporia (webbing supports, pallet lifters, hooks) and industrial plant machinery yards of Sotiraki, through the urban sprawl of Anagennisi and Elaionas towards the Gulf of Elefsina with its shipyards, refineries and gas flares – once the site of ancient religious mystery cults, now the city's western industrial fringe.

The islands of Salamis and Aegina are fundamentally unchanged. The seascape is the same as it was when the Persians were defeated. It's just a short stretch now to the furrowed wedge of the Corinth canal, a green sea ribbon ruled through its bottom. Now the destination is close enough to stir impatience. Now we're leaving mere history behind. We're moving into the realms of myth. Here in the eastern Peloponnese is Nemea, where Herakles killed the monstrous lion. Nemea – an actual place with its disused level crossing. Not too far away is Lerna, where Herakles killed the many-headed Hydra, and Stymphalos, where he killed the man-eating birds. We'll also pass Cyclopean-walled Tiryns, whose King Eurystheus gave the hero his twelve tasks, and fabled Mycenae, whence King Agamemnon set forth for Troy and to which he returned to be slain in the bath by cheating wife Clytemnestra.

Did any of this, or a version of it, ever happen? It doesn't matter. The stories adhere to the places, which do exist and which have existed under the same names for millennia. Myths were born here. These are the gnarled roots. This is the amygdala. Athens has the classical glory of Socrates and the Parthenon, Pericles, Plato and Demosthenes – but the Argolid is a pocket of prehistory: the kind where nobody knows any dates for sure. The dates are irrelevant. The events predate the ideographs of Linear A or B. These are the darkest recesses of culture and memory – ancient even to the ancient Greeks.

I know I'm close when I see the castle cone of Argos, Europe's oldest continuously inhabited city and one of its most wholly uninteresting. The bus used to crawl in single-file traffic through anciently twisted but concretely ugly streets for twenty minutes to the central bus station, but now I see they've built a utilitarian new station on the through road. It's a quick changeover.

And now, across the bowed head of the Argolic gulf, I can see Palamidi: the 200m high rock with its Venetian fortress glowing white in the sun. Just twenty more minutes.

I don't know how many times I've arrived here. The first time was as a sunburned teenager on a family holiday, visiting on a day trip from the nearby resort of Tolo. The second time, in my twenties, was when I arrived to live. There were multiple excursions all over the country – south to Crete, north to Florina, east to Athos, west to Ithaca – but always back along this same route. Twenty-five years since I last saw the place.

Palamidi's rocky bulk grows ever more massive until you can't see the top of it through the bus window. One Greek writer wrote that it was so high, so vertical, that his hat fell off if he tried to look at its peak from its base. We're into the plate-glass frontages, the angular balconies, awnings and show-rooms of the new town, which look like any Greek town from Thessaloniki to Sparta. The handful of backpackers we picked up at Corinth are hovering above their seats and looking around. Are we there yet? Are we passing it?

Not yet. We're very close. So close. I'm virtually off the seat myself with anticipation as the bus slows for what we used to call Death Junction and the locals *endekati* – the chaotic node where five roads meet. There used to be dust-filmed traffic lights that hadn't been switched on again since the confusion they'd first provoked. There was no indication of who had priority. Near-collisions and angry horns were a daily cac-ophony. Now I see there's a roundabout (installed in 2014) and civilised circulation.

This is the modern town's gate: the route out to Aria and Tolo, to Epidauros and the villages, to Athens and Argos. From here, we turn down Sidiras Merarchias and the memories start to flood. The park where I walked; the branch of the National Bank where I waited to deposit earnings; the gyro joints; the post office on the corner from where I sent handwritten letters; the Goody's burger restaurant that caused so much cultural hand wringing when it opened . . .

We turn left onto Andrea Syngrou and I can see other buses parked outside the tiny KTEL office wedged between cafes, pop-up shops and souvenir emporia. I'm off my seat. I'm ready.

Down the steps into engine-hot air.

I realise I'm in an ecstatic state. I'm again in a place that's existed in my mind, in my memories, for much longer than I physically lived here. It's a super-real sensation – a lucid dream state. I've returned somehow to myself aged twenty-five, standing at this same bus stop as if a third of my life hasn't passed in the interim.

While others dither over directions, retrieve backpacks and take taxis, I stride almost automatically, intuitively, to the corner and turn right down Plapouta street: my old street. A quarter century has passed and yet I feel I could close my eyes and feel it around me. The big Venetian building on the corner, the marble-paved road, the place that used to be the butcher's shop, St George's church, the hardware shop (now empty) where the assistant once muttered that I was a *malakas* because I was impertinent enough to handle something with the genuine intention of buying it. All but one of the shops along Plapouta has changed ownership.

Here's my old iron-railed, first floor balcony amid a cumulus of cerise bougainvillea and opposite it the still-ruined building. Someone else is living there now. A pair of shoes' toes peep over the edge. A child's coloured toy lies on its side. Strangers in my house.

I don't stop. I've been imagining this for a long time. I turn right at the end, past the still-ruined Agipgas building, and left at the Allotinó café where I used to drink. Now we're on the so called 'big road' of the old town, the bougainvillea bedecked and pedestrianised Vasileos Konstantinou. I move as in a dream, feet not consciously touching the ground, absently noting what hasn't changed (the ice-cream place, the photo shop) and drawn magnetically towards the polished marble of Syntagma Square: ground zero, the old town's centre for half a millennium. No time to stop.

I'm rising from impossible depths, rising towards the light and air and life of the surface. I can't stop. Twenty-five years of submersion can't keep me down and I can feel the blue-sky horizon beyond, the sea's shimmering mercury-mirror transparency. All that matters now is that first breath.

I cut across the square and pass under the plane tree – memories swirling now like starling murmurations – past the church, past the gelateria, and I cut across the corner of Napoli Di Romania café as I always did. Now I'm on the *paralia*, the sea immediately to my right, and the tiny Bourtzi castle is just there on its islet in the bay as it has been for over five hundred years. I approach Kondogiorgos cafe where I spent so many hours and choose a sea-facing seat one row back from the promenade. The furniture has changed but the view is the same. Timeless.

I order a large Greek coffee, medium sweet, and look out at the Bourtzi with its backdrop of Arcadian mountains and the calm cobalt plate of the Argolic gulf and I breathe. Twenty-five years telescope to this point as if I left it only yesterday. The air is soft. There's no sound of traffic – no sound at all. Only colour and light and the faintest breeze that doesn't even stir the umbrellas. My tall glass of water is opaque with condensation that soon forms droplets and melds with the table.

I'm in Nafplio again.

Nobody knows who Nafplio's first arrivals were, though its precipitous eminences and sheltering peninsula have made it an attractive defensive port throughout history. The ancient Greek words *naus* (ship) and *pleein* (to sail) suggest that the town has had maritime importance from the beginning. Some believe that the earliest inhabitants were Egyptians or eastern peoples brought to the area by the mythical Libyan king Danaus. A place called Nuplija is mentioned as Mycenae's port in the Egyptian mortuary temple of Amenhotep III in the early fourteenth century BC.

Mycenaean tombs (1200-1100 BC) have been found here, as have geometric period burial sites (900-700 BC). The town was part of a league of states centred on Poros in the seventh century BC but was attacked and plundered by neighbouring Argos in the sixth. It became the port of Argos and the acropolis was fortified around 300 BC. However, by the second century AD the Greek traveller Pausanias found Nafplio deserted and in ruins. The acropolis was refortified in the late Roman or early Byzantine period, perhaps in the third century AD with a second phase in the late fourth century after the earthquake of 375. These walls may have protected the town against successive waves of invaders of the Argolid: the Heruli in 267 AD, the Goths in 399, the Avars in 589 and Slavs in 746.

The Byzantine Empire took more of an interest in Nafplio from the ninth century AD onwards, after which the church of Agia Moni appeared near Aria and when one Nikephoros Karantenos was appointed general of the town. He probably never set foot in Nafplio, as he was busy waging war. In Brindisi, he beheaded a hundred corpses and shipped their heads back to Constantinople to impress the emperor. What a gift. What a smell.

Under the Byzantines, fortifications were repaired and augmented to better defend this port whose position made it an important base on Mediterranean trade routes. The problem with a large sea-based empire is covering the territory, so Byzantium granted the Venetian Republic free trading rights to Nafplio as early as 1082 in return for naval support. The potential value of the site must have got back to the doge and now this Argolic peninsula was on his wish list.

By the late twelfth century, the Byzantium-appointed ruler of Nafplio was Theodoros Sgouros, who in 1198 passed the title of *archon* to his son Leo. Political allegiances were cemented with Leo's marriage to the daughter of a previous Byzantine emperor.

Leo Sgouros deserves a digression for his homicidal hotheadedness. Known particularly for his temper and impatience with religion, he imprisoned the bishop of Nafplio. The bishop of Corinth fared worse, being invited to supper, blinded and tossed from the 600m high peak of Acrocorinth.

It was a historically seismic period. The Fourth Crusade had ended with the largely inadvertent sack of Constantinople and the dismemberment of the Byzantine Empire. Frankish warriors were heading south into Greece on the hunt for territory. Sgouros saw an advantage in the instability and decided to take Athens for himself. Characteristically, he attacked the town even as the Frankish warriors were invading it, setting fire to houses when he couldn't take the Acropolis. Frustrated in this attempt, he kidnapped the nephew of a senior churchman as a slave, later beating the boy to death when he dropped Sgouros's favourite glass during a dinner service.

There was no holding off the Frankish invaders, whose warrior Boniface laid siege to Nafplio in 1204. Sgouros fled to the fortified peak of Corinth and defied the besieging Franks for three years. Blockaded there, and without any possible escape, he did the obvious thing and rode his horse off the battlements into the void, colourful to the last. Apropos of nothing, sgouros means "wavy hair." His portraits show him with a short beard and very curly hair.

The Franks had Nafplio in their hands by 1212 and it became part of the fiefdom of Otto de la Roche, Duke of Athens. Thereafter the town was held by a variety of aristocratic Frankish owners (the Brienne, the d'Enghien) during which time Nafplio gradually became a dependency of the powerful Venetian Republic, finally being sold to Venice in 1388. The sale was complicated slightly by the Byzantine 'Despot of the Morea' Theodoros I Palaiologos holding most of the surrounding territory. Only five fraught years of negotiation persuaded him to leave. Alas, Nafplio's luck remained bad. A huge Turkish invasion by Ottoman sultan Bayezid I in 1397 saw Argos and Nafplio left heavily depopulated and the Venetians had to attract new settlers with the promise of forty acres of land and four acres of vines for each family, plus materials to rebuild the destroyed houses or build new ones. Many of those who responded were Albanians who had come south to escape strife in their homeland.

Thereafter, Nafplio was a territorial tennis ball between the Venetian and Ottoman empires, falling to the Turks in 1540, back to the Venetians in 1686, and back to the Turks in 1715 (game, set and match) until 1822 and the Greek War of Independence. It was briefly Greece's first capital from 1828 to 1834 after which the honour was transferred to Athens. That might have been the end of the story if the Germans and Italians hadn't occupied the town from 1941 to 1945 during the Second World War (WWII).

So, three thousand years of new arrivals give or take a few centuries. Nafplio has been, for most of its history, a defensive base and port in service of a strategic trading station. Its earliest visitors were soldiers, military engineers, slaves, merchants, mariners, builders, artisans and those servicing the strategic superstructure. Few of them initially expected (or even wanted) to stay. They were stationed there. They called it different names: Nauplia, Napoli di Romania, Porto Cadena, Anápli, Nauplie, Anabolu. The Peloponnese was known as the Morea for much of this time, named after the mulberry leaf (*morus*) whose shape it resembled.

As for the Greeks who lived there – almost perpetually occupied – we know very little about them before the nineteenth century. For centuries, they were in the minority, as populations arrived from Venice or Ottoman territory. Almost never do we know their identities. Thousands lived nameless. Thousands died nameless in battle, in accidents, executed, of disease and natural causes. Virtually no trace of them remains.

The town drew the young men of Europe on their Grand Tours from the seventeenth to the nineteenth centuries, though perhaps more to experience the decadence of late Ottoman rule than to see archaeological sites such as Tiryns, Mycenae and Epidaurus that began to be excavated and understood only in the nineteenth century.

Intrepid travellers came from around 1800, creating their cultural itineraries. As the Greek War of Independence drew to a close, Nafplio became the new nation's first capital and was, for a brief historical moment, as talked about as London or Paris. Prussian author Friedrich Tietz published a book in 1836 grandly entitled *St. Petersburgh, Constantinople, and Napoli di Romania*, tying this small Peloponnesian town into the nexus of European power and politics. Tourism – Nafplio's modern raison d'être – came only much later.

I didn't know any of this when I arrived the first time as a teenager on an excursion from nearby tourist resort Tolo. I saw the vast bastions, the towering castles, the ruined Venetian buildings, the converted mosques and Turkish fountains and I felt history around me in the narrow alleys, the bowed stepped streets, the scent of incense through church doorways and the fragments of ancient wall or cistern peeking through under-growth. It was also elementally Greece: the liquid sapphire sea, the wire-tensioned, rickety raffia chairs outside cafés, the hammered copper *brikia* at the end of their long brass handles and heavy with velvet brown coffee. Nafplio was living history, even if I didn't know almost any of it. It was a storybook brought to life. It was exotic.

When I came back aged twenty-five, it was with the same sense of wonder and expectation, the same general ignorance outside the bare facts my guidebook told me. The Internet was in its infancy. Google was created in the same year I came to live in Nafplio so there was no simple source for learning more about the place. No comprehensive history book existed in English. Still, I was now going to inhabit these streets and walk these battlements and become a part of the story. I didn't realise how much it was going to become a part of mine.

When were you happiest? I'm not talking about a landmark moment – the birth of a child, a wedding day, that threesome in Ibiza – but a period in life you'd go back to in a heartbeat, a golden age. That time when everything was good. The period that, if you had to admit it, was probably, really, one of the few times you felt like you were living your life rather than merely a passenger in it, tolerating it, surviving.

Maybe it was those university days where the only pressure was a deadline for a not very difficult essay and you lived among friends who hadn't yet been existentially atrophied by children and careers. Maybe it was your childhood of long summer freedom and bike rides and tree climbing and no thought of any future but the most unlimited, Astronaut, Racing driver, Princess. Mine was Nafplio.

I'd left university with no idea of what I wanted to be except, vaguely, an 'artist.' I'd worked in retail and sunk into jaded failure even before any real career could start. Nafplio was a leap of hope: an English teaching job I didn't especially want and wasn't remotely qualified for, but which gave me a licence to live in that historic town and travel in Greece. The drachma still reigned supreme and transport was cheap. I also had a tent.

It was a time of total fulfilment. I lived amid antique masonry, drank long coffees on shaded terraces, ate all that Greek cuisine could offer me, swam in the Argolic gulf, ambled the irregular streets, had sexual adventures and – best of all – became a part of Nafplio. I had my haunts and my patterns. I was recognised as a resident. I spoke a faulty but broadly functional Greek that made me feel unlike a tourist. Waiters would sometimes bring me my drink before I ordered. When the daytrippers and the travellers went home, I sat on my balcony watching the seasons cycle.

A year later, I left in search of other adventures in other countries but Nafplio felt more like a home than any other I had for a long time afterwards. The memories were so rich and varied. It was a place I could return to in my mind and inhabit again whenever I chose. Certain sites – the sheer Acronafplio battlements, the coastal walk, the squares, a deserted Karathonas beach in winter – were pristine, unchanging states of being I could flick through.

Most of all, that second-row seat in Kondogiorgos café facing the Bourtzi castle and the Arcadian mountains was representative of my whole Nafplio experience. It was a place for dreaming. It was a dream. I'd go there most mornings for a coffee before not preparing my classes, but on Saturdays I'd buy a magazine from the international newsagent in the square and spend a couple of hours or more there: sipping, riffling pages made slack with humidity, looking out at the view and imagining my illustrious future as a writer – probably the kind who'd redefine literature. A Joyce. A Faulkner. Maybe a Melville. Probably a Henry Miller.

The seat in Kondogiorgos became the epitome of my hopeful and fruitful future. When that future didn't immediately materialise, the view remained a beacon extending across time and age. I imagined I'd return there one day and sit at my usual place, order my usual coffee, but this time as a lauded author. It would be my prize – a promise I'd made:

a pact with the Bourtzi to face it again as an artist. After all, Lord Byron himself had gazed at this same view. So had Henry Miller. Patrick Leigh Fermor, too.

If during those decades after leaving, I occasionally met someone who'd been to Nafplio, I'd listen to their stories and memories with an indulgent smile and nod politely, filling in or correcting the names of the restaurants they'd eaten at. They'd merely met Nafplio in passing. I'd been married to her. She was mine. She was a part of my history. She was to me as Paris was to Hemingway, a "moveable feast" I carried with me always – a part of my life that had made me.

I later lived in different places. I met new people. I lived a whole other life, but Nafplio was always mine. At any moment, I could return to a café terrace or favourite restaurant or seat myself in front of a particular view. I couldn't share this detailed psychocartography with anyone, even those who'd been there and done the same things. Nor did I want to. More than one partner was jealous of the way I spoke about it, suspecting, perhaps, that there'd been some consuming and latently burning love affair I wasn't revealing. Nothing could compare.

Now I had come back to write a history of the town. I'm not a historian. I've written a handful of books set in Victorian London, which required months of research into primary sources such as online newspaper archives and antique books. I've also written about first-century Judaea and nineteenth-century lighthouses. But that isn't history; it's cherry picking. The job of the novelist is to pull out the juiciest stories, the most arresting scenes, the most evocative locations and slot them into a fabricated narrative. No footnotes or bibliography are necessary. No strict fidelity with the history books is expected. The reader should assume that it's all more or less true. And it is – more or less. It's credible. It *could* have happened.

So why attempt a history of Nafplio? And what kind of history? Nafplio has a lot. Military history. Political history. Social history. Maritime history. Archaeology. Folk history. The history of art. I aim to include little of each while recognising that others have already written good and very comprehensive books on the Venetians, the Greek War of Independence and the ancient civilisations. My intention is something else.

Consider the Bourtzi, sitting there elegantly in the bay. Every visitor gazes at it but what do we know about it? Your guidebook tells you that the Venetians built it in such and such a century and that the town executioner lived there. Do these meagre facts satisfy the imagination? I wanted to know what the bay looked like in 1470 or 1941. I wanted to know the stories and the secrets. I wanted to look out at the castle as I drank my coffee and understand its role in five hundred years of history. I wanted to *see* it all go by like a film projection.

Likewise, I wanted to walk the streets and see them as something more than generically old and exotic. Not only did I want to know the history of that mosque, but what happened in it through time and what it meant to the different people who passed through. Nafplio is now one of the prettiest towns in Greece, but its history is predominantly one of attack and defence, siege, slaughter and occupation. I wanted to know where the blood ran and what it looked like in the moment. If Lord Byron was here in 1810, what did he do? Did he make anyone pregnant?

Let's call it a psychogeographic history. The concept has its roots in the beard-stroking intellectualism of French Situationism, but it can be reduced (for my purposes) to getting pleasurably lost in the town and its history. The psychogeographer strolls and drifts without destination or purpose, allowing details to draw attention to themselves – the kinds of things you don't notice when you're going somewhere, or when you've lived in a place your whole life. Locals very often don't see things that tourists come to visit.

This history of Nafplio means becoming a *flâneur*, a sauntering observer in search of unexpected encounters or perspectives. It's an interesting way of experiencing a place. Psychogeography suggests that the whole history of a city is simultaneously present in its fabric. Not just the monuments and buildings – not just what remains – but everything that ever happened to everyone who was there.

The *flâneur* is a reader of a place, looking for stories and clues. It's exactly the same process as novelistic research: strolling through books and newspapers looking for personalities and details that deserve more attention – chasing fugitive clues across sources in a relay race of accumulating story.

My time in Nafplio as a young man had involved a lot of *flânerie*. I spent a year walking the streets and staircases of the old town entirely without purpose – merely to inhabit the place, to absorb it. Now, a quarter of a century later, might I meet myself in these same streets: another shadow of the past? My peregrinations, my memories and experiences in these alleys and culs de sac alongside the Turkish fountains and carved Viennese lions were as valid in Nafplio's history as the glorious entry of Bavarian King Otto, albeit less illustrious.

Nafplio has welcomed kings, sultans and empresses, artists, adventurers and heroes. I'm one insignificant person, resident for a single heartbeat of its myth-rooted history, but I saw things. I was a witness to tiny moments of its history. Millions have passed through before and since – most of them in the last fifty years. It's a palimpsest. It's a history that has been told by others, but not like this.

MAPPING

For my purposes, Nafplio is the peninsula that juts east to west out into the upper Argolic Gulf in the Peloponnese. That's to say: the rocky hill of Acronafplio that shows sheer cliffs to the south and shelters the twenty hectare old town to the north. I'll also be including a little bit of the periphery, such as the coast as far as Karathonas beach, the broad and ever-silting bay containing the Bourtzi, the colossal 200-metre-high Palamidi fortress overlooking the town, and Kolokotronis Park.

The old suburb of Prónoia just a few hundred metres to the east (and where I briefly lived) has its own fascinating history in parallel to the old town, but I'll be mentioning it only in passing. The new town, meanwhile, stretches out along the Argos road and is maybe five times bigger than the old. It's where the majority of Nafplio's Greek people live and it looks very much like many other modern Greek towns: architecturally utilitarian and predominantly concrete. Most visitors merely pass through on the way to or from Athens.

Arrival in a new town, whether for a short visit or to live, involves a period of mental mapping, sometimes called behavioural geography. It's a primal animal impulse to establish one's place and security in new terrain. In urban environments, you identify the route from the point of entry (a bus stop, a train station, a car park) to your base or accommodation. Next, you discern the location of the shops you'll need to feed yourself. Then, as you start to explore the space, you begin to map specific routes, buildings, landmarks or other features that tell you where you are in relation to your base. An actual map may initially help with this process, but a map is an abstract: a symbolic representation of the physical fabric. We instinctively map in three dimensions with our senses: the height of buildings, the width of a road, a sign, a

corner, a dead end. We unthinkingly calculate the most efficient routes and seek shortcuts to avoid a wasted ten seconds
during a late night *baklava* hunt.

When you stay longer in a place, your mental mapping
changes from the strictly functional to the more aesthetic or
hedonistic. It's a mysterious process. Why, for example, did I
choose Kondogiorgos as my café of choice when so many of
them crowd along the *paralia* facing the Bourtzi? There's very
little to differentiate them. Was it pure chance? Was the view
better there? Did a local introduce me to the place, thus
bestowing some imprimatur of authenticity in my mind?

There were and are many cafes in Nafplio, but I almost
never drank at Lyrikon (now gone) on Vasileos Konstantinou,
or Napoli di Romania, or at Sokaki behind the archaeological
museum. Other cafés were clearly used by a specific clientele,
such as Agora (also on Vasileos Konstantinou, now gone),
which was crowded with high-school students in the afternoons, or the café with wood-and-raffia seats opposite Alpha
Bank, which in 1998 seemed to be a traditional *kafeneio*, for
old men only. I seldom drank a coffee in the square because it
was "for tourists." Café Allotinó opened the year I was living
here and was just twenty metres from my door, so it, too,
became a regular haunt.

Likewise with the restaurants. My habitual choice was
mezedopoleio Noulis off Plapouta Street for lunch. For dinner,
I chose Kakanarakis or Omorfo Tavernaki in the port area, or
Noufara in Syntagma Square. Of these, only Noufara has gone,
which speaks for the quality of food. Why did I eat only at
Meraklís among the many restaurants of Staikopoulou Street? I
have no idea. Familiarity, perhaps. Once you eat at a good
place, you feel comfortable there and it becomes a fixture on
your mental map. Trying a new place comes with the risk of
disappointment. We are creatures of habit. I probably ate at
almost every restaurant and taverna during my year in Nafplio,
but at some stage the map becomes fixed.

Or rather certain points on the map become fixed: shops,
the post office, the offices of the utilities, the bank and cafés or

restaurants. The mental mapping continues the longer you stay and the more you become a part of it. You start to wander and drift as a *flâneur*, seeking new territory purely out of curiosity and pleasure. Now the town starts to become a part of you. You can visualise it. You have a feeling of it and for it.

My mental map of Nafplio was now twenty-five years out of date. The street layout hasn't changed in centuries, but many of the buildings and businesses have. Shops, inevitably, have changed ownership and products. My old street, Plapouta, had a traditional supermarket selling salted fish from huge circular cans and feta cheese from a barrel, both carefully measured out by a man in a white apron. It's abandoned now, the siesta shutters permanently fixed. Next door was the Singer sewing machine shop, whose leather-jacketed owner used to spend hours standing and smoking in the doorway. I never once saw a customer leave or enter the shop, though it seems to have moved rather than closed (to the new town near the park). The old hardware shop on the corner by St George's Square has gone, too, and was one of my favourites even if the woman who worked there hated me for some reason. Maybe she hated everyone. Inexplicably, the shop below my flat that sells flags and embroidery paraphernalia remains. So, too, does the Odyssey bookshop in Syntagma Square, selling much the same range of books today as it did in 1998.

Maybe you live in Nafplio or used to. Maybe you're planning to go or did many years ago. Maybe you got this book as a Christmas present and couldn't care less. Whatever. It's time to map the town to get a sense of its shifting limits since the Mycenaean period.

More of today's Nafplio was under the sea in Mycenaean times. The junction of *endekati* was a shoreline and much of the land between it and the old town was also underwater, including the old train station. At this time, and for a couple of millennia afterwards, there was only the rocky peninsula of Acronafplio. No lower town – no streets or squares. The sea to the south washed the foot of the hill as it did to the north. For this reason, all early construction was on Acronafplio. Probably for the same reason, the tombs of early inhabitants were in Prónoia, where it was easier to dig and less prone to erosion. The town's cemetery is still there.

It's possible that the Byzantines started to extend the land northwards at the foot of Acronafplio using alluvial landfill. It's equally possible that the ever silting harbour started to deposit swampy land there. By 1380, the shore was roughly along today's Papanikolaou Street, passing St. Spyridon and going south of Syntagma Square towards the ruined swimming pool complex of the Amphitryon Hotel. This makes sense because the tiny church of St. Sophia and the *Frangoklisia* (today's Catholic church) both have Byzantine origins and are built on the slope of Acronafplio.

In 1388, the Venetians inherited a town with neglected fortifications that may have been damaged by the Frankish siege in the previous century. A tower opposite today's Kapodistrias Square was connected to a length of ruined walls and a gate on the eastern land front. The investment required was large and Venice was slow to act, but in 1470, amid an increasing Ottoman threat, new governor Vettore Pasqualigo arrived with engineer Antonio Gambello to kick start a significant building programme. They brought the necessary workers and materials with them.

Much of the work was focused on strengthening Acronafplio's defences and protecting the port by building the Bourtzi. Walls were also to circle the town along the seafront and the land. However, when commander Bartolomeo Minio arrived in Nafplio in 1479, he saw that the town was still in a relatively unprotected state, its land and sea walls incomplete. Nor were there sufficient builders with the skills to finish them. He spent three and a half years bringing in more craftsmen and materials from Venice to complete the masonry work. They worked day and night, but the immense scope of the job meant that it stretched into the next century.

The new walls described the limits of the lower town while also expanding it. Minio saw that he would have to build on marshland and that this would require some particularly Venetian know-how. They were much more experienced in reclaiming land from the sea than the Byzantines and in order to make the level areas of the lower town fit for construction, they began using a combination of alluvial filler and the same method they had mastered at home: wooden pilings.

The Venetian system involved sinking between six to ten oak or pine pilings with sharpened ends into every square metre of mud or swamp selected for building. These pilings were ten to thirty centimetres in diameter, depending on what they needed to support, and were driven between eight and ten metres into the ground according to soil conditions. The hammer was a huge two-handled iron cap that fitted over the top of the pile to be lifted and dropped by two human pile drivers. The pilings, once in place, were entirely encased in mud and wouldn't rot. Nor would they shift, move or allow sediment to seep between them because the spaces in between were filled with crushed stone.

The multiple pilings would then be sawn flush across the top and topped with two or three layers of five-centimetre-thick larch or oak battens, creating a level base. Courses of limestone blocks were typically laid on the battens then the courses of brick or other materials could begin the intended structure. A single building might require a month of work merely to sink the pilings.

Some urban planning would have been part of the overall building scheme. Today's Syntagma Square was laid out in around 1500 and the fact that the old town's so-called 'big road', Vasileos Konstantinou, runs directly into the centre of it at the eastern end is unlikely to be a coincidence. Warehouses, workshops and housing were also needed.

Most tourists don't realise that they're walking on a platform of sixteenth-century Venetian wooden piles, though the locals know. It is said, and I have felt it, that rough seas can make some of the lower town vibrate at a low frequency. How would it react to an earthquake?

There was a huge seismic event on the 22 April 1928 with its epicentre at the Corinth isthmus. Three thousand houses were destroyed in Corinth, twenty people were killed and the whole of nearby Loutraki was levelled, with not a single house remaining. In Nafplio, some buildings fell and dust clouds covered the town. The first shock was a magnitude 5.25 and the second 6.3 – moderate to strong. Perhaps Nafplio was far enough away on that occasion to avoid worse damage, or perhaps the Venetians did excellent work. Indeed, the region has been hit by earthquakes that would have been felt in Nafplio in 1837, 1858, 1948 and 1999.

The Turks made few changes to the Venetian structures when they took over Nafplio in 1540, either too complacent of Ottoman power to worry about invasion or content with the fortifications as they were. Their focus was to turn the town into a liveable Turkish possession, which meant fountains, bathhouses, public buildings and mosques. Maps of the period show a lot of empty space within the walls, with most buildings concentrated around the internal perimeter. Many buildings ruined by the siege had presumably been demolished and cleared.

Turkish visitor Evliya Çelebi noted in 1667 that the lower town had around 1600 residences, the larger of which looked like palaces to him. Some of the houses were uncleared Venetian ruins from the siege and bombardment of 129 years earlier. He also wrote that there were many mosques, at least three of which were new (which is to say not converted from Christian churches). The mosque that is now the Trianon in Syntagma Square would have been one of them, as it is the town's oldest. Çelebi describes two mosques in the town square, each with large minarets.

Delineating the limits of today's old town means talking about the walls of the second Venetian period, which were partially augmentations of the first-period walls and also new ones that would finally encircle the town, containing it for the next three hundred years. The first Venetian period had seen fortifications concentrated mostly upon Acronafplio (see **Castles**) but the second initiated a massive programme of reinforcement for the town and for Palamidi.

Having just taken Nafplio back from the Turks in 1686, Captain-General Francesco Morosini knew precisely where the weak points lay. Moreover, the nature of warfare had changed in the intervening centuries, with gunpowder weapons now much more powerful and accurate. Nafplio needed better walls, particularly on its land flank where a besieging army could mass with heavy guns. The plans came together in a piecemeal fashion between 1701 and 1711.

First to be built was the Dolfin bastion, named after Nafplio's governor (1701-1704) Daniele Dolfin. This was on the town's northeastern corner, replacing the old tower inherited from the Franks or Byzantines roughly by the site of today's Kapodistrias Square. It was designed to cover the land front and the eastern harbour. Alas, constant silting soon deposited more land around this intended sea bastion, reducing its effectiveness. The detached Mocenigo bastion was therefore built just to the north (where today's high school is) demolishing in the process the marine bastion from the first Venetian period. A small, protected harbour basin was created on the bastion's inner, southern face.

The land wall south from the Dolfin bastion also needed to be made stronger. Work started in 1706 and included the Land Gate (just south of today's 25 Martiou Street) that was reconstructed around 1999 on the original's foundations. A roadway of seven arches would eventually lead to this gate over periodically boggy ground and a wet moat that had been created in the early sixteenth century and perfected in the eighteenth. The reconstructed gate retains the original Venetian lion atop it, though not the original drawbridge that would be pulled up each evening around 7.00 p.m. You can see the slots on each side of the reconstructed gate where the chains descended.

The new land wall and gate had to connect with the fifteenth-century Castel del Toro on the edge of Acronafplio, so the Grimani bastion was built on Nafplio's southeastern corner (to the left of the Land Gate), rising in three huge tiers to join with the walls of Castel del Toro. It's still there today, scrubby and overgrown but still hugely impressive. The distinctive stonework, angled backwards and rusticated on the lower part, was probably how the whole land front appeared in its heyday and was designed to deflect the impact of cannonballs.

The walls then continued around to the west, following today's road up to the Arvanitia car park before rising to the cliff heights and walls of Acronafplio that mark the southern extremity of the peninsula. The Venetians also cut a deep right-angled ditch into the rock around the eastern edge of the Grimani bastion, further separating the peninsula from Palamidi's slopes. The sharp masonry corner at the road fork between the Arvanitia car park and the road up to the derelict Xenia hotel was then the edge of the town, falling away to the sea. There was no level ground where today's car park is, just a staircase down to the water.

We pick up the town walls again at the remaining Five Brothers (*Pente Adelfia*) bastion, named for its cannons facing the sea approach. A large, arched gate with foot-polished cobbles still passes under the bastion and through the wall. One nineteenth-century visitor refers to this as a sluice gate and perhaps it allowed water to run out of the town during heavy rain, but mostly it was a sea gate for when the Land Gate was closed for the evening.

From here, the town walls ran along the sea line behind Akti Miaouli, encountering the colossal Cistern of the Port on the site of today's ruined Amphitryon pool and then the bastion of S. Theresa/Moschos on the site of today's Philhellion Square. Thereafter the wall passed roughly along Ipsilantis Street to connect with the line of Amalias, where another sea gate existed, and finally back to the Dolfin bastion to complete the loop. Portions of the Amalias wall were uncovered in 1934 and in 2013 during road-surfacing work, the latter leaving a stretch of Venetian foundation exposed, revealing part of an original arch and drainage works.

The area north of Amalias and outside the walls became the marina district where warehouses would be concentrated, but this was the shape of Nafplio for hundreds of years hence: an enclosed and fortified town that would host the second Ottoman occupation, the Greek War of Independence and the early years of statehood. The amount of human labour involved was immense. Digging a deep trench through rock around the corner of the Grimani bastion was a gargantuan task in itself. The walls were metres thick in places and solid. Perhaps fifty years and incalculable man-hours were expended in putting a stone ring around Nafplio's old town.

The masonry's gigantic dimensions were one of the reasons why the walls remained for so much of modern history, even after they became a disadvantage. Threat of invasion passed after the Ottoman and Venetian empires faded, but the bay was still prone to silting and remained a source of fever. The town couldn't breathe. Filth accumulated. Even today, Nafplio can be exceptionally humid at the height of summer, its eminences trapping evaporating brine and stilling the wind. Nor could the town grow within its lapidary curtain, hemmed in by sea and cliffs on three sides.

Demolishing the walls would turn out to be almost as much work as building them had been and would require a significant amount of labour. Fortunately, or unfortunately, Nafplio's nineteenth-century profile would be as a militarised prison colony. There would be plenty of men, willing or unwilling, to wield a hammer and push a wheelbarrow.

Work began in the late 1800s. The S. Theresa bastion next to the Napoli di Romania café came down in 1865. Most of the sea wall went in 1867 to open access to the harbour, while the vast walls and gate of the land front were removed in 1894-5 with the help of convict labour, during which time the wet ditch was filled in. The Dolfin bastion followed in 1928 to make way for Kapodistrias Square and finally the colossal Mocenigo bastion fell in 1932.

The walls came down gradually and erratically. Old photos show stretches remaining along the sea, isolated bastions standing briefly naked and the land wall a gap-toothed grin. Some structures were harder to eradicate. The enormous, eight-metre-high eighteenth-century cistern close by the Five Brothers bastion had been a part of the sea wall and remained useful as a cistern for most of the nineteenth century. Its eventual demolition would take almost eighty years thanks to various quarrels and the interruption of WWII.

The cistern was one of the few Venetian structures whose destruction was questioned on historical preservation grounds. Perhaps the requirements for air, light and better access to the sea were sufficient justifications for nineteenth-century municipal councils to rip down the walls. Today, the Venetian fortifications are one of the main attractions and characterising hallmarks of Nafplio's old town. We can only wonder what it would have been like if the walls had remained as they have in other European towns such as Lucca, Carcassonne, Ávila, Sienna, Toledo or Óbidos.

Much remains: Acronafplio's perimeter walls and sundry structures; parts of the Castel Del Toro; Palamidi's forts and curtain walls; the Grimani bastion and the Five Brothers bastion; the Bourtzi. These lend a lot of charm and historical flavour. Even without its complete circle of walls, the scope of Nafplio's old town is limited by the peninsula it occupies. You feel that you're within it when you enter the streets.

As you'd expect from a town that has been invaded and besieged so often, building and rebuilding has been constant throughout history. Nevertheless, there are patterns to Nafplio's development. The oldest structures were built on Acronafplio because that was initially the only land available. Little evidence of these remain on the hill because its military significance meant the limited space was better used for batteries, barracks and prisons. Many Turkish houses existed here during the first and possibly the second Ottoman periods.

The northern slopes of Acronafplio, characterised today by the neighbourhoods of Psaromachalas and Vrahateika, contained the next wave of houses, connected by steep, stepped streets zigzagging erratically around the hill's contours. Look at a map and you'll see very few straight lines. Again, there was nowhere else to build until the Venetians started to fill in the lower town in the sixteenth century.

Accordingly, the next wave of building was on the newly acquired flat land, roughly north of Papanikolaou and Staiko-poulou streets, where many of the town's distinctive stepped streets begin. Those that survive are Venetian and Turkish constructions, such as the Trianon mosque, the Vouleftikon, the current archaeological museum and other large buildings like the Armansperg mansion on the corner of Plapouta and Syngrou streets. Wherever buildings of this period were dest-royed in bombardments or simply fell to pieces through age, newer eighteenth and nineteenth-century houses have been built, though sometimes badly. They have aged worse than the Venetian and Turkish structures.

The final phase of building was north again (where else?), generally past Vasileos Konstantinou Street. This was the rev-olutionary period beginning in the late 1820s, when first Greek governor Ioannis Kapodistrias attempted to turn this historical patchwork of a town into Greece's first capital with a concerted building and repair programme. The damaged Ven-etian aqueduct carrying Nafplio's sole source of fresh water from Aria was one of the first priorities. You can still see some of its remaining arches at the back of the summer cinema near *endekati* and behind the fire station on 25 Martiou.

Much building work was neoclassical in style: the grand residence (the *palataki*, burnt down in 1929) built for Kapo-distrias then used as King Otto's palace, some of the buildings of Syntagma Square, the first high school in Three Admirals Square and the customs house on Bouboulinas Street. Such structures were praised by contemporary visitors for their taste, but others observed that they were hastily and badly built. In the meantime, many of the town's older buildings remained. One nineteenth-century visitor described houses cheaply made of lath and plaster, albeit charmingly painted on the outside with landscapes, maritime scenes or animals.

King Otto continued Kapodistrias's work, maintaining and updating the military infrastructure. More houses and factories were built. It was during this period that visitor Godfrey Levinge wrote that, "Napoli di Romania is the best town in Greece," noting the flourishing and well supplied shops along either side of Vasileos Konstantinou, which connected Syntagma and Three Admirals squares.

Since the late nineteenth century, Nafplio has filled in its gaps according to whatever regulations allowed at the time. Some buildings have been sensitively and thoughtfully renovated, many of them as hotels and guesthouses. Others have been pulled down and replaced. Some ugly houses have sprung up where nowadays they wouldn't be allowed by urban planning and architectural control committees. I'm thinking of one particular blocky reinforced-concrete bunker of a house near Psaromahala. It's well cared for (I'd live there in a heartbeat) but it's an architectural insult to the area where it sits. Apparently, the owner wanted to build an extra floor on its flat roof but was told the entire building would have to be demolished before any further work could be done. It was probably built before (or in flagrant disregard of) regulations that prohibited such modern structures.

The resulting town is architecturally eclectic. Walk its streets, squares, alleys or staircases and you'll drift through five hundred years or more of buildings. Here, a mosque; here, a medieval Turkish fountain; here, a Byzantine church; here, a roofless ruin with shutters askew and supporting walls bulging alarmingly into the street. There, a beautifully restored nineteenth-century house; there, a ruined doorway beyond which 2,000 years of stonework is revealed; there, an eighteenth-century sentry box you can go and stand in, pretending for a moment that an invading Ottoman force is about to swarm the Land Gate. The streets of old Nafplio are endlessly changing and engaging. It's a place made for mental mapping. Let's go deeper inside

SQUARES

Nafplio's Syntagma Square, not to be confused with its riot-friendly namesake in central Athens, is the centripetal heart of the place: the focal point around which everything else is measured. Each old-town visitor and resident navigates according to its location and knows the streets surrounding it – crossing it, skirting it, cutting its corners, passing along its edges. It's Nafplio's second island after the Bourtzi: a world in itself, self-contained but inseparable.

Like everyone else, I've sat under the plane tree and drunk a coffee as I watched the local children kick footballs into the café terraces, overturning drinks and smashing glasses. I've crossed the russet marble in every conceivable direction, completing every angle in a complex geometry of invisible lines and arcs. I've cycled across its deserted, gleaming surface in the dark of winter nights and walked blinded by its glare at the height of summer. And yet the stories of its many buildings, both current and lost, were a mystery to me for a long time. It was just "old." Just charming.

There are more old photos of the square than of almost any other part of Nafplio, so we can see its many personalities over time. Before photography, the water-colourists, sketchers and engravers couldn't resist the Trianon and the old houses where the National Bank currently stands. It would be easy to assume that most of the structures around the square are roughly of the same era, but every building has a story to tell. Not all of them are talkative. Let's start from the beginning.

The Venetians set the space, if not its final dimensions, in 1500, building on reclaimed swampland with vertical wooden piles and alluvial fill. They called it the Piazza di Armi (parade ground). More informally, it was known in their dialect as the *foros* – the forum – and doubled as a marketplace for goods and gossip. Later, it would be called Place de Platane, Plateia Platanos, Stratonas Square, George II Square and Ludwig Square. The people never liked that last one and compelled King Otto to change it to Syntagma.

The Turks, meanwhile, used the square as an administrative centre and established its *serai* (government offices) here. There's also some suggestion that public executions under the Ottomans may have been carried out from the branches of its principal tree.

For most of its history, Syntagma Square was known as Platanos Square for the plane tree(s) within it. Perhaps you're already familiar with the stately old plane tree in the northwest corner, the seats and tables of café Kentriko set out under its gnarled branches – but this tree is not five hundred years old. Thus begins the first mystery.

A photo of the square from 1907 shows a young plane tree in the same corner and also a twin tree opposite it towards the Vouleftiko. The morphology of the branches in the northwest tree is the same as the tree in a 1947 photo and in a 1968 photograph. Given that today's tree looks quite old and has a lower branch supported by a wooden strut, we might surmise that it's the same tree as in 1907. The species can live for several hundred years if not damaged or diseased. However, neither this tree nor its vanished twin can have given their name to Platanos Square in the early nineteenth century. They would have been mere saplings. Is it possible the new tree was planted on the site of the old one?

Many nineteenth-century travellers refer to Platanos Square without telling us anything about a plane tree. Could it be that the tree existed in an earlier time and simply left its name? There are certainly historical incidents related to a notable plane tree in the square. For example, Theodoros Kolokotronis mounted a large stone under the tree (probably a walled enclosure around it) to address the populace after he returned from the Troezen Assembly, at which Nafplio and been chosen as the new capital and Kapodistrias as its governor. Noted educator and intellectual Georgios Gennadios famously addressed a large crowd under this same plane tree to raise money for a national subscription. During the fight for independence, illiterate locals would come to the square and have their grievances recorded by clerks in the shade of the tree. But where was it?

The answer appears to lie in the accounts of Italian visitor Count Giovanni Pecchio, who came in 1825. He described a drinking fountain that flowed from the stately trunk of the plane tree in the centre of the square. He also noted that the surrounding cafés were wretched (he *was* Italian). What happened to this tree? The last mention of it seems to have been around the time of Pecchio's visit, when the town was embroiled in civil conflict, overpopulation, disease and starvation. Maybe it was cut down for firewood. Maybe it was simply old and died of disease. Could Theodore Kolokotronis have ordered it cut down, as he had with the plane tree in Tripolitsa (now Tripoli) town square that the Turks had used for hangings? Much more likely is that it was damaged in the bombardments of 1827, when revolutionary fighter Theodoros Grivas decided to take Palamidi and bomb his Greek rivals in the lower town. An image of 1829 shows no tree and Prince Hermann von Pückler-Muskau (see **Presence**) mentioned in 1836 that the square had everything but a plane tree. The only modern hint at the original tree is a small raised circle in the centre of the modern square, a black cube of marble sitting on it. Some anecdotal accounts suggest that a sundial once occupied this space, but I've found no evidence of that. I'm more inclined to believe that this circle was intended to mark the place where the stone wall encircled the first plane tree when the current layout of the square was established in the 1980s. Whatever the current vestiges, this central point was where Kolokotronis addressed crowds in 1827. As for the black cube of marble, there's no clue as to its significance and I suspect it was put there to stop vehicles driving over the top of the circle. There were a couple of ornate cast-iron lampposts in the square from the 1940s but one of them was destroyed in the 1970s when a council vehicle backed into it.

The square has had many trees that have come and gone. The late nineteenth and the twentieth centuries in particular were the great tree-planting eras as the square became more leisure-focused – a place for the evening *volta* or promenade rather than for drilling troops. A row of trees went down both sides of the square between the museum and the Trianon at various times in history, though it's difficult to see from photos what species they were. One visitor at the Hotel des Etrangers wrote that they were fragrant pepper trees, which seems unlikely.

At some stage, these trees were cut down and the plots replanted with new ones because they are saplings again in photos of the late 1960s. A road went around the sides of the square for most of the twentieth century, so this could have been connected with resurfacing or widening. By 1980, there would be no perimeter road and only one tree: today's venerable specimen.

You sit under the old plane tree drinking your coffee and you look around at the buildings: Venetian, Turkish, neoclassical, modern, ruined, vanished. It's the history of the town in microcosm. There have been coffee houses here since at least the start of the nineteenth century and almost certainly under the Turks, who liked to relax with a long pipe and glass of sweet tea. Visitors recorded many restaurants and coffee houses in Place de la Platane during the 1840s. Then, as now, they seemed to gather along the north side. Old photos show the chairs and tables dotted about the square, reached by waiters crossing the road from the cafés in the buildings.

I used to drink my *elliniko* or frappé and idly wonder what functions the buildings had throughout history. My rudimentary historical knowledge told me which ones were Venetian or Turkish, but that wasn't much to go on. Wouldn't it be cool to sit at my table and range my gaze around that marble rectangle knowing its secrets? Let's do that now.

Today's Archaeological Museum was built by the Venetians in 1713 during the tenure of naval procurator Agostino Sagredo (according to the Latin inscription on the façade) and was first used as an arsenal or warehouse. We don't know how or if the Turks used it, though we do know they had a distinctive aesthetic and a different understanding of space. They built a lot of their own administrative buildings and it seems likely that they used the large, strong museum as a warehouse, or possibly a treasury. Later, it became a barracks and was the home of Nafplio's artillery from the nineteenth century, housing up to 300 soldiers. As the town scaled back its military capacity, the building became a military club until around 1929. In 1941 the Germans used it as their investigations HQ and by the late 1940s it had become the museum it is today. Many old photos show sentry boxes and soldiers gathered in front. The passage along the south side of the museum that now contains a huge and ancient marble bathtub was walled up during the late nineteenth century, possibly as a small courtyard or storage space.

From 1897, there was a memorial in front of the museum commemorating the 8th infantry losses of the Greco-Turkish war. It was an obelisk with a cannon each side of it and one in front. The sculpture was moved in 1933 to the out-of-town army camp at Polygono, but the cannons may have remained for a time. Another photo shows them displayed at the opposite end of the square.

The huge building currently being noisily renovated (2022) in the corner opposite the plane tree is known as the Viga. It was built in 1878 on land that belonged to Theodoros Kolokotronis's son Gennaios and served as a private house until it became the printing office of the *Argolis* newspaper. The original printing presses were still sitting dusty in the lightless basement in 2019. During 1929-30, the building was briefly a café and a barber's before becoming a military officers club. In 1941, the Italians took it as an HQ and detention centre for the carabinieri. From 1945, it was an officers club again but soon fell into disrepair. Despite coming under the care of the Ministry of Culture in 2000 it remained a ruin for a further twenty years and something of a civic embarrassment.

It will be interesting to see what becomes of it now.

The next building, now housing the Kentriko café on its ground floor, is clearly relatively new, though maintaining a semblance of neoclassical styling. An entirely different building appears on this spot in early twentieth-century photographs – a grand structure with two wings east and west of a recessed façade. One 1907 picture shows the word *xenodoxeio* painted on the inside of the west wing, but no hotel name is shown. It's another tantalising clue. Could this have been the Hotel d'Europa where Prince von Pückler-Muskau stayed in 1836 and was woken at 5.30 a.m. by the town's artillery drilling? He says that they were doing it directly in front of his hotel, which would also have put them in front of their barracks. For some reason, this building was demolished, perhaps after burning down, and was replaced with the current one, whose façade is flush with the other buildings of the square's north side.

An alley slips down the side of the Kentrikon building and the next structure along is the Noufara building, probably dating from the late nineteenth century. From 1974 to 2014 it was the Noufara restaurant, whose lofty ground floor tinkled to the sound of the resident pianist. Smart waiters served Greek and Italian food in a stately, slightly old-fashioned way. I remember eating there at midnight one evening (spaghetti al pesto) and getting into an argument with my roommate over a comment I'd made. We argued a lot. Before the place was Noufara it was the Grand Café of Smyrna but beyond that its history is vague.

The reddish two storey building beside Noufara is from the 1950s and currently houses a pharmacy, which always reminds me of something my Nafplio students told me. In their slang of 1998, *farmakeio* meant "pricey" – owing to the typically inflated prices of pharmacies in general. They were probably lying to me, the little shits. They delighted in offering me oranges they'd pulled from the decorative but uncultivated trees of the streets (very bitter) and called me "miss" instead of "sir" just to irritate me. Most of them failed their English exams.

Squares

We can't be sure what stood in the spaces occupied by the twentieth-century buildings on this side, though French visitor Theodore du Moncel noticed around 1843, "the strange architecture of some houses, mainly those located in the square, with decorative skylights in the Turkish style of the Middle Ages." He doesn't say exactly where, although some sketches of ten years previously show buildings of this sort on the south side where the bank currently stands.

Now it starts to get interesting. The current Hellas restaurant has been there for around thirty years in a building from the second Venetian period (1686-1715), although only the first two floors are Venetian. The third was added after 1839 (images before show only two storeys) and this may be when the building's second floor started being the Mykinas hotel, run by Ioannis Thermogiannis. For some reason, Heinrich Schliemann (who excavated Mycenae) decided not to stop in this hotel when excavating nearby Tiryns in the 1880s, but there was an even more notable visitor.

One day in the 1890s, a smart gentleman called at the Mykines and asked for Nikos Thermogiannis, the proprietor's son – a noted multi-linguist, author and educator. Was Nikos in trouble? Not at all – the gentleman represented a certain lady whose yacht was moored in the harbour. The lady was requesting a guide to the local sites for a week or two and had heard that Nikos was the man for the job. The lady in question was Duchess Elisabeth Amalie Eugenie, Empress of Austria and Queen of Hungary. She was then in her fifties and travelling extensively incognito with a group of ten intellectuals and language teachers.

Nikos was in his twenties and grabbed the opportunity. He and his father welcomed the empress at a reception in the hotel and the lady was escorted about the regional sites of Epidaurus, Tiryns, Mycenae and the rest. Thereafter Nikos accompanied her on her travels as a teacher of modern Greek and was still employed by her in Vienna when she was assassinated by Italian anarchist Luigi Lucheni. The assassin's preserved head was on public display in Vienna until 2000.

Did young Nikos walk Syntagma Square thereafter having tasted the finest wines, the choicest banquets and the richest culture of Europe's capitals? Did he, like Neil Armstrong, feel that the greatest part of his life was already over and nothing else could compare? He went on to become a highly respected writer with a street named after him (in the new town) and a very smart family monument in Nafplio's cemetery. As for the hotel, it operated until around 1920.

The Trianon mosque is the square's oldest building, built during the first Ottoman occupation (1540-1686). A Turkish visitor to Nafplio in the 1670s mentioned the mosque and noted that it had a cistern beneath it – a necessity in a walled town accustomed to sieges. Every large roof was an opportunity to collect rainwater.

When the Venetians took the peninsula again, Francesco Morosini gave the mosque to the Franciscan monastic order and dedicated it as a church of St Anthony. In 1715, it was to become a mosque again and hosted the faithful until 1822, when Theodoros Kolokotronis and the Greeks stormed into the town after a year long siege. Thus began a hundred years of multiple uses.

In 1823, the building was the headquarters of charity efforts to help the many orphans, widows, poor and starving created by the war. A couple of years later it was a boys' school, with 150 young and orphaned lads studying under the airy dome where prayers had been read and where men had kneeled for the last century. Sometime in the late 1880s it was a magistrate's court before becoming a theatre in 1893. In 1901 an important agricultural congress event took place in the space and the town was full of people who had also come to see the Kolokotronis statue unveiled in the park.

Around this time, structural changes were made according to its modern use and to manage acoustics. A false ceiling was put in to conceal the dome in 1915 and a mezzanine of reinforced concrete was constructed. The front portico was also filled in between the arches to create more internal space.

The building officially became the Trianon cinema in 1937. I remember watching the occasional film there during the winter months, and though I have no recollection of the cinematic entertainment, I recall the birds flying around inside the auditorium. I remember that the screen seemed to be made of bed sheets sewn together and that there was quite a big hole in it so that some of the action simply vanished into a black ink-blot. I also remember that the predominantly teenage audience (my students) didn't stop talking and rustling packets and throwing things off the mezzanine for the entire film. They were genetically incapable of being quiet. Occasionally, in class, I'd tell them that they could all go home early if the whole group could stay quiet for one minute straight. Not once did they manage it.

Since 1993 the building has multi-tasked as an exhibition space, the cinema and a theatre. As such it's highly characteristic of Nafplio as a whole – one of those buildings that has changed with the times, changed its religion, changed its function.

A large neoclassical monument surmounted by a cross is shown in front of the mosque in many old photos. This contained the bones of Demetrios Ypsilanti, one of the early revolutionary leaders and a besieger of Nafplio in 1822. He died of illness in 1832 and his brother had the monument made in Vienna before shipping it to Nafplio. Its location, however, blocked the façade of the mosque and it was moved to Three Admirals Square where it remains today.

In that southeast corner is the square's only current hotel, the Athena (opened 1969) and next to it is the building I always think of as the Dodoni house. While it has sold Dodoni ice cream for the last thirty years or more, the structure is one of the more pristine examples of late nineteenth-century neoclassicism and was a branch of the Athens Bank in the early twentieth century. Photos from around the 1930s show that the façade originally extended twice its current width with those fine old stone balconies across the front. These were evidently two adjoining buildings constructed at the same time. The westernmost one became the Hotel Des Etrangers (*Xenodoxeion ton Xenon*) recommended in the Baedeker travel guides of 1889 and 1894. Its ground floor was the Olympia restaurant.

By the late 1960 or early 1970s, the hotel was abandoned and rotting, its windows boarded or broken and its façade blackened with mould from a broken gutter pipe. History has shown that this beautiful neoclassical building could have been maintained as well as its neighbour, but it was demolished and replaced by a much less attractive building in the late seventies or early eighties – the one we see today with the weird stone arches on the ground floor and home to the Odyssey bookshop/newsagent.

Now for a mystery. We know that revolutionary hero Nikitas "The Turkeater" Stamatelopoulos, more usually known as Nikitaras, (see **Heroes**) had a house on the square, but there's some disagreement over where it is or was. Some have suggested the Dodoni house or its neighbour as candidates. Others have offered the site of today's Alpha Bank. Again, old photos provide some very useful clues.

There was an alley shortcut alongside the old Hotel des Etrangers, as there is today alongside the Odyssey bookshop joining with Staikopoulou Street. The next building along was a huge block that looks old even in early photos. What we know of the Nikitaras mansion is that the government used to meet there before the Vouleftiko was repaired enough to serve as a parliament and that trials were held on the first two floors. This puts construction of the house necessarily in or before the 1820s even though many of the neoclassical houses were built after Kapodistrias's arrival in 1828. Certainly, the building in the photos is large enough to serve these purposes and it looks sufficiently old. It could have been a Venetian structure constructed at the same time as the Hellas building. The architecture is not dissimilar. But was it the Nikitaras house? We'll come back to this.

The big old building was gone by the early 1930s and there

was only a scrubby patch of land where the national bank would soon be built in 1936. This is the ugliest and most incongruous building on the square – the world's only known example of Minoan Revival style from architect Nikolaos Zoumboulidis (though apparently the work was not completed according to his wishes). I had an account with the National Bank and remember standing in line at this branch to deposit money, listening to other Nafplio residents bitching about the wait and arguing with queue jumpers who arrived every few moments and pretended not to notice the others. One old man laughingly asked me if I was gay as he jumped the queue while pretending to know someone inside. Happy days. During WWII, the bank's basement was used as an air-raid shelter.

The national bank occupies the space of another famously vanished house – that of Kalliopi Papalexopoulou, the Nafplio heroine who's completely unknown outside Greece (see **Heroes**). Early-twentieth-century photos show the house shuttered or with a few broken windows. There are balconies on the first and second floors from where Kalliopi exhorted the people to reject Otto's rule. A staircase runs up along its west side and a walled garden continues along the square to the corner opposite the south end of the museum building. An even older photo shows a partially ruined structure on the garden site, its high arches suggesting a warehouse or other storage facility. Kalliopi lived in the house until she died, aged one hundred, in 1899.

One thing is clear: the two houses on the current National Bank plot were gone by the early 1930s and the garden, too, had been cleared. Both were likely abandoned or derelict by the time they were removed. It's worth noting that all of the buildings mentioned so far on this south of the square did not exist under the Ottomans. Indeed, an 1834 engraving by German architect Ludwig Lange shows the Turkish *serai* buildings filling all of this side.

And the Nikitaras house? It can't have been any of those on the south side because none existed in the 1820s. The museum was already built at the west end and so was the mosque at the east. That leaves only the north, where we have Kentrikon, Noufara and the pharmacy building. There is one final clue, albeit a maddeningly ambiguous one.

In 1875, a large fire broke out in a house on Syntagma Square and threatened to take many others with it. The town's fire fighters managed to bring it under control, but the damage was serious. The house almost certainly needed to be demolished, and possibly also the neighbouring structures. Reports of the time noted that the burned building was the famous house. But which one!

The Viga could be a candidate since it was built three years after the fire. Why would Kolokotronis's son have built the house only then if he'd owned the land previously? Let's remember that Nikitaras was Theodoros Kolokotronis's nephew, so maybe it was a family plot. The truth is that any of the current houses along the north side could have been where he lived. Any except Noufara perhaps, which looks like it might have been built a little earlier than the rest. For some reason, there are very few photographs and apparently no early paintings of the square's north side. It's a tantalising historical absence.

One important building remains to be described. The Vouleftiko is not on the square but dominates its southwest corner. According to local lore, the original mosque was built by an aga in penance for the murder of two naïve Venetian youths who approached him with a request. Their father had buried treasure on the site during the previous Venetian occupation and they had come to dig it up. On finding the treasure, they were murdered for it. True story? The names of the youths have been recorded (Andreas and Guido) and their father was reputedly the wealthy merchant Petro Loredanos. It certainly seems likely that there are undiscovered family hoards in a town that has been so wealthy and so besieged. The aga in question apparently fell off his balcony and was killed while watching the mosque's construction.

People assume the Vouleftiko is very old, but an Ottoman

survey of the town taken in 1715 does not mention it among the other mosques. Construction was probably around 1730, using limestone from a quarry northeast of Nafplio. The lintel of one of the upper west doors is reputedly fashioned from a column taken from the ancient site of Mycenae. Its lower floor follows a commercial plan (ten rooms, numerous doors for shops) while the upper part, reached by an exterior stone staircase, is the mosque. At the rear is a three-storey madrasa, or religious school, that forms a courtyard between the two buildings

Muslims worshipped here for almost one hundred years before the structure was heavily damaged in the siege of 1821-22. It seems likely that Nafplio's mosques – highly conspicuous symbols of Islam – had their domes targeted by the Greek artillery. Thus, the Vouleftiko was almost in ruins when the Greek forces entered the town in 1822 and couldn't operate as the new parliament building. The executive bounced around a few other places until the decision was taken in 1824 to repair and re-use this large space so close to the square. Military engineer Theodoros Vallianos drew up the plans.

By 1825, the mosque had become the new parliament building, with a repaired upper gallery for public attendance and square paving made of Maltese stone, known to be very hardwearing. They were planning for the long term future of Greece. The revolution kept stopping and starting, however, and in 1827 a projectile fired from Palamidi smashed through the new roof to kill deputy Christos Gerothanasis, who was taking part in a meeting.

The building also doubled as a court, most notably in the 1834 trial for treason of Theodoros Kolokotronis. Around the same time the lower rooms and the courtyard operated as a prison. When the capital and the government moved to Athens, the Vouleftiko was left without a definitive purpose. For a while, it served as a ballroom and as a storage space or museum for archaeological finds (1915-32). The front courtyard was still littered with large architectural pieces such as column drums and capitals in 1998 and the building lay empty for a long time. It was under restoration for even longer and was always closed when I lived in Nafplio. It remains closed most of the time nowadays, except when in use for exhibitions or other important events.

Buildings often have a life of their own. They age. Plants grow in their gutters or in the niches of their roof tiles. They sometimes settle or sink with subsidence. Rain damage, humidity or salt eats away at their fabric. Walls bow and wooden staircases twist helix-like. My house on Plapouta had such a staircase. Every ascent or descent came with the added spice of not knowing whether it'd all rip from the wall that day and you'd break a leg. My flatmate did actually fall down the uneven steps while rushing to answer a phone. Incredibly, the call was from an aunt whose last call had also caused the flatmate to run, fall and injure a knee. We went to Argos hospital with a frozen octopus wrapped around her ankle and I still remember the doctor's face when we removed the towel to reveal a limply looping grey tentacle.

The Vouleftiko had such a comment to make on the third of December 1910, when a part of its stone stairway tumbled into the street killing two people: a shopkeeper called Koulopoulos and a soldier called Michaelaikos. Grainy newspaper images of the incident show the rubble piled in the road. Neither man could have imagined on that winter morning the possibility of a Turkish mosque, built 180 years previously by a penitent, balcony-tumbling aga, crashing out of nowhere to end their lives. Nor could those hopeful young Venetian boys seeking treasure have guessed that their quest would have ended the way it did. No doubt the story hasn't finished yet.

Visitors see Nafplio for only a fraction of time. It's easy to think that the square is always the same: the cafés, the kids running about, the visitors crossing and re-crossing with maps or phones in hand. It's a different place in the rain, marble shining and cafés closed, wet leaves blowing about your ankles. Sometimes, it's black with people for national and historic celebrations such as the dedication of the Ypsilantis monument, the 1930 centenary of independence, political rallies or Easter celebrations. Troops drilled here for decades, marching in formation as local boys ran ahead of them. In 1941, it was a car park for dozens of allied vehicles, its surface wrenched up in trenches. King Otto strolled here, as did the empress of Austro-Hungary and countless, nameless others.

Before we leave Syntagma, here's a final image for you to ponder as you drink your coffee. Imagine sitting in the square on the morning of Sunday, 27 September 1831. It's early, around 8.00 a.m. You hear a shot echo across the town. Then another. You hear massed voices shouting and another shot. The voices come closer, reverberating around the square and a group of people emerge from beside the Trianon mosque. They are dragging a body that leaves a thin blood trail across the square as they run, still shouting and execrating the corpse, kicking it, spitting on it. They are on their way to throw this dead man from the parapet of the S. Theresa bastion into the sea. He was Konstantinos Mavromichalis, who five minutes previously had assassinated Ioannis Kapodistrias outside the church of St Spyridon.

Syntagma is not the only square, of course. The nineteenth-century town was bisected by Vasileos Konstantinou Street that runs between the two principal squares, Syntagma to the west and Three Admirals Square, initially known as Fountain Square, to the east.

Three Admirals square originally occupied the northeast corner of the town, bound on two sides by the Venetian walls and with the sea on the other side of those walls. It attained its current layout in the early nineteenth century according to the plans of engineer Stamatis Bulgaris and was oriented around the large neoclassical residence (now gone) that was built in 1829 for first governor Ioannis Kapodistrias. Early visitors noted the number of smart new neoclassical structures along the square's south side, many of which remain important historical firsts.

Modern Greece's first high school was one of them, though it's a little inaccurate to call it that. A few of the town's buildings were being used as schools before this one was built, so maybe it's better to call it Greece's first purpose-built high school as part of a state programme of education. It doesn't have quite the same ring to it, though. In typical Nafpliot style the building has since become the current Town Hall, whose previous incarnation was near the customs house on Bouboulinas Street.

Further along to the west is Greece's first pharmacy, already in place when Kapodistrias's residence was being built. The current building is newer, dating from around 1850, but the space functioned as a pharmacy until 1972. Its proprietor was an Italian called Bonifatios Bonafin, an old school friend of the first governor and the man who would embalm Kapodistrias after his assassination in 1831. A marble plaque on the façade says as much. The building was bequeathed to the Orthodox Church when it ceased to be a pharmacy and has operated as an electrical goods store since then. Nafplio's municipal council bought the building from the church for €585,000 in 2017 and hopes, with the Panhellenic Pharmaceutical Association, to turn it into a museum.

The monument in the centre of the square is the Ypsilantis memorial that used to sit in front of the Trianon mosque in Syntagma Square. It was moved here around 1850, about the same time that the square's name changed from Fountain Square to Three Admirals in honour of Codrington, van Heiden and de Rigny – the "Great Power" heroes of Navarino.

The square marks the start of Vasileos Konstantinou, which locals still refer to as the main road or the big road (*megalo dromo*) even though it's a tiny pedestrianised alley. Its historical importance is due to various factors, not least it being the principal thoroughfare joining the new governor's (later, the king's) residence to the Vouleftiko and Syntagma Square. This was also the embassy district. The Russian ambassador's house was opposite the *palataki*, the privy council president's house was just round the corner on Plapouta, and no doubt there were others established in new or renovated houses nearby. For these reasons, it was probably one of the first streets to be properly surfaced after the ravages of the 1820s and it was soon lined with prosperous shops – something that hasn't changed for almost 200 years. Everyone who comes to Nafplio walks down the street at some point.

St George's Square on Plapouta Street was my local square during the time I lived in Nafplio. There is nothing in particular there – no café, no restaurant – apart from the church, so I passed it almost daily without stopping. I did spend one magical Easter inside St George's when the Holy Fire is received from the tomb of Jesus at Jerusalem's Church of the Holy Sepulchre. It is said to rise miraculously from the tomb every year at Easter (only Orthodox Easter) and is passed from candle to candle across the world, then from person to person in Greek churches, the space filling with light, smoke, incense and hot wax dripping. "*Christos anesti,*" say the congregation: Christ is risen.

Some sources say that St George's was built in the first Venetian period (1380-1540) and maybe it was, but the floor plan is oriented towards Mecca as with the town's other mosques, so the Turks must have demolished any previous structure. Certainly, the arched portico looks very like the mosque in Syntagma square. When Francesco Morosini victoriously entered the town in 1686, he attended St George's church for a eulogy and the building once again became a place of Christian worship. It remained so until 1715 when it became the mosque of Sultan Ahmed III. Each time it changed religion, the minaret (pictured in Thomas Hope's late eighteenth-century drawing) became a church bell tower or vice-versa. An etching of 1834 shows both the new bell tower and the massive column of a truncated minaret behind it.

A few illustrious Nafpliots spent time in St George's, which is considered to be the town's cathedral. Dimitrios Ypsilantis was buried in the church until his bones were removed for the monument in Three Admirals Square. Though Ioannis Kapodistrias worshipped and was killed at St. Spyridon, his funeral was held at St George's and his embalmed body lay here for six months after being on display at his residence. King Otto also visited as part of his triumphant entry into Nafplio, though this was mostly for appearances. He was a Catholic and the church in 1833 was Orthodox.

Just to the rear of the church is a ruined, roofless Venetian building from the first Venetian period that may have been a religious school around 1712 and which has since been a printing house, an orphanage and around 1824, the Ministry of Education.

Saint Spyridon square is Nafplio's smallest but possibly its most notorious open space. It was here, on Sunday, September 27 1831, that first governor Ioannis Kapodistrias was assassinated in the church's doorway (see **Heroes**). A supposed bullet hole from the incident is preserved in the masonry beside the door, protected inside a tiny glass-fronted case. It doesn't look very much like a bullet hole, but we can assume that a hundred fingers probed it and that the weather eroded it before it could be protected. With a little imagination, it could certainly be a bullet hole.

There are a few very smart neoclassical houses on the square and I remember that the large one on the east side had a piano that someone used to play in the evenings. (The first piano was brought to Nafplio in 1828 by Ioannis Kapodistrias – his own instrument.) The centre of the square used to have a venerable pine tree and a bronze bust of Nafplio-born writer Angelos Terzakis, but both were removed during repaving work in 2022. The south side, comprising the grocery store and house of the Koulourides brothers and its neighbour, was entirely derelict for many decades. Both have now been beautifully restored and St. Spyridon Square is today the town's most attractive residential square. (The bust of Terzakis is due to return, apparently.)

Though it seems like a hidden niche today, from 1706 the square was on Nafplio's main and most direct thoroughfare from the Land Gate to Syntagma Square. Most people arriving or leaving would have passed this way. The church itself is older, constructed in 1702 on the site of a previous church damaged in the 1686 Venetian siege of Nafplio. A plaque on the east side of the building attests to this.

A second-period Ottoman fountain is built into the corner of the old Koulourides grocery. Its inscription says that Aga Mahmoud had it built in 1734-5 for the use of horses, which suggests the road was a well used route and possibly the first open area to stop after passing through the city walls. A trough would originally have stood at the base of the arched recess and the large dimensions suggest that the fountain stood alone. The patchwork of different masonry, particularly on the edge by the staircase, shows centuries of repairs. Another, larger Ottoman fountain is directly in front of the church.

It's interesting to note that the first three red marble steps on the way up to the Catholic church are the same stone as the steps of the large house and the steps down towards Angelos Terzakis alley. All must have been part of the same programme of works, very probably repair work after one of the heavy storms that periodically turns the stepped streets into waterfalls.

The next two squares were created when the Venetian bastions that stood there were demolished in the nineteenth century. Kapodistrias Square is at the eastern end of Amalias Street near Three Admirals and features a white marble statue of the man, erected in 1932, just over one hundred years after his death. Confusing markings on the ground appear to show the location of the previous Dolfin bastion. It's barely a square at all really – more an open corner between Sidiras Merarchias and Syngrou streets. You get the impression that they needed to put the statue somewhere and this spot was available at the time. It's a pity. Kapodistrias had as much effect on the modern fabric of Nafplio as two competing empires did.

Philellinon Square in front of the Hotel Grande Bretagne came into being when the S. Theresa/Moschos bastion was demolished in 1866. The grey obelisk monument to the French philhellenes that now occupies its centre was erected in 1903.

Like Kapodistrias Square, it's more of a vacant corner. The expanse of pale marble makes it as bright and hot as a nuclear flash in summer and dull on an overcast winter day. Half-hidden under a tree in this square is a tiny bust of Mandó Mavrogenous, a remarkable woman (see **Heroes**) who lived in Nafplio during the fight for independence. It seems rather an insult that she should be tucked away here amid the foliage in someone else's square. I'm sure I don't remember noticing the bust the whole time I lived in Nafplio.

Other squares that are not really squares include Aristotle Onassis Square, a pedestrianised road behind the high school where the annual book fair occurs, and Lakka Square, now a car park in Psaromahala.

As we saw in **Mapping**, Nafplio's urban structure came together in a piecemeal fashion over history, dictated by topography and available land. Of all the town's squares, only Syntagma seems to have been intended as a square from the beginning. It's the only one that's rectangular, while the rest are defined by the position of various buildings that have come and gone over the years. Most of the modern squares (post-1850) were previously covered with other structures.

Three Admirals Square is an unusual case, tucked away as it was in the corners of Venetian walls. Was it always the empty space that offered itself in 1828 as the germ of a new capital? It seems odd that such a large area would have remained unused for so many hundreds of years. Engravings from the late sixteenth and early seventeenth centuries show houses in this corner, but that could have been artistic license. There is a record of coffee houses occupying the space that would soon have the *palataki* built on it, so we might infer that there was a small square here. There was, after all, a sea gate through the wall in the northwest corner of today's Three Admirals Square and a small open space would have made sense. The same thing existed inside the Land Gate.

Kapodistrias is credited with extending and widening Vasileos Konstantinos from its start in Syntagma Square to the edge of the town at Three Admirals. It's not too hard to imagine that whatever existed there previously was swept away by the new palace and the new urban programme. As for St. Spyridon Square, it looks like the kind of space where traffic would whorl and eddy as it entered the town – already a clear space in 1734 when the horse fountain was built. It's so prettily anonymous today, but we can imagine it as a place where newly arrived or departing travellers shared news of the road. Were there bandits in the Dervenakia pass? Was there impassable snow on the road to Tripolitsa? Were the Turks or Greeks encamped close to the town? Was the road to Argos boggy after the recent storms? Now, there is only silence and the very occasional drip of Aga Mahmoud's fountain.

CASTLES

Nafplio is physically characterised more than anything else by its castles: the Bourtzi, Acronafplio and Palamidi. Almost all visitors throughout history, whether arriving by sea or land, have remarked on the impressive aspect of the town's fortifications, which seemed to make it impervious to outside attack but in fact made it highly prone to attacking itself.

Of course, many other towns in Greece have Venetian fortifications (Corfu, Koroni, Methoni, Nafpaktos), but they don't have three different ones so aesthetically situated, rising in scale and punctuated by colossal bastions or towers. Each has its own history, stories and secrets. Let's begin with my favourite and follow in order of height.

The Bourtzi (meaning tower in Turkish) is the unofficial emblem of Nafplio – the one structure that instantly calls the place to mind, like Corfu's Mouse Island, the Acropolis in Athens or Navagio beach in Zakynthos with its shipwreck. It's been called jewel-like and Cubist by some writers and its aesthetic charm is undeniable. Seen from the *paralia* along Akti Miaouli, the castle appears to be a sculptural work rather than a defensive fortification. Its harmony of verticals and horizontals, its turrets and towers, its arches and swallow-tail crenellations seemed designed to delight the eye rather than repel invaders. The very lack of symmetry between its bastions and batteries occupies your gaze where perfection would soon tire it. Like a multi-part puzzle, the pieces somehow fit together though they don't seem to match.

From above, the Bourtzi looks like a ship leaving port, its concrete harbour a wake. This is because its western battery is pointed like a prow to deflect seaborne cannon fire. Squint a little and its footprint also looks like a WWI British Mark V tank (as featured in *Indiana Jones and the Last Crusade.*) It's a different aspect again from the north, where most ships couldn't pass due to the shallowness of the bay. Here, the profile is more saw-like thanks to a semi-circular barbican with more of those swallow tail merlons (the gaps in between are called crenels in fortification parlance.)

The Bourtzi is ever changing according to the light, the season, the time of day. I sat looking at it for a year. It is brown or grey in dull weather. It's beige in the midday glare and yellow, orange or gold in the setting sun. It's a silhouette against the twilight mountains and incandescent in its bathing floodlights. When heat haze blurs out the background, it seems closer. When the distant mountains are pin-sharp in the midwinter wind and their crests heavy with snow, it seems close enough to touch. It reaches out across the early morning bay as a mirrored image, while in the evening its floats on lilac-violet ripples. Waves occasionally crash against its rocky fringes, shooting spray.

Construction began around 1471 under the supervision of Antonio Gambello and the fortress was known to the Venetians as Castello dello Scoglia (of the rock) or Castello a Mare. They may also have heard the locals call it the island of St Nicholas or St Theodore, possibly from a previous chapel on the site. It would have been crenellated throughout with those swallow-tail battlements, which were designed to provide cover for archers. For the same reason, the central tower was originally higher to get a better angle on passing vessels. However, as military technology developed and gunpowder made cannons the weapon of choice, the central tower was lowered after 1525 and a new parapet with embrasures for heavy artillery was added.

What are we actually looking at from the shore? From the left (west), we start with the prow-like gun battery, which would have been full of cannon able to cover the sea approach through strategically positioned gunports. Next is the lower horizontal wall of a platform that occupies much of the castle's central portion and runs around most of the central tower.

Deep beneath the two floors of this odd-sided hexagonal tower is a cistern to collect rainwater and sustain soldiers during a siege. There's also a staircase running up the outside of its western face, though this can be hard to see from land. Continuing east, there are two low-level bastions on either side of a large, arched door. This was the sea gate, protected by the tower through which its staircase rises emerging onto the platform. It would have been difficult to land here unless the sea was relatively calm.

The arch to the left of the tower and the three arches to the right are modern additions to the castle from the 1930s. Finally, the eastern end is another battery, from which extends a thin modern quay and a landing stage to serve the small boats that sometimes take people out to the Bourtzi. It seems there may have been some kind of landing basin there when the castle was in defensive use.

The north part of the castle is rarely seen unless you can circle it by sea. It's also much changed from the original, with a skirt of quay built around it and some low, modern structures built against its sides. There's another entrance on this north side, presumably for when the wind made landings difficult at the south gate. This one is more highly fortified with a semi-circular, crenellated barbican around it, a gate tower above and a courtyard with gun ports inside. As an extra level of security, the Venetians built a *porporella*, an underwater obstacle of submerged stones, around the castle to stop ships coming close enough to land.

According to local sources, parts of the castle (probably the main tower) were built with removable stairs so that soldiers could withstand attack until the very last moment. Today, the east and west batteries and the main tower are closed to visitors so it's difficult to get a sense of what they're like inside.

It's easy to forget that this most picturesque of castles saw a lot of action. Its men and weapons were employed in the first siege of the Turks (1537-38), the Venetian retaking of Nafplio (1686), the Turkish comeback (1715), the War of Independence

(1821-29) and the WWII German invasion (1941). The latter two in particular caused a lot of damage to the structure. In 1821, an international group of soldiers stormed the Bourtzi to slay the sixty or so Turkish soldiers who would have been there, along with citizens who had fled there to escape the Greek bombardment from Palamidi. The Nazi forces, in their turn, spent a few days dropping bombs on the town and its defences, raking the walls and the sea with machine-gun fire from their Stukas.

The island ceased to be an active military fort around 1865, though a picture from the early twentieth century shows a uniformed man on duty. It was also, famously, the official residence of the state executioner and his assistant from around 1833. (See **Punishment**.)

Photos of the Bourtzi from the early 1900s show a very different outline. It looks like a ruin. The sharp lines and smooth surfaces have been eaten away by shell strikes, gunfire and erosion. It is pitted and crumbling into the sea. All of this changed in the 1930s, when German architect Wulf Schaefer oversaw the Bourtzi's renovation and transformation into a hotel. The clean lines of a cruise ship returned and new structures were sensitively added using the same (or indist-inguishable) stone.

The hotel operated from around 1939, was reconstructed and expanded in 1951 and closed in the mid-1970s, when the government refused to renew its lease. There's scant evidence of what the hotel was like, though a few tantalising glimpses of it appear through history. The English writer Dorothy Ratcliffe was one of the first guests and wrote about the hotel in her book *News of Persephone* (1939). Patrick Leigh Fermor stayed there with his family and was pictured by his wife sunbathing atop one of the batteries. Greek singer and politician Nana Mouskouri consummated her first marriage there with her second husband Jules Dassin in 1966.

The hotel has been described by people who saw it as charming, elegant and deluxe. It had just twelve rooms, situated in the east and west batteries, plus a restaurant. Few photos survive, but the main group of characters in the 1958 Greek film *The Man on the Train* stay at the hotel and we get to see the interior. The décor of the bedrooms features partial wood panelling and white plaster laid thick around each individual stone for a strange "Swiss cheese" effect. Iron-railed balconies with pot plants are visible through the heavy masonry walls, while each room has a door with a square of frosted glass. Despite the general luxury, each bathroom shower has an opaque plastic curtain (through which we see some rather risqué female silhouette work from director Dimos Dimopoulos).

Patrick Leigh Fermor and Nana Mouskouri may have been the most famous residents, but the Bourtzi's most flamboyant guests came in 1941 when the German pilots from Argos airfield were billeted in Nafplio's best and newest accommodation. The thirty Luftwaffe flyboys (two or more to a room) were soon engaged in May's Battle of Crete, taking their Bf 109s, Bf 110s and Stuka dive-bombers across the Aegean daily. They'd rise early each morning and take trucks to Argos. Each evening, they'd return and spend the evenings partying on the 400-year-old terraces – drinking, dancing, smoking. Strains of laughter, champagne corks and *Lili Marlene* drifted across the glassy harbour and around the burned-out wreck of the troopship Ulster Prince to the darkened curfew streets of the old town. Fewer of the initial thirty returned each evening, having gone down in flames over Souda or Heraklion. Others lay entombed in their cockpits at the bottom of the sea. Finally, there were just twelve: singing harder, drinking more, laughing with tears in their eyes. Live now, for tomorrow we die.

After the hotel ceased operation in the mid-1970s, the Bourtzi was briefly a café that clearly relied too heavily on transport to and from the town quay. All commercial use ended in the 1990s, apart from the occasional trips made by small boats from the quay on the edge of Philhellinon Square. I went on one of these in the summer of 1999 and it was a largely depressing experience. The military architecture remains impressive, especially if you like to take black-and-white photos. The view from the west battery at sunset is astounding. But the place was filthy: litter piled in corners, the smell of urine and worse, a particularly large and healthy looking rat scuttling along the base of a wall. Was this what 500 years of illustrious service had come to? A stone trashcan? A fortified toilet?

There are currently plans to renovate and turn the castle into a museum. That would be great, but I wouldn't hold your breath. If other stories in this book demonstrate a pattern, it's that change in Nafplio can take anywhere between twenty and a hundred years.

Acronafplio is something of a paradox. I was once up there sitting by the clock tower, looking out over the old town's roofs, when an American tourist called to me from the cobbled road. "Excuse me? Do you speak English? We're looking for the castle."

My answer, inevitably, was: "You're standing on it." The truth is that very little remains of Nafplio's acropolis when you consider how much construction used to exist here. The walls and towers you see from below suggest that there must be a whole fortified complex up here, but then you take the weaving road up past Arvanitia and suddenly you've arrived at the Nafplia Palace hotel. Where was the castle in between? What's left today is mostly the perimeter walls and a few scraps of what used to stand here. Satellite views show an expanse of scrubby brown earth and the trace footprints of buildings fallen or demolished over seven or eight hundred years.

This is to be expected. Every new empire in Nafplio focused its building and rebuilding on Acronafplio. First forts, then houses, then forts again, then barracks and prisons and hotels – everything replacing everything else. And seasons of relentless bombardment in between. Picturing Acronafplio has to be a process of historical reconstruction.

The earliest structure on the hill is a stretch of polygonal wall, dating from the third century BC, that originally stretched from the peninsula's western tip and along the crest above what would one day become the old town. The ancient entrance gate has long been absorbed into sloping earthwork and high walls of Acronafplio's eastern edge, where we now see a small parking area on the tight upwards turn after passing the long-derelict Xenia hotel.

The Byzantines simply built on top of these walls and put their entrance to the acropolis in the same place, adding three semi-circular towers in the third and fourth centuries AD. Two of these flanked the main gate. So Nafplio would remain for about nine hundred years hence until the coming of the Franks in 1212.

Unusually for Nafplio, the invaders agreed to share the peninsula with the Byzantines. At this time, remember, Acronafplio was Nafplio. No lower town existed – only sea and possibly swamp. Two castles were thus established, the eastern third of the acropolis going to the Franks and the remaining western two thirds to the Byzantine Greeks. To be on the safe side, the Franks built a north-south wall between their part and their neighbours'. There was, admittedly, a gate between the two for free movement, but also a tall Frankish tower by the gate in case arrows needed to be fired. The stub of this tower remains (and close by it a later Venetian pyramid-roofed powder magazine). The northern end of the Franks' wall also had a tower, but this was later turned into the campanile of the Venetian church of San Marco. The church has gone but the campanile remains as the clock tower looking over the old town. I spent many an hour sitting up there, thinking impressive thoughts and hoping a beautiful girl might walk by and ask me about them. Instead, I was asked, "Where's the castle?"

One question of cohabitation lingers. Did the Greeks have to enter the east gate as they always had and pass through the Frankish part to reach their own? It wouldn't have made much sense security-wise. Allan Brooks discusses the possibility of a gate in what is now an overgrown patch by the northwest corner of the Nafplia Palace property. There is a walled-up Venetian gate here in the angled wall of the Dolfin demibastion, but it could stand on the site of an earlier Byzantine structure.

One wonderful mystery of the Frankish building programme was connected to the additional work they did on the eastern gate around 1291-1311. We can see the towers today by the small parking spot, but the gate work involved decorating the interior with a spectacular series of frescoes that the inhabitants enjoyed for around 150 years as they entered or left the acropolis. The Venetians blocked up this gate in 1463, possibly preferring the disputed north gate down to the port and nascent town. The frescoes then passed entirely out of memory. The Venetians were ousted in 1540 by the Turks and would not return again until 1686, by which time anyone who had known of the frescoes was long dead. They remained buried all through the second Turkish occupation, the War of Independence and the Nazi bombs.

The gate itself was unknown in modern times until 1935, when the German architect Wulf Schaefer surveyed the town's historic structures. WWII interrupted that project and it wasn't until 1957 that the gate chamber was excavated and the frescoes seen for the first time in 650 years. Depicting saints and warriors, they retained almost all of their colour, clarity and brilliance. How they remained in such good condition during 150 years of use – horses, carts, flamed illumination, people brushing them – is another mystery entirely, unless the population of Frankish Acronafplio was minimal. The gate has been restored and you can find it just opposite the scenic Venetian gate (see below) to peek through a metal grille at the remains of the frescoes.

The Venetians initially did little other than patch up the existing walls when they arrived in the fourteenth century. When war broke out with the Turks in 1463, however, it was time to make some changes. The east gate (with the frescoes) was bricked up and filled with soil, while the whole eastern end of Acronafplio became a steep, angled earthwork around the Frankish towers to deflect cannon shots. The Venetians then built a new gate overlooking the protecting southern cliffs. It's now a popular photo spot on the left-hand side of the Acronafplio road, just after the lookout spot above Arvanitia beach. Many believe it must have been a window because it just sits on the edge of the precipice, its stairway or supporting structure having tumbled away into the sea.

The next Venetian construction work was a defensive wall across the width of Acronafplio: the Gambello traverse. You can see it on the left when looking up the road from the aforementioned gate: a low semi-circular barbican and an imposingly lofty, angled wall with a swallow-tail parapet. The entrance was within this southern/left-hand complex and you can still venture inside the arched gate if you don't mind litter, rats and toilet paper. I often used to walk through these fortifications and sit on the artillery platform looking out at the spectacular view. Did the Venetian soldiers appreciate it as much, or were they bored watching the sea day after day for an invasion that might never come?

There was also an additional concealed gate at the other (town) side of the traverse. This has been mostly destroyed by the curve of the modern road but if you look down, you'll see the top of its arch at ground level. What appears to be a drainage hole was a secret entrance.

The biggest Venetian project of this period was a considerable extension of Acronafplio itself to the east: the Castel del Toro. Previously, the hill had effectively ended with the east gate of the Byzantines and Franks. New perimeter walls were added, extending the acropolis fortifications towards a huge round tower at the hill's new easternmost point. You pass this tower on the way to the Xenia hotel from the Arvanitia car park. A flight of steps leads up to its barred door from the road, though these southern walls would originally have been along the top of the cliff overlooking the shore.

A fortified gate was also built into the Castel del Toro on the opposite, north side with access down to the town. The work took some time and may have lasted from around 1470 to 1482. It's still there (defaced with graffiti by a moron) beside the little car park below the eastern earthworks. You can additionally access it from the town by taking the stepped street up from St. Spyridon Square (by the Turkish fountain), passing the Catholic church on your right then turning left at the top of the stairs. The arched gate with a carved lion of St Mark and shield above it invites you into a vaulted passage, which has a "murder hole" directly above your head for the pouring of hot oil or dropping of rocks on invaders. Was this ever used on an unfortunate Turk, Venetian or Greek? Did a body once lie on this spot with his skull smashed in or writhing in flames?

The arrival of the Turks in 1540 resulted in relatively little work on the fortifications. It was hardly necessary after the frenzied building programme of the Venetians. Rather Acronafplio, named *Its-Kale*, "inner castle," by the Turks, accumulated houses: around 200 with clay-tile roofs according to Turkish visitor Evliya Çelebi in 1667. There was also a mosque with a minaret on the hill.

The re-arrival of the Venetians in 1686 involved a siege and bombardment from Palamidi, which would have damaged some of the same fortifications they had built a hundred years earlier. These had to be repaired, and more were added: an artillery platform above the old east wall, a battery on the south side of the Castel del Toro, a large barracks on the site of today's Nafplia Palace hotel, and the Grimani bastion built over the end of the Castel del Toro (see **Mapping**). I recommend Allan Brooks's book for more detail on the military engineering involved in these fortifications.

Perhaps the most interesting Acronafplio addition of this period was the new monumental north gate known as the Sagredo gate after Agostino Sagredo and situated immediately below today's Nafplia Palace hotel. Its construction required a long stairway from the centre of the lower town, the last stretch leaping over rocks in a series of arches. The steps remain, taking you up to a platform with two flanking, pyramid-capped pillars in front of an arched gate. A pediment sits atop it and there's a mess of infantile graffiti all over it. It's not possible to enter, but a stepped, vaulted corridor within the gate begins immediately to the right and continues upwards through Acronafplio's walls to what would have been the site of the 1690s barracks. It's likely that the corridor originally belonged to the walled-up gate in the Dolfin demibastion and it remains visible from inside the hotel grounds.

At the far western end of the peninsula atop towering cliffs, the Venetians also added a gun battery and a gate known as the Morosini gate, which led down to the sea via a vertiginous stairway. This was added to provide direct access to the sea from Acronafplio at a time when the inner harbour was most likely silted up. The arched gate is today walled closed.

Despite all of these fortifications, the Turks took Acronafplio again in 1715, just a couple of years after many of the new structures had been completed. Again the Turks would build atop the hill. As well as erecting mosques and houses, they reinforced their *Its-Kale* and Palamidi with 400 cannon, determined to keep it in their hands this time. But the next besiegers wouldn't be the Venetians, and nor would they arrive for another hundred years.

Cue 1821. Cannonballs again assailed Acronafplio from Palamidi and the Greeks took back the peninsula taken from them in 1212 by the Franks. Theodoros Kolokotronis famously raised the flag of freedom on the ramparts before going off for a spot of murderous looting. A new age was about to begin for the hill.

Significant nineteenth-century change came with the arrival of the new governor Ioannis Kapodistrias in 1828. German officer Carl Wilhelm von Heideck took over as commander of Nafplio's military and quickly assigned Acronafplio to fifty Spetziot soldiers under Captain Nikolaos Goudi. The first priority was to repair the defences destroyed in the 1821 siege against the Turks and in the 1827 civil chaos (see **War**). Then they needed a military hospital. The town hospital in Psaromahala (see **Absence**) had been built in the fourteenth century and, though much repaired, was straining to serve even the civilian population of a town famed for its fevers and plagues.

With Nafplio now the nation's first capital and also a major military base, it needed a hospital for its troops.

Heideck chose Acronafplio due to its good air and presumably because there wasn't much space inside the old town. The site of the two-storey hospital appears to have been a semi-ruined Venetian barracks, which would have offered ready foundations and a good location in relation to Acronafplio's gates. Construction was quick and the hospital was in operation by August 1828. Just as well, because business was brisk. More than one hundred people per month were being admitted by December and more staff had to be employed. The town's central pharmacy also had its head-quarters here.

One historical document gives us a fascinating glimpse into these vanished lives. In March 1831, the hospital's nurses included Nikolaos, Ioannis, and Georgios. Spyraina and Georgina were the cooks, Violeta the dishwasher and Dimitrios was the mule driver. The foreman of the institution was responsible for day-to-day operation, orderliness, financial management and the movement of patients. All of them have been dead for more than a hundred years, but we might imagine poor Violeta scrubbing *fasolada* from the bowls, Nikolaos changing a bandage and Dimitrios wielding the switch to encourage his mules up through the Sagredo gate.

Heideck's solutions for funding the hospital without dipping excessively into state funding were innovative if perhaps a little Germanic in their efficiency. Sick soldiers would have a part of their pay docked while they were patients and a part of the bread intended for them would instead be sold. It was probably unpopular among the men, who might have mutinied if they'd felt better. Regardless, the hospital had been commandeered for the exclusive use of French troops by May 1832.

The arrival of King Otto in 1833 saw another burst of construction. He added to the military hospital and built more barracks atop Acronafplio. Even after moving to Athens, the king ordered the general repair of all the fortifications and bastions of Acronafplio, plus new cannon to equip them. This seemed to make sense, given Nafplio's history, but the next attack would not come for 108 years and by then the whole history of warfare had changed. The German attack of 1941 would come from the sky and in armoured, petrol-driven vehicles – something the Turks, Venetians and revolutionary Greeks could never have imagined.

King George I of Greece came to the throne in 1865 and from this we might date Nafplio's switch to a militarised penal colony. As well as adding more barracks and large rainwater collection tanks to Acronafplio, he began to create more prisons in addition to those of Palamidi. Another large prison was added in 1884. What had for centuries been a defensive acropolis of last resort was now a walled island of detention for military and political prisoners, or prisoners of war from the various fronts Greece fought on.

The profile stayed the same during the WWII occupation, with the Germans adding modern gun emplacements, an underground bunker and an observation post on the cliff edge.

All of this would change, as it always had. The modern road up through Acronafplio was built in 1935, during which all surface structures of the Castel del Toro were demolished, leaving a largely flat area. This site was then almost totally covered by the now derelict Xenia hotel in 1961. Indeed, a new era of hotel construction cleared away the majority of Acronafplio buildings (regardless of their historical interest or significance).

There's nothing left of the military hospital or the Venetian barracks. Look at a satellite image of the peninsula and you'll see traces of the Frankish north-south dividing wall with its ruined tower, the Venetian powder magazine and some low-level scrappy foundations. Continue on the road past the Nafplia Palace and you'll reach a turning spot with a hopeful H painted on it for helicopters. Maybe some do land here occasionally (Athens celebrities visiting for the weekend?) but the place is more commonly used by young people who come here to make out.

Among the pleasures of today's Acronafplio is exploring what's left. You can walk up through the town and enter via the Castel del Toro gate, or ascend the road from the Arvanitia car park. If you don't mind entering the long grass, the litter-choked hole and the occasional extemporised toilet, you can pass through the overgrown "garden" of the Xenia hotel to the Castel del Toro complex and enter its warren of fifteenth-century staircases and tunnels, which in turn will take you to the sixteenth-century convolutions of the Grimani bastion. The Gambello traverse offers similar entertainment, beyond which you can kick around in the dry scrub, stumbling (sometimes literally) over the foundations of a Frankish tower or WWII circular gun emplacement.

There's a genuine sense of Indiana Jones style adventure in entering such spaces, though you do so at your own risk. Nobody knows what subsidence and the occasional earthquake have done to the inside of the hill over a thousand years. If that seems too risky, climb the steps to the Sagredo gate from the Hotel Leto in Psaromahala, where you'll also see a stretch of third-century BC wall.

The views from Acronafplio are also amazing. As you emerge from the Castel del Toro gate, you can look to your left over the rooftops of the old town. Walk up and around the bend for an aerial view over Arvanitia beach and the Argolic Gulf, then continue up to the bell tower for another great old-town view. The vista from the clock tower just further round the bend is higher still, looking down on Syntagma Square. It's a route I used to follow a few times each week for exercise and inspiration. Thereafter, you can retrace your steps or continue to the Nafplia Palace and take one of the two lifts down to the subterranean passage that brings you out at Lakka Square.

Your first glimpse of Nafplio is Palamidi. You see it even before you arrive at Argos on the road from Athens. Its castle complex of eight forts joined by huge walls hugs the contours of the peak and can look like some colossal mythological beast sleeping there. I spent many summer evenings sitting in cafes and waiting for the rays of the setting sun to strike the hill, turning it yellow, copper, brass and finally into a dark carmine ember. Then the floodlights snap on and it seems suddenly to hover in the sky – an alien craft observing the town.

Now, as in the past, the easiest way up to the castle is the road that approaches from the south. This is where Venetian field marshal Königsmark and later the Turks attacked in 1686 and 1715 (see **War**). Arrive in the car park today and you first face the Epaminondas fort that was unfinished when the Turks arrived in 1715. The large, arched entrance gate is partially concealed by the edge of its protecting bastion, which originally would have appeared much taller and imposing. The car park has been built up and around it, widening the area before the gate.

The vaulted gate passage turns to the left and you go through a series of massive gun platforms to the interior. What lies within Palamidi is a complex system of military engineering that I'm not going to explain in detail. Allan Brooks knows more and has done it better in his book, which I recommend to anyone who wants to identify each arch and stairway. Here's a general guide.

Turn immediately to the left, climb the hill, then turn left again by the imposing face of the Fort Themistokles bastion – in the direction you just arrived from by car – and you'll pass through the *Doppia Tenaglia* (Fort Achilles): a large and apparently empty rectangular space. It was here that the Turks exploded a mine in 1715 and terrified the resident Venetian soldiers sufficiently that they all ran down to the town, voluntarily abandoning the Peloponnese's strongest castle so it could bombard them in Acronafplio.

Continue in the same direction (southwards) and you reach the Turkish bastion (Fort Phokion). Why the multiple names? The Venetians named the forts after their commanders, but the Greeks changed these names after the War Of Independence to recognise Greek heroes. The Turkish bastion was built after 1715 to close the remaining weak point in the castle's fortifications, possibly using the Venetians' uncompleted plans. Importantly, the guns point in the direction from which Königsmark had invaded in 1686 and taken the Ottoman held castle. There's not much to see today apart from cactus, dry grass and a glimpse of a square door leading to an underground cistern. This part of the castle has barely been touched for hundreds of years.

Rather than retrace our path to the main entrance, let's instead teleport back down to the town and approach Palamidi as the adventurous do: up its famous staircase of 999 steps. Is the number correct? Others claim 857, but it depends what you call a step and exactly where you start counting – if you care. You may also read some fanciful story about Theodore Kolokotronis breaking the thousandth step with his horse's hoof, though it's not entirely clear why he would ride a horse up 1000 steps or position himself at the top and start jumping the animal around.

The steps begin just after the café/bar on Polyzoidou Street, which leads up from 25 Martiou to the Arvanitia car park. Note that the covered tunnel structure you see rising up the lower slopes is not the staircase, as many new arrivals assume. It's a caponier – a structure from which gunners could cover the Land Gate approach to the town. I ventured inside it one winter day in 1999 and found it full of thousands of plastic bottles, drinks cans and used toilet paper.

The stone staircase existed before the Venetians built the main castle complex in the eighteenth century, although the initial stretch dates from 1935 when the road was built. Previously, the stairway was more direct and started from beside the Grimani bastion. Today's route takes you through an arch and towards the caponier before starting to zig zag up and over the rocks. The views from the stairs are astounding and ever changing as you switch direction and rise – a mere promise of what awaits you on the battlements.

Almost at the top, you face an arched gate built into the base of the Maschio tower. This was the defensive lower entrance. From here, you begin to ascend the grand stairway to the main castle.

The small pyramid-roofed building you see as you ascend is an old Venetian powder magazine, situated separately to avoid getting caught by fires and roofed in this way to deflect cannonballs. The staircase eventually takes you alongside the structure, which is further surrounded by a protecting wall. Its original iron shutters are still over the windows. There is a near-identical twin magazine on Acronafplio.

A ramp from the third landing leads up to the wall walk, but you'll need to enter by the main gate if you want to see inside the castle. The main, arched door is found at the end of the final landing, whose stones are polished by hundreds of thousands of visitors over the last few centuries. It's safe to say that more people have climbed these stairs and entered the castle in the last hundred years than in the previous five hundred. This particular route would historically have been used only for direct pedestrian access to the town. All other supplies and large bodies of men would have gone up the south route by horse, mule and cart.

On entering the castle, you're immediately in the walled Venetian parade ground with its double row of loopholes for muskets. The colossal fortification beside you is the St Girado bastion/Fort Andreas, which has its own large, arched entrance gate to the north, partially concealed behind a bastion edge. A relief carving of the lion of St Mark sits above the arch, but this entrance was designed specifically for dissuading, then killing, unwanted visitors. It has a murder hole like the Castel del Toro gate on Acronafplio and used a portcullis and loopholes at the end of its passage to fire on invaders inside. The bell tower of the nineteenth-century church sits atop the gate. Fort Andreas is essentially a massive artillery platform covering the vulnerable east and south approaches (the modern road and traditional invasion spot).

According to popular lore, Theodoros Kolokotronis was imprisoned in a tiny, pitch-black cell inside Fort Andreas. There's even a sign pointing to the cell door. This particular part of the castle did operate as a prison in the nineteenth century but the purported Kolokotronis cell looks nothing like any of the others on Palamidi. It was probably a storage area that some enterprising guard a hundred years ago told gullible visitors was the site of Kolokotronis's cruel punishment. People were obviously asking, and nobody seemed to know for sure where it had been. Even Kolokotronis himself wasn't specific in his memoirs, though we do know he shared it with another man. You can imagine the conversations visitors had with the guards back then: "Kolokotronis? Ah, yes. He was kept here in this tiny dark hole. If you'd like to enter, I can sell you a candle for ten lepta . . ." The consensus among historians is that he was held in the Miltiades bastion, which was a dedicated prison block in the nineteenth century.

Though it all seems like one castle, it was conceived as multiple forts. The St Agostino/Themistocles fort begins where the St Girado bastion ends, stretching up along the ridge to a huge gun platform at its highest point. Two Venetian barracks were built along this stretch but they were demolished in the 1950s and barely a trace remains. The walls between the two forts are not especially high because they're protected by the geography of the hill. Its gun batteries point to the southwest – again, the vulnerable rear approach.

This is pretty much the Palamidi experience: walking from fort to fort, climbing steps, exploring doorways, peering through loopholes and gazing into murky cisterns. It's a mystery to most. You really need a detailed map and some good description to understand what you're looking at, which also means understanding the difference between a revetment and an embrasure, a casement and a terreplein. It's all military architecture. The pleasure for most people is feeling the history in the gigantic walls and getting lost inside the massy stone labyrinth. It's barely possible to imagine hundreds of cannons firing at an invading fleet or a besieging army. The air would have been white with smoke, sharp with gunpowder and totally deafening. The occasional cannon may have been badly cast or previously damaged and would explode in a burst of superheated bronze shrapnel.

Life must have been very dull for the soldiers, whose life (as now) was often a case of simply waiting for the next enemy action. History has shown that the majority of them waited for their whole lives, for generations, between sieges. In the meantime, their days were occupied with the soldier's routine: reveille, drills, duties, watches. The views were spectacular, but these men were eagles above the world, floating, drifting with the clouds as nothing happened year after year. They paced the walls. They stood in sentry boxes. The cannons stayed mostly silent unless, rarely, someone important visited and there was a salute.

Palamidi was always separate from the town – a no-go zone for the general public. It hadn't been the basis of the town as Acronafplio once had. When early visitors came in the late eighteenth and nineteenth centuries, they had to request permission from the Turkish or Greek authorities to enter this sensitive and largely secret military base. Before the age of flight, only the people officially allowed up here knew what it looked like. Even when permission was granted, it wasn't always to the entire site. The Miltiades fort, for example, was always a particularly secretive part of the castle.

Miltiades (known to the Venetians as the *bastione staccato*) is roughly in front of you if you enter from the upper car park and to the east of forts Andreas and Themistocles. It is a colossal pentagonal bastion whose gun batteries cover the land approach and the other forts to its west in case they were overrun. The bastion is not always open to the public, perhaps because it's unsafe, or perhaps because of its problematic political history (see **Punishment**).

An outer door leads to the north courtyard, from where the main gate takes you into the inner courtyard. This was originally an open space but walls were added from the nineteenth century to create cells and observation decks for the prison guards. You can also see the tall, walled up arches with the doors and circular windows of yet more cells. Perhaps this fort was chosen as a prison block because it was distant from the others and further away from everything, even more remote than the Bourtzi. An elaborate system of drainage channels around the fort gathered all rainwater that fell and carried it to a large cistern. It's strange to think of the guards and prisoners filling a cup in August that had fallen from the sky in April or May.

Imagine how it must have felt for the prisoners approaching these lofty, impenetrable walls built for war – these walls that derived from imperial might. The men would have arrived on foot after entering the main gate from the road and felt the masonry rise around them. This would be their world for the next twenty years or until death – whichever came first. Some faced execution. The only sky they'd see for decades was the rectangle above the inner courtyard. Life would continue down in the town. Perhaps the occasional smell would rise on the breeze to torture them with memories of liberty: Easter's roast lamb, hot coffee beans, citrus fruit being loaded at the dock – just a scented filament in the air. Then gone.

Fort Leonidas is the lowest of the castle's separate units, lying to the north of Miltiades and known to the Venetians as the *piattaforma*. It was (guess what?) another gun battery, with its cannons ominously trained over the new town. The area would have been largely unoccupied in the eighteenth century however, and was where any invading army would have to approach or encamp. There are three enormous Venetian cisterns here, which would have served the castle and possibly also the lower town in times of need.

Palamidi remained a purely military base and prison complex long into the early twentieth century. It wasn't designated a tourist site until 1962 and repairs to the fabric were not made until 1969. Today, it is one of the most complete examples of Venetian military architecture anywhere and the views are spectacular at virtually every turn.

I remember once remarking to my students (presumably during a rare lull in the screaming chaos) that I'd been up to Palamidi the previous weekend. "Why?" they asked me. Why would I do something like that? Many of them had never been up there – not even on a school trip – though there was an annual excursion to Argos's castle, Larissa, which has a monastery close by. Monasteries are different; they deserve a visit, even if none of the kids had any serious interest in religion. Neither had any of them been to the Bourtzi on a boat. Maybe children are the same everywhere, but they had very little interest in the remarkable history of their town and the physical evidence of it all over the place. They knew Theodoros Kolokotronis's name because it has vaguely rude connotations in Greek (wiping one's bottom with a rock?).

But I shouldn't judge. It was enough for me at the time to know roughly which structures were Venetian or Turkish and to appreciate the general quality of "oldness." Later, I'd understand that around seventy per cent of my understanding of Nafplio's history was actually the product of my overactive imagination.

PLEASURES

Modern Nafplio is a destination known for its pleasures. For this reason, and also because of its relative proximity to Athens, it's one of the few Peloponnesian towns that has high visitor numbers all year round. The food and the drink are not hugely different or better than any other place in Greece – it's the ambience that keeps people coming.

Part of Nafplio's special character is its historic fabric. Many Greek towns have their Byzantine church, their old mosque, their castle, their classical site, but few have so many of these things in such a small area (and with multiple famous ancient sites just a few minutes away). You stroll on marble paved streets beneath vivid bougainvillea and neoclassical balconies, and suddenly you're in a medieval square or on the steps of a mosque. You pass an Ottoman fountain. You look up at Venetian fortifications and you get lost in tiny Byzantine alleys joined by staircase streets. Here is Greece's first parliament. Here is a spot where Kolokotronis once stood or died. These are the steps that Staikopoulos climbed to victory and eternal fame. It can seem like a historical theme park: all of Greece's history condensed into one small peninsula. It's romantic. It's interesting. It's beautiful.

And that's just for the Greeks, who are already accustomed to Mediterranean charm. To the peoples of continental Europe, Nafplio can seem almost absurdly attractive. To sit and drink a coffee in Syntagma Square by the museum or on the *paralia* looking out at the Bourtzi is a genuine travel experience. There are so many spots in the town where you pause and think quite seriously that you'd like to give up your job and move here forever just to see these sights every day.

Nafplio hasn't always been so attractive, as you'll see in the rest of this book, but it has always had its pleasures. Since visitors first started coming, they have noted the coffee shops where merchants and soldiers would smoke and drink. Friedrich Tietz in the early 1830s mentioned one such café built like an Italian villa and situated in a garden just outside the Land Gate. It was first named Café Kapo D'Istrias but later became Café Liberal. There's still a café on the same site today though it doesn't look like an Italian villa. French writer Lamartine noted the coffee houses in the port area that were built on stilts extending into the sea. He wrote: "These floating coffee houses and platforms are occupied by several hundred Greeks wearing the most pretentious and also the dirtiest costumes." He wasn't easily impressed.

Most of the early foreign visitors to Greece were unfamiliar with Greek cuisine and ingredients, gazing in horror at sea urchins, squid and octopus. They tended to eat at the French and Bavarian restaurants established to serve the various international soldiery. Like the British budget tourists who arrived in the 1980s, they wanted to eat fried eggs and chips rather than *spetzofai* or *kokoretsi*. Mousaka was OK because it looked a little like shepherd's pie, while *keftedes* were quite similar to burgers. It's funny to think that there's now barely a restaurant in Austria or Britain that doesn't sell feta cheese or *tzatziki*.

Obviously, there's a difference between visiting and living in a place. Yes, the ambience remains charming and there are always great places to eat and drink. But that soon becomes your normality. So what are Nafplio's day to day pleasures?

Walking is an underrated Nafplio activity, made pleasurable by the general lack of traffic in the old town. You park at the port or get off the bus and then you're mostly free to stroll aimlessly, discovering streets and shops and cafés. Walking up to Acronafplio and around the battlements is easy, with plenty of things to explore and places to stop. A climb up to Palamidi is more demanding but worth it for the magnificent views.

The evening stroll has long been a classic Mediterranean ritual. In Italy, it's the *passeggiata*. In Spain, it's the *paseo*. In

Greece, it's the *volta*. You don't need to have a purpose or destination – you walk to show yourself as part of the town and to encounter other people doing the same thing. Traditionally, it was a way of viewing and selecting future partners. Mothers would take out their primped and prettified daughters to show them off, while men would prance and preen and pretend they didn't know they were being watched. In some Greek villages today, the men gravitate towards one area while the women and children go to another. "Visiting parties" then move between the two.

Increasingly in recent years, older Greeks have taken to walking as exercise – probably on the advice of their doctors. The Mediterranean diet is great, but not if you spend the whole time at home watching TV or sitting in a bar with a cigarette and a *tsipuro*. If you go out strolling early in Nafplio, you may encounter the occasional paunchy man, his gut tautly encased in sporty Lycra, or a couple of grandmothers wearing jogging shoes as they gossip without pause.

Nafplio has a couple of good places for a more sustained stroll. The first of these is the coast walk, which can begin below the Five Brothers bastion and continues below the cliffs towards Arvanitia beach (see **Tour**). The creation of this path was funded in 1895 by the Archbishop of Argos, Nikandros Delouka. His aim was to give local people a place for a pleasant stroll outside the town. Part of the route involved creating an arch through the rock, a task that fell to a young lieutenant engineer named Ioannis Metaxas, the same who went on to become Greece's virulently anti-communist and authoritarian prime minister of the 1930s. Perhaps for this reason some people still call the arch the 'despot's cave.'

The track was and is prone to erosion and assault from the sea. I remember walking along it in mid-winter 1998 and seeing waves breaking over the lanterns of the lamp posts near the arch. The path was repaired in 1926 and widened so a small car could pass, but it wasn't paved until the mid-1980s.

In 2010, two large boulders of around two cubic metres rolled down the cliffs during a January rainstorm. It happened at night and nobody was harmed, but the coast walk was closed thereafter and barriers were set up to prevent access. A geological study showed that large parts of the walk, particularly from the sea-swimming pool to the light beacon, are considered very dangerous and prone to rock falls. The suggestion was to add wire-mesh barriers above approximately half of the path to protect walkers, though these nets would impair the natural aesthetics of the area. It hasn't happened yet.

On 14 August 2019, part of the cliff behind Arvanitia beach collapsed and tumbled onto the path, sending up huge dust clouds. Some people filmed it and uploaded it. The faulty barriers remain in situ, but walkers continue to habitually step around them and use the path as they always have. I've done the same because I love the route. If people are crushed by a rock fall, it's their own fault because they passed the barriers, ignored the signs and accepted the risk – an eminently Nafpliot solution.

The walk offers gorgeous views down the Argolic gulf and of the opposite coast down to Astros. In winter, the mountains of Arcadia are heavy with snow, the air is sharp and the visibility astounding. On arrival at the Arvanitia car park, you can loop back down to the town and arrive near the Land Gate or you can continue along the coast, which is what you should do.

The next stretch takes you past the ruined building beside the beach and onto a rough gravel track lined with pine trees, eucalyptus, laurel and fragrant bushes whose combined scent is intoxicating. This continues straight for a while, high above the sea, then dips to a tiny and usually deserted pebble beach with transparent water. The path rises again from here and continues to Karathonas beach, a wide swathe of gritty sand that has remained a virtually undeveloped wilderness for decades. When I lived in Nafplio, there was no bar or café here, only the concrete ruin of an abandoned building at the northern limit. In winter, barely a soul visits. I was never really a beach person when I lived in Greece (or now). I couldn't see the point of going somewhere to lie down on some sand and do nothing. Swimming in a pool is cleaner and more convenient. Still, I walked to Karathonas regularly during the colder months for exercise, an eight to ten kilometre round trip. I also came to catch octopus early in the spring and summer mornings, swimming in the shallow water and pulling the animals by hand from under rocks or from their "gardens" to prepare and cook them later at home.

Many visiting beachgoers don't know that there is a "secret" church inside the cliffs behind the beach. Look for a flash of white paint among the crags and head towards it. A door (if open) leads inside a natural cave whose tortured rocky contours have been turned into a tiny, incense-scented Orthodox church complete with icons and candles. There's also another small chapel at the southern end of Karathonas where the track ends.

One final image from the coast walk. In 1482, during the first Venetian period, seven ships arrived at Nafplio after being caught and damaged in a storm. Since the port didn't have ship-repairing facilities, the vessels were hauled up onto the sand at Karathonas to be repaired, their crews camping wild in the manner of today's campervan nomads. It's something to imagine as you lie on your sun lounger or towel.

Another popular place for strolling in Nafplio is Kolokotronis Park between the old town and the new town, roughly from Polyzidou Street to the *endekati* junction. This area was under the sea or was swampland for much of the town's history, with solid earth only between the Land Gate and Aria along the foot of Palamidi. It was here, in peacetime, that the locals would stroll during the evenings, following the dusty, tree-lined road towards Prónoia.

The townsfolk would sit on rocks in the shade talking, listening to a musician, gossiping and flirtatiously watching each other. The warriors would prance and charge their horses, showing off their skills in their *fustanellas*, fezzes and embroidered tunics. On Sundays after church, the ladies would walk in their jewellery and their fine dresses. King Otto would also occasionally ride out, splendid but impossibly young in his blue uniform, accompanied by his guard of lancers and followed by the three beautiful daughters of Count Armansperg.

The area outside the Land Gate developed slowly, partly because it was conceived by the Venetians explicitly as a killing zone. The guns of the Dolfin bastion to the north, the Grimani bastion to the south, the caponier at Palamidi's feet and the gun battery above the gate itself were all pointed at this terrain. Everyone approached the town from this direction, but so would an invading army. It made sense to keep the surface area small for maximum artillery annihilation.

The Turks added more soil to the area and attempted to create some kind of park or garden. Turkish traveller Evliya Çelebi commented in 1668 that the area outside the gate was dedicated to commerce, with fifty shops and a large bazaar each Sunday. Alas, it became a no-man's land after the Venetian walls came down during the first decades of the twentieth century. Photos show a featureless rubble field, although one very early picture seems to feature a cooperage on the site with a large pile of barrels stacked nearby. Executions were also carried out here on occasion, either with a guillotine or by firing squad.

With the walls coming down, there was more reason to extend the land towards the sea for additional building space. Perhaps more importantly, the town's increased importance as Greece's second city necessitated a train station, which was built in 1885 and started its first services to Athens via Argos and Corinth in 1886. Early photos show crowds of people waiting or disembarking from these regular trains, but what they faced on leaving the platform was a stretch of barren, undeveloped land up to the Land Gate. When Englishwoman Isabel Armstrong arrived by train in the late 1890s, she found the Land Gate "transformed into a hanging garden of campanulas" as the old Venetian walls were gradually consumed by nature. This station closed in 1963, to be replaced by a hideous corrugated metal shed in the port area in 1993. The original rails, which were presumably preventing effective road planning, are still visible in various parts of the town leading to the first station.

I occasionally used the train to or from Athens, but it was frustratingly slow due to the century-old infrastructure. The train accelerated out of the station in Athens and then seemed to spend the next seven hours gradually decelerating as it got closer to Nafplio, arriving slower than continental drift after an agonising final stretch from Dervenakia. It was, however, ludicrously cheap to travel by train before the euro and therefore popular with gypsies, who seem to be universally hated in Greece.

I recall distinctly that two gypsy women and their children once got into my carriage and that the other people unsubtly moved to other carriages, leaving me alone with the gypsies. Keen to show my liberal credentials and lack of racism, I offered them an extra bottle of water I had in my rucksack. They laughed and asked me for money instead. Then one of the women spat at my shoe when I refused. I didn't leave the carriage, but I wanted to.

The unveiling of the Kolokotronis statue in 1901 was another opportunity to do something with the open wasteland east of the town. They couldn't just put the statue amid gravel and rubble, so a rudimentary park structure was laid out around the sculpture: flowerbeds and stripling palms, some of which will have been trampled by the massive crowds that day. This work fell into disrepair almost immediately and the land returned to its natural state: dry and barren in summer, marshy or waterlogged in winter.

Not until 1930 was any further attempt made to create a park. There were plans to landscape the area and some new planting took place. Benches and lighting were added. It was a period of greater activity beyond the old town perimeters, as more of the old fortifications came down. The Dolfin bastion fell in 1926 and the Mocenigo bastion in 1932. The new courthouse had been built in 1911 and the Nikitaras monument would soon be followed by Kapodistrias's in a square of the same name. New Nafplio was taking shape outside its fallen walls.

For a while, the park became a cool and shaded place to walk at the weekend or in the evenings. It was popular until the 1970s to have photos taken amid the trees by professionals who worked there every day. Apparently, most Nafpliot families have at least one such picture in their collections. I remember that it was indeed a cool place to sit under the pines during the heat of the day or to walk at night away from the captured heat of the town.

The park was looking a little shabby and worn even in 1998, its flowerbeds bare and the gravel walkways puddled or overgrown with weeds. The economic crisis hasn't helped, of course, and keeping a park irrigated perhaps wasn't the town council's number one priority when people were having their pensions and their electricity cut. The benches inexplicably disappeared for some time. The flowers died. The trees were simply felled rather than trimmed. In the meantime, the seats and tables of the cafés and gyro shops on Sidiras Merarchias impinged on the northern fringes of the park.

In 2020, Kolokotronis Park was officially named a protected historical monument, though there was no apparent improvement by 2022. It's still a pleasant place to stroll, though it looks a bit ragged, a bit neglected. It could be a wonderful place.

Nafplio is a coastal town, of course, but beach life is a relatively modern pleasure. For most of history, beaches were places to be feared – places of shipwreck and of the dangerous sea. Most people couldn't swim and there was trepidation about what lived in the water. Tietz in 1833 was terrified of swimming in Nafplio, citing the dangers of jellyfish, octopus and snapping turtles that could cut a one-inch-diameter wooden rod with their beaks. Beaches were also places to throw a town's rubbish in the knowledge that the tides or the waves would take it. Native islanders in Tahiti and other idyllic Pacific islands used their beaches as toilets or refuse sites well into the twentieth century. Sea bathing, however, became popular from the start of the nineteenth century as a health treatment – initially among the higher social classes who did no physical work and were weak and sickly. Of all places, the trend began in England, with its freezing seas and minimal summers. Later, the benefits of sea air and saltwater spread to the larger population, though we still can't speak of "beach life" in a modern sense. Nobody was strolling the shore in their bikini or Speedos in an age when public nakedness was scandalous or irreligious.

Nafplio had a head start in bathing as a daily pleasure thanks to the Turks, who brought their tradition of the *hammam*, or hot bath, to their various dominions. Nafplio had at least three of these during the Ottoman occupations and they were used by foreign visitors. Traveller William Gell visited one around 1804 and recorded it in detail (the same process experienced in the modern bathhouses of Istanbul):

"It is better for a stranger to visit these places when they are not crowded by the inhabitants. The first apartment has a fire in the centre, and round the walls are several sofas, or rather beds, which have clean sheets and blankets. Here, when the bather is stripped, a cotton cloth is wrapped round him, and he is conducted in wooden pattens through several vaulted rooms, each hotter than the last, to a chamber, where he is placed upon a wooden platform about the size of a door, and raised four inches from the pavement. Here a profuse perspiration is rubbed off by one of the attendants, who likewise performs the ceremony of champooing for those who wish it. After this, a bason full of lather is brought, and the bather is rubbed with a soft brush made of an oriental plant. He is then left alone with a bowl, with which he pours upon himself warm or cold water, both of which flow near him into a marble basin. On clapping the hands, the attendant brings a fresh dress of cotton cloth, which is wrapped round the waist, and another in the form of a turban is placed on the head. He is then reconducted to the first apartment, where he is placed between the sheets, and drinks a cup of coffee while he is drying. It is said to be perfectly safe to leave any sum of money in the pockets while bathing, and that no instance of theft ever occurred at a bath."

Gell was misguided about the latter point. A police report of 1826 records the theft of a woman's pearl from such a *hammam*, while in 1827 some foreign volunteers were murdered for their possessions while in the bathhouse (see **Fantasists**). One of these bathhouses has left traces in the modern town. You can see the remains of a domed structure close by St. Spyridon on Papanikolaou Street, which was joined to a larger complex now forming part of the Catholic church's buildings. Another was on Vasileos Konstantinou.

It's not clear if the Greek inhabitants used these facilities, which were such a part of Islamic culture and society. We know that they did adopt certain elements of clothing (the fez, the turban) and other habits (the *komboloi*, the long pipe) so perhaps the baths were also part of this assimilation over centuries. After 1822 and the eradication of the Turkish population, their baths continued in business, as shown by the above crimes committed there.

By the 1860s, the sea bathing craze had reached Nafplio and a bathing complex was created just below the Five Brothers bastion. It was built of wood and raised above the surface on stilts. Access was via a raised walkway from the quay pointing at the Bourtzi, though it was made of rocks and sand in the 1860s. Inside, there were twelve individual bath cubicles with seawater that must have been raised in buckets or pumped mechanically. The bathers were not actually in the sea but in its water. There is also a suggestion that certain mineral-rich waters were brought in from other parts of Greece (e.g. the volcanic springs of Thermopylae).

We should remember that most of Nafplio's fresh water came from Aria via the aqueduct and was stored in large cisterns. Rainwater augmented the supply in the winter months. It's unlikely that there was sufficient water for 6,000-10,000 people to bathe in a bathtub at home every day. Nor was that kind of bathing normal in the nineteenth century or for much of history. Even some of Europe's royalty bathed just once a month if necessary, and there's a story that Queen Victoria's clothes had partially grown onto her torso because she'd worn them so long without washing (them, or herself). They had to be cut from her in preparation for her funeral. So a sea bath might have been the only bath that many Nafpliots could enjoy.

These wooden baths were still in use in the 1950s, having served the town throughout the WWII occupation. They were probably in a poor condition after almost a hundred years of sun and waves and were demolished in 1959 to make way for a more substantial structure on a concrete base. These plans were opposed by locals, who complained that the proposed new building looked like a barracks rather than a bathhouse.

Still, the new baths were built and began operation in 1960, offering standard seawater, hot seawater, mineral baths and various proprietary treatments. The place remained highly popular into the 1970s and had a bar and café on a wooden platform over the sea. The children would dive from the platform or play in the new circular pool alongside the building while the parents enjoyed an ouzo or *mezedes*.

At some stage in the late seventies or early eighties, the bathhouse ceased to operate. Perhaps its lease had run out and a new tenant couldn't be found. More likely is that beach bathing had become more popular with the loosening of morals and the advent of greater international tourism. Social bathing habits had changed and, besides, the town's water supply was much more modern. Saltwater bathing became a historical curiosity and swimming took over.

Nafplio has at least three beaches. Four or five kilometres along the coast is wild Karathonas, while stony Neraki is about halfway along the same coast that has many small coves for swimming. The "official" town beach, however, is Arvanitia.

There are two theories about the name, which is etymologically connected to Albanians. The colourful version is that Gazi Hasan Pasha led five thousand Turkalvans (Muslim Albanian mercenaries to whom he owed money) to Palamidi and threw them over the cliff, turning the sea red with their blood. Memorable, but unlikely. It's relatively labour intensive to transport five thousand men up the road to Palamidi without any of them wondering why they were being escorted to an impregnable fortress-prison. "Yeah – just leave your weapons behind. You won't need them." And how do you organise throwing five thousand people off a cliff? By threatening them with guns? Just shoot them in the first place and save all the logistical problems!

The other theory is that there was an Albanian settlement based on the beach. We know that the Venetians had brought in a large number of Albanians to compensate for population depletion among the Greeks who didn't want to pay heavy taxes. We also know that the Turks used them as mercenaries and in the Ottoman army. Sixteenth-century maps actually show a settlement of Albanians at Arvanitia beach. So it's pretty much "case closed" on that question.

Whatever existed on the beach in the sixteenth century, it was empty for most of Nafplio's history. The Venetian fortifications ended abruptly with the southern corner of the Grimani bastion and the land simply fell gradually away to the sea. There was no road up to a car park at the beginning of the 1930s – only the deep ditch cut through the rock by the Venetians. The land beyond this cutting (now the car park) was initially a barren incline – no trees. The rock-cut ditch was filled in to create a road in 1935 and it appears from photos that an area of level land was established where the car park would be. Still, no trees existed. Arvanitia was just earth descending into a rocky shore – not remotely attractive or comfortable for bathing even if anyone had wanted to.

Before there was an organised town beach, the car park area was briefly a square that hosted two tavernas on its eastern side. One belonged to Kripa and the other to Katerinakos.

Since there were no other houses around, it was a good place for music and raucous late-night entertainment. Many of the dockworkers would come when the cafés by the port closed.

The design for the beach was paid for by the Greek state tourist organisation (EOT) and designed in the late 1960s by Kleon Krantonellis. Part of the scheme was also to plant the whole slope to the beach with pine trees to provide shade and to prevent erosion. A path would snake down from the car park to the pebbles, avoiding too steep a gradient. In recent years, it appears that this path cuts across a water table or a sewer so that malodorous black liquid occasionally seeps down part of it, puddling horribly by the sides.

By 1969, the beach facilities were in place. The design was very much of its time: a concrete gateway down from the car park, concrete path, concrete platforms for sunbeds, a concrete terrace for bars and restaurants, and concrete changing rooms with exterior showers. There also seems to be an area marked out as a football pitch or other activity field that is now scrubby and overgrown. The place has been repaired and renovated regularly since 1969 but is essentially the same.

Arvanitia remains popular all year round. In winter, a group of pensioners meets to swim almost daily. According to them, you don't notice the sea getting colder if you swim every day. In summer, the beach is full all the time and more so on Sundays. It's a cool place for the town's young people to show off the work they've done in the gym and to hang out with a drink. It's also a popular haunt of the *kamakia* (see **Tourism**).

I never liked Arvanitia much in summer. It's small and can feel very crowded, especially on the pebbles. But if you go a few metres to the west, there's a stretch of flat limestone rock that's good for sunbathing and which has a rickety metal ladder for sea access. A staircase goes up through the pines from here to the coastal walk. I used to come here most afternoons in the summer for a swim, drying off on the rocks before walking back along the path for a siesta at home. I remember the crystalline, salt-caked depressions in the stone and the sensation of seawater drying on hot skin.

I was once propositioned at the top of this staircase by an old local gigolo. Hairy chested, balding and paunchy, he used to walk along the rocks stopping at every sunbathing woman, staring down at her body, complimenting her beauty and asking if she'd like to accompany him on his moped to a "secret beach" along the coast. They all said no all the time, but he did it every day regardless and I assumed that he must have been successful one time out of a hundred. I was returning home one day after my swim and he was sitting on his bike at the top of the stairs. "There's a secret beach along the coast," he said, tapping the saddle behind him. "Do you want to come?" I guess being bisexual doubled his chances of success. (I didn't go.)

Another of Nafplio's pleasures is the yearly cycle of festivals and holidays, of which there are many – sixteen national holidays in 2022 compared to the UK's eight. Some of these are the same (Christmas and New Year) but others like *Oxi* (No) day or Clean Monday retain the delight of novelty for the non-Greek. *Oxi* Day, 28 October, commemorates the occasion when Prime Minister Ioannis Metaxas rejected an ultimatum given to him in 1940 by the Italians under Benito Mussolini. They wanted permission to enter and occupy Greek territory and Metaxas said no, triggering a bloody war in the north. He actually responded with a slightly longer response, but the best Greek responses throughout history have been anecdotally short, as in King Leonidas' response to the Persians' demand to lay down Spartan arms: "Come and get them!"

In October, *Oxi* day can often be rainy. The schoolchildren parade through a gauntlet of umbrellas then everyone floods inside the cafés, whose windows steam opaque. I remember returning from one freezing cold, sleet-sodden *Oxi* Day in the mountains of northern Greece to find a dark-eyed girl called Anastasía waiting outside my door, her hair and clothes soaked. She needed warming up. That was a *Nai* (Yes) afternoon.

Easter, too, is a wonderful time. There's the magic of the Holy Fire and the nocturnal church services, but best of all there's the *kokoretsi* and the whole roast lamb cooked for hours on the spit. One nineteenth-century visitor recorded how the streets of Nafplio ran with blood as countless lambs and goats were slaughtered. The smell was later replaced by the smell of roasting meat and pies made with the offal. Bells rang and guns were fired in celebration. Various people were killed this way, including one man who came out on his balcony to see what was happening. Is there another town in Greece with so many random deaths?

The foreigner takes part in these things as theatrical performances, observing and participating in an illusion of belonging. I attended weddings whose guests smiled at me while wondering who I was and why I was there. I sat through long Orthodox services as an atheist, enraptured by incense and by music I didn't understand. I spent one night with the sole monk in a semi-ruined canyon monastery in Epirus, drinking *tsipuro* and eating stale bread with a single candle on the table, talking about the power of the spirit at Athos. Always an impostor. Always an intense pleasure.

Everyone has his or her own pleasures in the end. For me, it was a double *elliniko metrio* with a Bourtzi view; it was a slow walk down the coast to Karathonas, drunk on the perfumes of pine and eucalyptus resin; it was the August sunset slipping over Palamidi; it was the old town's Cubist roofs from the Venetian clock tower. And more than any of these, it was eating at my local *mezedopoleio*: Noulis.

There are other restaurants in Nafplio, I suppose. Mine will always be Noulis. The menu today is the same as it was twenty-five years ago – I have it memorised and can order without it. It's Greek food, but Greek food entirely without flaw. A few times each week (or day), I'd go there alone or with others and order two or three more plates than I should have, eating it all anyway. The beauty of *mezedes* is that you can fill the table with different flavours and dart between them as you reach planetary mass. A fork of *horta*, a swipe of *fava*, a sardine or prawn picked up by the tail . . . Bread soaked in oil. I believe the happiest moments of my life have been spent in the narrow alley terrace of Noulis's place. I'd happily die there, suffering an embolism after eating everything on the menu. That would be my ideal way to go.

Nafplio was and is pleasure. I've seen a bit of the world, but Nafplio is still the place I think of most. Maybe it was my youth and relative innocence – a happy accident of coincidence and consequence.

PRESENCE

Not as many people live in the old town as they used to. For various reasons, the population is around sixty per cent lower than it was in the 1980s. The truth is that it's not an especially liveable twenty-first-century town because it was laid out in the sixteenth century when horses, mules and carts were the only forms of transport. Many streets are pedestrianised and/or have strictly controlled vehicle access, while others (particularly in Vrachateika and Psaromahala) are narrow, steep, twisty and just inaccessible except by motorbike. Most of the car parking is on the seafront. All of this makes life difficult for young families and the elderly.

Another factor in the population depletion is that old-town property prices are disproportionately high (c. €500,000-€1,300,000, even for derelict buildings). Such prices are aimed at international buyers looking for a part of the dream. The buildings also often come with strict guidelines on how they can be renovated and decorated. It makes sense for a family with a legacy house in the old town to rent it as accommodation and/or retail space and to live off the proceeds in a cheaper, more modern house in the new town.

Nafplio can seem full in the summer months or if you visit at the weekend when the Athenians or Corinthians are in town, but the place can feel almost empty during the week and out of season. It's a purely modern condition. Visitors from the eighteenth century onwards have described a population between 6,000 and 10,000 living purely within the Venetian walls. This may have doubled at times of war with the Turks. In 2022, the permanent old-town population is around 3,000 with another 13,000 living in the new town.

These are just numbers. The problem with history is that it seldom gives us a sense of what it's like to be in a place. Dates and battles, buildings and notable residents are accumulated facts but the human history is usually in the decades and centuries where nothing happens except the day-to-day business of eating, working and sleeping. Nafplio has passed around three thousand years doing just that. There were Venetians who lived and died there without ever experiencing a siege. Same with the Turks. There were Nafpliots who barely ever saw a foreign visitor and others who have grown up watching badly dressed pale people pulling a juddering suitcase down Plapouta Street while staring at a phone.

What was Byzantine or Ottoman Nafplio like? How did it smell? What was it like to pass Kapodistrias or King Otto in the street? The early sources for such information are few. Most visitors were there for a reason (e.g. to assess or build new fortifications) and didn't record the kind of things we'd like to know. Other more idle visitors had their own agendas and interests. Even the people who lived there and saw it and recorded it in their memoirs (Heideck, Kolokotronis) tended to focus on their legacy rather than where to buy the best *bougatsa* or how they passed a cool spring evening. We generally have to wait for the Grand Tourers and the European writers of the nineteenth century before we get a real sense of what Nafplio was like and how it looked. But let's give it a go.

We can condense the first few thousand years into a general summary. Nafplio was originally just the fortified rock of Acronafplio. The population was necessarily small due to limited space and most of it would have been concentrated around the top of the gulf or today's Prónoia district. That's where the ancient tombs have been found and where most people lived – farming their land, fishing and mastering crafts such as pottery. The acropolis, as in most ancient civilisations, was the redoubt of last resort: a lofty viewpoint where the sea breeze sighed around the masonry. Maybe there was a temple or some other cult centre on the hill now buried beneath Venetian masonry or a modern hotel. Maybe people came here in wonder to commune with their gods.

The Franks and the Byzantines were largely limited to Acronafplio, too, though their efforts to control silt and make a harbour suggest they were expanding the town and its importance as a trading centre. The tenth and eleventh centuries in particular saw Nafplio thrive as a centre of silkworm cultivation and silk making. Distant ship-owners may have had agents here to oversee loading and unloading, warehousing and possible selling of goods on the local market. But Acronafplio wasn't a place to support a large population and the land around the peninsula was always at risk of invasion. It was still an outpost of a distant empire: a source of goods and a stopping place on longer trade routes.

It would have felt like the end of the world to someone from Constantinople or Smyrna – a beautiful setting, but primitive and lonely. Everybody would have known everyone else by name. Maybe they commiserated with each other and spoke about home. When the Franks decorated the gate to their castle, it was an attempt to bring just a little art and culture to this fortified colony. Visiting Venetian captains, however, looked at the location and saw greater potential.

The first Venetians would have experienced a pretty sad-looking place that had been in decline throughout the Frankish period. After all, Nafplio had been sold to them by an aristocratic family short of money and then raided by Theodore I Palaiologos before the Venetians could take possession of their purchase. Acronafplio was unguarded and virtually in ruins, while Palamidi was just a big hill, possibly with a lookout post but no considerable fortifications. It's likely the local land-based population had little or no idea of what existed beyond the horizon. This was their entire world.

A huge amount of building was done in the fifteenth and sixteenth centuries (see **Mapping**). Nafplio at this time was a town of builders, carpenters, labourers, cooks and other essential workers such as bakers, butchers and plasterers. The town was not self-sufficient. It was increasingly surrounded by encroaching Ottoman possessions. Grain and other essential supplies had to be bought from the Turks, as did the kindness of not invading at any moment. Large amounts of baksheesh were thus paid to local potentates in an always tenuous and contingent peace. Living here must have seemed a temporary condition for many. They would return home once their work was done.

Amid all of the building work and sea traffic of this time, there was also much tension. With Nafplio in the middle of Ottoman possessions, there would have been a mood of expectation in the town. The talk would have always returned to the question of when. When will the bribes not be enough? When will the Turks decide to make their move? Are they waiting for us to finish the fortifications so they can invade? Meanwhile, bad weather or bad relations might mean no bread for a month. Though it lasted around 150 years, the first Venetian period was an uncertain one and, for many, Nafplio remained an outpost or a stop on a longer route.

Still, the town was taking shape. Syntagma square was in place, as was Vasileos Konstantinou, St George's Square and many of the streets in Vrahateika. Offices, barracks, warehouses and armouries were built and the increasing population required more houses. For thirty years, the old town reverberated with the dull thunk of iron hammers on pilings, the cough of the two-man saw above its pit, the endless chink of stonemasons' chisels on thousands of stones, the squeak and rattle of ropes running through the wooden blocks of cranes. Ships would have been arriving regularly in port from Venice or its other markets with fresh timber, fresh tools, fresh hands. Dock workers would have carried barrels and bales to and from ships by day and drunk heavily by night, as dock workers generally have through history. It's very thirsty work.

It was starting to look and feel more like a town by the end of the first Venetian period. People stayed here because it could support them with its markets and its jobs. People came from Venice to oversee their trade, their fortifications, their military forces. No doubt others decided to stay and take advantage of the growing possibilities in this newly-walled

town. Abel Boyer wrote in 1696 that a "vast number of strangers of several nations" lived in Nafplio. It was an exciting place
to be – a place with a future. Money could be made here. The
town was populated with new residents, go getters, self start-
ers, pioneers. They were all watching it grow.

Many of the Venetian soldiers in Nafplio were from the
"several nations" mentioned by Boyer. There were Albanians,
Italians, Dalmatians, Germans, French, Flemish and Batav-
ians. Venice didn't always pay them with money but granted
them land to farm and the right to pass their land to their
children. It's true that these lands could be taken back at any
time by the Venetian overlords, but that doesn't mean they
were. Many Nafpliot families today can trace their family line
back to these land-owning Venetian mercenaries.

With its growing population, the town had bakeries and
slaughterhouses whose smells would fill certain neighbourhoods. There would have been a fishy part of the harbour and
places where the catch was cooked over fire. Oil extraction
from olives would have cast its special aroma across the town
at harvest time. Somewhere, wine was being made. It was a
town of smells. But what about the native Greeks who'd been
here all the time, living on the land around the peninsula since
Agamemnon was king?

Well, the Greeks didn't like the Venetians very much. Partly
it was a question of religion. The Venetians were Roman
Catholic and not well-disposed towards the Orthodox Church.
They changed most Byzantine churches into Catholic ones.
Also, from the very beginning of Venetian ownership, the
governance of Nafplio was arranged around three things:
efficient collection of public revenues, the rendering of proper
justice and the assurance of defence to consolidate and
maintain Venetian sovereignty. The town was always going to
be an imperial possession and Venice's presence an occupation. They imposed strict taxes on their dominions and were
diligent in collecting them. Initially, the Venetians took account of local sensitivities by permitting an advisory body made
up of local representatives, usually prominent members of

society. This seems to have become less effective and more difficult the longer the Venetians were in Nafplio. In 1445, the town sent a complaint to Venice that the system had largely broken down and that they weren't being consulted. Later, they complained that they shouldn't pay any more taxes, or that they should receive a rebate because the fortifications they'd paid for hadn't been finished according to schedule.

The overall result was considerable depopulation as local Greeks fled abroad or to other parts of Greece, often preferring the slightly more relaxed Turkish rule. Early figures show that Venetian Nafplio was unable to meet its revenue targets throughout much of the fourteenth and fifteenth centuries because there weren't enough people to pay them. Argos, with its much bigger population at the time, had to cover its neighbours' costs. The Turks had attacked the region in the summer of 1397, sacked Argos and captured the entire population as slaves. The Venetians were obliged to bring more people from home and from Albania to do the necessary work in their dominion, further diversifying Nafplio in the process. It became the dominant of the two towns from this point.

The second half of the fifteenth century saw much instability as the Argolid was invaded first by marauding bands of Albanians and then by the Turks. This disrupted agriculture and the economy of the town. Going beyond the walls, which were still under construction, was a dangerous activity. War with the Turks eventually broke out in 1537. Nafplio resisted a fourteen-month siege but in the peace treaty of 1540 Venice was forced to cede the town to the sultan.

The Turks added little to the fortifications because the Venetians had done it all for them. As more experienced empire builders, the Ottomans knew that the key was to make the town a home rather than an outpost. Accordingly, their building programme concentrated on fountains, bathhouses, public administration buildings and mosques. Later, they added alluvial soil to the swampy land outside the gate and turned it into a park area for evening strolls. They also brought in an entirely new population from Turkey, presumably offering them incentives to relocate. These Turks arrived in a ready-made town and continued living as they had always done: going to the market or the bathhouse, fishing, farming, trading. Maybe the streets were unfamiliar at first, but the walls contained everything they needed to create neighbourhoods, form friendships and build families. Nafplio was just another part of the empire in which everyone was Turkish.

In 1667, Evliya Çelebi described a walled lower town of forty-two royal towers and five gates. Numerous military and political commanders of the region were based in Nafplio, some of them living to a degree of opulence that became famous. The palaces of Mcryologlu and Seyhi effendi were two outstanding examples for Çelebi. He also mentioned 200 shops, three inns and a small bazaar containing artisan workshops. The residents dressed colourfully and elegantly in multi-hued felts and were often accompanied by their slaves in the street.

For the Greeks who had remained or returned, it may have seemed a fairer rule. The Turkish authorities sold the houses of Greeks or Venetians who had fled the town, but protected and respected the property of those who stayed. The latter group also received some tax exemptions. Çelebi refers specifically to the district of Psaromahala, "the quarters of the infidel," in the west of the town, where the Greek merchants lived. He counted seven of their churches in this place, though it seems only the Venetian chapel of the Holy Apostles and possibly the Byzantine St. Sophia remain. Some Greeks, such as doctor Romios Michalakis, became well known and highly respected.

And so Nafplio continued as normal for the next four or five generations as a Muslim town. The call to prayer would have sounded from the town's various minarets five times a day and ships would have arrived in port from Asia Minor. The locals would have drunk tea and coffee while smoking their long Turkish pipes and handling their prayer beads to make calculations or count the names of Allah.

Plague would occasionally sweep through the town, either brought in on the ships or carried over from the ever-present swamp at the head of the bay. It's not clear exactly what these recurrent plagues and fevers were (see also **War**). Bubonic plague would surely have wiped out most of the population, and maybe it did. Many nineteenth-century visitors complained about the quantity of lice and vermin in the town. Malaria is another possibility given the perpetually silted-up bay, though typhoid and cholera are equally likely in a walled town with its water stored in cisterns and its occasional siege. Friedrich Tietz noted that ships were often held in port under quarantine in the 1830s, while Thomas Hope in the late 1700s remarked on Nafplio's healthy mosquito population in his novel *Anastasius*. We can assume that the town's medieval hospital would be occasionally overcome with cases and that, periodically, scores of bodies would have to be buried according to the Muslim religion.

Where did all of the Turkish dead go in the 148 years of their first occupation? There must have been a cemetery unless every cadaver was shipped back to a grave in Asia Minor (unlikely). More likely is that whatever Turkish cemetery existed had its markers, if not its corpses, removed and was wiped from the historical record. There may be thousands of nameless bodies lying under a patch of land near Prónoia or under new Nafplio. It's another mystery.

The Venetians were caught up in one or more of these illnesses when they approached again in 1686, Encamped between Tiryns and Nafplio, they were stricken with plague but still managed to take the town back for more of the same unpopularity they'd enjoyed previously. A whole population was moved out and a new one came in.

Let's stop for a moment and imagine what this does to a town. Many in history have been attacked or sacked multiple times (Jerusalem and Rome are the two most obvious examples), but the original population tends to trickle back after the fires have stopped burning and the marauders have moved on. In the case of Nafplio, whole populations were explicitly replaced, either in concerted marine exoduses or wholesale slaughter. The Venetians didn't want any of the enemy in their walled town and nor did any Roman Catholic want to live under Islam. At various points in its history, immediately after 1540, 1686, 1715 and 1822, Nafplio would have been a ghost town, most of its population having fled or been eradicated. Houses and religious buildings stood empty. Shops were closed or smashed and looted. The streets were peopled only with soldiers still high on the heat of their blood-lust and the temporary hiatus of all ethics and morality. Then, slowly, everything would start again and anew, but not with people who had lived there before. They had all died long ago. It would begin with a whole new population.

The Turks had brought their own people in 1540. Morosini would move Greeks from Ottoman-besieged Athens to Nafplio after 1686 to make up the necessary population of workers, farmers, stevedores, bakers, shoemakers and the rest. Most would have arrived to see it for the first time: the lofty Palamidi, the imposing Acronafplio, the impressively walled and bastioned lower town. After the tiny settlement of Athens with its smaller population (around 4,000 even in the 1830s), this was like something out of a fairy tale. They were going to live here? Houses and businesses would be allocated in this ready-made, though somewhat damaged, new town.

Morosini allowed his men to buy property in conquered towns on their own terms, so many Venetians also became owners of buildings in Nafplio. It was another reason for more people to come from Venice to settle and enjoy the facilities created by vanished generations. For a few years, everyone would be a stranger to everyone else. Every neighbour was temporarily unknown. Everyone was a new arrival until the wheel of time could make all of it into normality again. At least, for thirty more years.

Does a town retain some psychic imprint of what it has seen? Thousands have died from disease or violence in Nafplio. Each new siege and wall breach resulted in the slaughter of the garrison, indiscriminate rape and massacre of anyone who hadn't managed to escape – anyone who spoke a different language, wore different clothes and worshipped a different god. When the newcomers arrived, did they feel any echo of the people whose scent still lingered in the bed sheets and whose bodies had occupied the furniture? Or does all such presence vanish with the bloodstains?

We don't know for sure what Nafplio was like under the second Venetian occupation, but we can guess. Look at the architecture that remains: clean lines, precise brickwork, good drainage and water supply – form following function. If the main square wasn't paved at this time, it was certainly clean and clear. The principal streets, too, must have been mostly free of trash, or at least designed so that water could run through and clean them. Their town was a place to live, but it was also a mercantile centre. It was a social machine that had to work.

As the Venetian's capital of the Morea, Nafplio was busy. An engraving of 1713 shows the lower town now full of houses and we can surmise from the quantity of these houses, shops, factories, barracks and warehouses that the population was large. Ships' crews would have further caused numbers on the streets to ebb and flow. It was a town at work: making, storing, selling. Things were always moving. There was news to share in the coffee houses about political developments and imminent cargoes, rumours and predictions. It was an age of empires and Nafplio was tied into the network.

When the Turks returned in 1715. They found a well-established marine trading town. But this Ottoman occupation would be different from the last because the empire had changed. It was in gradual decline and its centres of power had shifted north to Thrace and the city of Thessaloniki. Internally, the great power had become less organised, more corrupt, and had replaced administrative efficiency with brute force. Its military imposed order on local populations and used punishment to compel obedience. Still, the fall of Nafplio was important. Sultan Ahmed III came in person from Constantinople with bejewelled swords of honour and fur cloaks as gifts for the military leaders.

Greek regions such as the Morea later became increasingly

cut off from Constantinople and were run as personal estates, stagnating throughout the eighteenth century. The once flourishing trade routes shifted more towards Smyrna or Constantinople and Nafplio tended to belong to an older pasha or one sent there in disgrace in lieu of decapitation. One early nineteenth-century French visitor found the richer Turks bloated and happily drinking wine or eating pork in contravention of their holy book.

But Nafplio was an Ottoman town again. The minarets pulled down by the Venetians were rebuilt and the calls to prayer went out. Camel trains crisscrossed the mountains, their bells tinkling through passes between Nafplio and Tripolitsa or Corinth. The Venetians had gone, but any remaining Greeks fared badly. They were not part of the official administration and did not have the same rights as Turkish residents, though they were obliged to pay a head tax and a tax for being permitted to follow their own religion. Families were also obliged to give a son to the Turkish military, a measure sufficiently unpopular that some mothers would cripple a child to prevent him being made a Muslim.

Such measures resulted in considerable depopulation as the Greeks fled the towns to the mountains. Some became *klephts* (armed bandits) roaming the hills and robbing anyone, Turks or other Greeks – to stay alive. Many more went out to the Greek islands or even further to Romania, Russia, Italy, and Austria. It was the start of a diaspora movement that helped to build a powerful collective Greek identity. People in the countryside bonded over popular songs, the Orthodox faith and their language. The *klephts* formed into clans, which would later become private militias in the fight for independence.

The few Greeks who stayed in Nafplio often became Ottomanised as they had previously, adopting habits such as the bathhouse, the long pipe, coffee drinking, *komboloi* and Turkish dress. Some nineteenth-century arrivals in Nafplio were surprised to see members of the new government wearing turbans or fezzes and baggy trousers while reclining on divans. For others, converting to Islam proved a relatively pain-free way of avoiding the worst taxes and of accessing the various benefits of being a "Turk."

Nafplio gradually became a backwater as Tripolitsa gained more importance. The population would have been much lower than under the Venetians. A census taken soon after the 1715 re-conquest revealed no civilian population at all – only military personnel. Most had fled or been killed, though more Turks would arrive from around Greece and from Asia Minor. Before long, it was a Turkish town again. One early nineteenth-century visitor discovered a population of 4,000 mostly Turkish inhabitants who, when questioned, had no knowledge of the town's history before their arrival.

Foreign visitors began to arrive in the early nineteenth century while Nafplio was still an Ottoman possession and from them we have descriptions of the town. William Gell was there around 1804 and mentions that although the town was abundantly supplied with fresh water, its port was heavily silted up. The Turks hadn't bothered to keep it open as the Venetians occasionally had. The town's residents were suspicious of any foreign visitors. Soldiers would demand to see any paintings or sketches of castles, suspecting that an enemy nation was collecting intelligence. This said, consuls and vice-consuls of various nations were living in Nafplio even before it became the first capital – possibly to keep an eye on trading interests. The French in particular had been very active traders via Nafplio since 1700. As for Greeks, there were very few and they tended to be shopkeepers. Gell described the townsfolk as the most barbarous in Greece.

William Leake was there around 1806 and found the town very quiet. There was a Turkish garrison of around 200 men, a governor, a judge and a customs collector. He describes the port not only as silted-up but also full of mud and rubbish so that only the smallest boats could enter the harbour. Life proceeded at a slow pace. Transportation was with horses, donkeys, and carts. Most town Greeks didn't own or couldn't ride horses, though the mountain Greeks and *klephts* were highly adept riders. This was the Nafplio experienced by Byron on his youthful travels, and though we don't know what he did while here, we might suggest he was thinking of the town in the second canto (stanza 77) of *Childe Harold*.

> The city won for Allah from the Giaour,
> The Giaour from Othman's race again may wrest;
> And the Serai's impenetrable tower
> Receive the fiery Frank, her former guest;
> Or Wahab's rebel brood who dared divest
> The prophet's tomb of all its pious spoil,
> May wind their path of blood along the West;
> But ne'er will freedom seek this fated soil,
> But slave succeed to slave through years of endless toil.

To enter Nafplio in the early nineteenth century was essentially to enter a Levantine town. Blind, maimed and reeking beggars gathered around the Land Gate and on the rocks near the sea gates. There were many coffee houses and the air was thick with imported Turkish tobacco. Most houses were built of lath and plaster, sponges for humidity, their upper stories extending over the streets on struts to block out the sun, trap bad smells and prevent rain from washing the filth away.

Almost every foreign visitor at this time mentions how much Nafplio's airless streets stank within the walls, how much vermin there was and how heaps of rubbish lay uncleared around the town. The Venetian fortifications had mostly fallen into disrepair – water-stained, masonry enweeded, bushes peeking from parapets – though the battlements everywhere remained porcupined with cannon.

It sounds bad, but these observers were coming from France, Germany and England. They brought their standards and expectations with them. This was the normality for the long-term residents, many of whom had no idea how old the "ancient" fortifications were or who had built them. Such things were lost in the dimness of time – and irrelevant anyway. They were accustomed to living in towns whose millennia of history sat rotting around them and whose stones or pottery occasionally emerged from the earth. It's a condition that persists today across countries like Italy, Greece, Spain or Palestine and it can seem outrageous to visitors not accustomed to such cohabitation with antiquity.

I remember once showing a native of Florida around the acropolis of ancient Asine on the edge of Tolo, a tourist resort close to Nafplio. I knew that there was one part of the hill where erosion and animal activity occasionally revealed shards of Mycenaean or Geometric era pottery. Sure enough, close to a rabbit warren, my American guest was able to pick up a small piece of pottery with a figure painted on it three thousand years previously. The finger marks of the original potter were still on the interior of the clay. Here was a piece of ancient history just lying there on the ground for anyone to pick up. Meanwhile, in Nafplio, there was a fifteenth-century castle gate, a third-century BC polygonal wall, and sixteenth-century Venetian cannons just sitting there. In public! Where anyone could touch them. Not even in a museum.

The siege of 1821-22 and the chaos of the 1820s (see **War**) saw many buildings destroyed by bombardment or deliberately by the Greeks, who didn't want to live in a town with minarets or Turkish houses. The Arabic-inscribed fountains survived solely because they provided water. The streets were heaped with rubble and littered with dead bodies. Meanwhile, the countryside around the town had been stripped bare by Turkish troops who had cut down the orange and olive trees to leave a barren wasteland.

Being in Nafplio at this time must have been both exhilarating and terrifying. The Turkish population of around 4,000 was gone: fled or murdered. It was a town on the axis of history – all normality suspended. Visitor Charles Frankland was impressed by the Greek fighters with their long, dark hair past the shoulders, their vivid red caps, their pleated *fustanellas* and their flamboyant gold-embroidered jackets. They seemed to spend all their money on their silver-inlaid Albanian rifles and muskets, charging about dramatically on horseback with sabres drawn. It was conflict as performance.

Young volunteers had also arrived from around Europe to aid in the fight for independence. These philhellenes stayed wherever they could, sometimes sleeping on floors, and were to be found together in the coffee houses. Meanwhile, the town was, according to one observer, all "ruins and misery." Ten to fifteen thousand people (mostly refugees) soon crowded inside the walls, dying of disease and starvation. Dust clouds curled from the denuded land outside the gate and from the peak of Palamidi.

Traveller Thomas Trant visited in the late 1820s. He recorded that on entering through the Land Gate, he found himself in a "narrow, dirty street full of people and from whence the sea breeze is excluded by the upper stories of the houses projecting one above the other until they almost meet." There were no sewers at the time and "the filth collected in the town is so abominable that I cannot think of it without abhorrence." He was also surprised how little evidence of the Turks remained. "No other country," he wrote, "after ruling a country so long a space of time, left such slight traces behind them as the Ottomans." His summary: Nafplio was the "most impure, offensive" town he had ever visited and would not long remain the nation's capital. It had been created as a defensive port – not as a place to live.

Trant was one of the few foreign visitors to comment on Nafplio's women, writing that they were highly suspicious of any non-Greek man attempting to speak to them. The younger girls were simply invisible – not allowed out onto the open streets where they could be coveted or worse. These women were intelligent, accomplished and eager to join a higher level of society at dances or in conversation, but they felt a crippling sense of inferiority and feared the worst derision would come from their own people. Almost all would marry men chosen by their parents, possibly at the time of their birth. And love? asked Trant. Was there no place for love? "We never love," replied the young girl he was speaking to. "We know not what love is." He noted, too, that many of the common women were broken by hard work, childbirth and many hours out in the sun – appearing old at twenty. The seasoned traveller was obliged to conclude, "I believe that there are few countries where woman is less respected than here."

The arrival of Ioannis Kapodistrias in 1828 initiated a much needed period of cleaning and building (see **Squares** and **Heroes**). By 1832, about fifty new public buildings had been constructed and the nearby suburb of Prónoia had been planned. Becoming the capital changed Nafplio society, giving it more northern European customs, a more cosmopolitan spirit, and a sense of civil society that included salons where guests discussed art and politics. Not everyone was convinced. French statesman and author Alphonse de Lamartine visited in 1832 during the Kapodistrian period and described it as a "wretched town" whose buildings were provincial and nothing special. He also noted soldiers lying all day in the shadows of the "rickety walls," and in the town's streets and squares, their costumes "rich and picturesque."

Kapodistrias's short period of order was the prelude to the regency period of King Otto, when Nafplio would briefly and gloriously imitate Vienna or Paris. Warships from around the world were in port and Europe's governments sent their ambassadors or consuls. France, Russia, Prussia, England, Denmark and Westphalia had official representatives in town.

The most beautifully decorated house was said to be that of the Russian ambassador in Three Admirals Square, though a close second was that of privy council president Count Josef Ludwig von Armansperg, whose house remains at the beginning of Plapouta Street, around the corner from the bus station. It's the huge three-storey Venetian building with the shutters closed and an impressive (chained-up) doorway. The third floor was added in 1831 in anticipation of an important resident and the façade has been renovated since, though the interior remains a ruin, its floors and ceilings unsafe.

Inside this grand abode, guests enjoyed the finest European decoration and a ballroom where local ladies used to come to catch a military husband. Englishman George Cochrane was present at one such soiree, which took place over three huge rooms measuring thirty by twenty feet. There was no dancing on this occasion, but the various military officers, their wives and around three hundred Greeks listened to music played by the three Armansperg daughters Louise, Sophie and Caroline. Sorbets were distributed and everybody went home at the civilised hour of 11.00 p.m.

Incidentally, Count Armansperg was originally part of a council tasked with running the new Greek state while the young King Otto was still only seventeen. After Otto reached eighteen and took control, Armansperg had little faith in the young man's judgement and operated virtually independently in many matters. Things reached a critical state when Otto briefly returned to Bavaria to get married and Armansperg asked the king's personal physician to send letters to Otto's father Ludwig claiming the young man was insane and unfit to lead. The count lost his job over this.

Nafplio in the 1830s was a town of parties and international hobnobbing. The military officers of the various nations would dance waltzes and gallopades in their dashing uniforms, the ladies in their silks and velvets. Diplomats would meet in clubs or private residences and talk politics as they played whist or *ecarté* over pipes and fine spirits. King Otto himself might have joined the dance amid a rustle of whispers and glances. Would he find his queen at one of these parties?

Meanwhile, the common soldiers came on shore leave from their many vessels to enjoy the cafes and bars established along Vasileos Konstantinou and in Syntagma Square to serve them. The Russians were least likely to be seen on the streets. The English were most likely to be drunk and starting fights (no change there; their descendants would later be holidaying in Faliraki.) Restaurants had also sprung up serving French or Bavarian cuisine for homesick soldiers who couldn't stomach the local food. Visitor Friedrich Tietz recoiled in horror at the Greek appetite for horribly inky squid, the salty olives or the *horta* that looked like a collection of common weeds to him.

Life in Nafplio was more normal than it had been for at

least a decade. The street markets sold greens and fish, onions, calamari, sea urchins, snails, courgette flowers, garlic, cucumbers, olives, spinach, asparagus, thyme, mint, honey and lamb – everything you'll see in today's Wednesday and Saturday markets (except the lamb).

With apparent safety conferred by a European monarch and military personnel everywhere, the town attracted many international residents during this time – particularly those engaged in trade. Different languages were heard in the cafés and through open windows. It was, after all a period of building, renovation and improvement. A painting of 1834 shows the area around the Five Brothers bastion neatly paved throughout, soldiers chatting and smoking in the sun.

And Acronafplio? Since 1822, the hill had been a dedicated military base accessed via the Sagredo gate – a town within the town that everyone below could see but none could enter. In this sense, Nafplio was a divided urban space for much of its history. People would have lived an entire lifespan never knowing what it looked like up there in the Castel del Toro or amid the hidden walkways within the walls and turrets.

Perhaps this is one of the aspects that makes Nafplio such an endlessly intriguing place to live. There are always these prohibited or enclosed mysteries in plain sight. Where does that doorway lead? What was that arch? How can you reach that bastion? Was it like this in medieval hill towns where the populace looked up at the lord's castle, wondering but never imagining what life was like inside?

Though now grander than any other Peloponnesian town, Nafplio returned to becoming a relative backwater after Otto moved the capital to Athens at the close of 1834. Kapodistrias had done effective work and the king continued to invest in making the town more liveable. Englishman George Cochrane was here in 1837 and saw it much improved from his visit the year before: "a pretty garrison town, well cleaned, and as in quite as good order as any town on the continent, of a similar size." In 1821, it had been wholly Turkish. Now, according to Cochrane, "the town is composed of the officers of the garrison with their wives, and the merchants of the place; which are many, for Napoli is a place of great commerce, it being the emporium of nearly all the produce of the Morea."

Cochrane lived very well during his stay. He met socially with Bavarian Madame Karbouni, daughter of the town's commander Colonel Strong, and dined with French artist Masson, whose Greek butler brought them roast turkey stuffed with currants and chestnuts and an accompaniment of excellent wines from Naxos. Dessert was ice cream ordered from the local confectioner. On another social call the next day, he heard about a grand ball held recently at which sixty Greek ladies had been dancing.

One of Nafplio's more colourful early-nineteenth-century visitors was Prince Hermann von Pückler-Muskau, a wealthy German aristocrat who became a publishing sensation with his travel books. He passed years travelling in Africa, Europe and the Levant, including an entire year spent touring most of Greece. He stayed in Nafplio and had a lot to say about it.

His first impressions were bad: "Nafplio has almost completely lost its Greek character and resembles – with the many soldiers in the German style and the Bavarian colours – a Bavarian garrison town." On the other hand, he praised its neat cobbled streets and picked up a bargain when a shifty-looking Greek man turned up at Pückler-Muskau's hotel with two large leather knapsacks containing precious stones, old coins and other curiosities. Among these latter items was an alleged signet ring of Constantine the Great (fake) and the notebook of the last Byzantine emperor, embossed in gold to prove its authenticity. It is unclear how much of this booty was stolen.

Pückler-Muskau also tells some stories about the Bavarian military, who held much higher ranks in Greece than at home and earned much higher salaries. Their burden was to work with the Greek artillery, which lacked the required Germanic discipline. On one occasion, the Greek gunners filled their cannons with fireworks instead of gunpowder and enjoyed the colourful explosions as their officers screamed at them. Teaching Greek teenagers was a similar experience for me.

In 1841, the French historian Jean Alexander Buchon visited and called it a well-built place with the appearance of a
western city. Its streets were paved, its squares were planted
with trees and Kapodistrias's legacy was some of the best
buildings to be found in European cities.

Like Trant twenty years previously, Buchon also took an
interest in the ladies, observing that, "the women have adopt-
ed the habits of France; many speak our language in an elegant
manner, and some would not pass unnoticed even at our most
brilliant receptions, not only for that kind of intense and pure
beauty which they received from their great-grandmother
Helen, but because of the comfort and perfection of their
manners, which seem so natural here compared to the women
of France."

The Land Gate still closed at 7.00 pm (or 6.00 or 9.00, depending on the time of year) as it had for around 140 years. Late
arrivals could sometimes take a small boat around to the
marina gate near the Mocenigo bastion, though von Pückler-
Muskau was locked out when he came after dark in 1836,
commenting, "Nafplio is governed even in time of peace as if
the whole country were in rebellion or as if a Turkish army
were approaching." Buchon was also forbidden access, noting,
"The sun is down, you are not to enter Nafplion any more; and
you will be obliged to repay the pleasures of your day's excursion by going to find shelter in some dirty inn or caravanserai in
the suburbs."

It's worth mentioning that the road between Nafplio and
Argos was one of the few paved roads in the entire country at
this time and also possibly its busiest. The traffic looked more
like a constant procession. Around 1843, Frenchman Theodore
Du Moncel wrote: "At all hours various carriages depart from
one city and the other [...] It is a strange contrast to see this
movement in a country where, all around, you hardly meet
human existence."

Let's experience arriving in the town as traveller Jane Loftus
did in the 1860s. Her steamer from Athens anchored in Nafplio
one rainy November day and she was carried to shore by a

small boat, the harbour being silted up again. The boatman brought her to the channel cut along the walls from the Dolfin bastion to the Land Gate and she entered there, noting the Venetian lion. An old painting from Carl Heideck offers an intriguing inside view of the gate as she would have experienced it. The passage through the town walls was oblique, as suggested by the modern reconstruction, and delivered the traveller into a small courtyard. To the right was a doorway leading along the land wall towards the Dolfin bastion, while to the left was a small sentry hut with the town guard on duty. There was also another, identically sized internal arch alongside the entrance that probably contained stairs to the gun battery above. Between the two arches was a Turkish fountain with an inscription and a water trough for animals.

If Loftus walked straight, she would have passed along Papanikolaou Street towards St. Spyridon. Her first impressions? The streets were wet and dirty, as was the small hotel her guide had chosen for her. They ate in a cramped dining room in which dogs bothered them throughout the meal for scraps. Later, they were unable to sleep because the whole town was celebrating the arrival of the king and queen at Athens.

The next day was also cold and wet but she and her party were led to the top of Palamidi's zigzag stairs by a soldier, who passed them to another soldier for a tour of the fortifications and prisons. They also visited Acronafplio. It's a brief but fascinating glimpse into a Nafplio that was accustomed to welcoming paying visitors even at this early stage. The notionally private military installations were sufficiently relaxed to let almost anyone in. The soldiers clearly had a system worked out whereby they would pass the visitors between their respective jurisdictions and share a part of the fee negotiated by the dragoman.

A few nineteenth-century tourists mentioned the dogs of Nafplio, which were also notorious for barking all night. It's something I remember from the late 1990s. Smaller provincial Greek towns tended to accrue a pack of stray dogs that would roam benignly in search of food. The children named them and some people would give them scraps. It seems to be the same today. If you explore Nafplio with Google Earth, you'll find stray dogs in various places around the town, usually sitting in the shade and looking at the camera.

However, these packs tended only to exist in the winter months. When summer and the tourists came, they would abruptly disappear. In their place, the ever-present cats still weave around the table and chair legs for a sardine skeleton. One afternoon, I was sitting at a restaurant table in the street and a cat jumped up into the plant pot beside me for a crap, staring at me intently the whole time. Such are the experiences of living in Nafplio.

By the 1860s, the town had started to demolish the Venetian walls. Nafplio was opening up to allow more air to circulate and starting to grow beyond the masonry that had circumscribed it for centuries. The Baedeker travel guide of 1895 called Nafplio, "a beautiful and healthy town with handsome new buildings." Finally, we're approaching the age of popular photography, which shows us a town with paved squares, surfaced roads and level streets. People strolled and sat in the cafés. Nafplio's old town of 1900 was not so very different to the one we see today. The layout was the same. Some buildings fell or burned and were replaced (see **Absence**). It was not yet a tourist destination but it was in gradual transition. War would merely pause that development for four years.

I lived in Nafplio for a short time. I knew the experience was only ever going to be ephemeral – a year or so – and I treated it as my only chance. I wanted to truly inhabit the old town and spend all of my time walking here, eating here, swimming here – being a part of it.

It's what anybody does when they arrive in a new place. There's a period of novelty. You visit the museums and the castles and you eat at the recommended restaurants. You do the things you'd do as a tourist because you don't know any better. Your concept of the place is derived from prior impressions or a guidebook. This phase passes after a month or less and you actually start to live in the place. You probably stop doing many of the things that tourists do, partly because only tourists do them. You start to feel that you belong.

Part of that belonging is spatial, as discussed in **Mapping**. Part of it is sensory. You learn the sounds, the smells, the textures and tastes of Nafplio. I remember the bell and the pre-recorded commentary of the *trenaki* (little tourist train) passing below my balcony; the hot smell of Staikopoulou kitchens ventilated onto Kapodistriou; slippery Syntagma paving; the jasmine in the Vrahateika gardens and orange blossom in March; incense from St George's open doors; iced ouzo on grey-veined marble table tops. I remember watching December storm clouds from the Five Brothers and looking down at patchwork roofs from Acronafplio. I can still call upon a sense of *being* there.

And If I'd stayed five years? Ten years? If I'd been born there? Some of my students couldn't wait to leave for Athens or Thessaloniki, where the action was. What could they do in Nafplio? Work in a bar, a hotel or the family restaurant? The history of the town was largely irrelevant or even invisible to them. The Grimani bastion was merely something at the periphery of their vision that they passed on the way to the beach. Syntagma Square was a place to kick a ball. Nafplio for them was their friends and their family and school. They'd have to leave and travel and return to know that they'd already seen one of the most attractive and interesting towns in their country and never realised it.

Or maybe not. I write this in a different Mediterranean country, where I've lived for a few years now. The novelty took a while to pass – perhaps a year. But there are regular reminders that this is not the UK. Palm trees are still exotic. Riding my bike through an orange or olive grove is still exotic. Ordering from a menu in the native language is still exotic. There's no winter here – not winter as I used to know it. Maybe it's just me. I'm a romantic.

ABSENCE

Every old town builds upon itself. The manner of that building depends on the history of the town. Fire, inundation and earthquake can totally erase a place, as can a concerted military sacking (*viz.* Jerusalem 70 AD). Religion, too, occasionally wipes infidel traces clean. Sometimes, whole areas are rebuilt with an opportunity to remodel, as with Christopher Wren's London after the Great Fire or Baron Haussmann's modernising programme in Paris. More often, a town is rebuilt in a scattershot manner as buildings are lost or replaced, demolished or dilapidated by time. Medieval structures built mostly of wood soon vanish, while stone persists. Almost always, vestiges and strata remain.

Nafplio's history is one of multiple sieges and occupations, which leave an interesting footprint on a town. Such places soon develop walls and castles, as we've seen. Bombardment from the sea, from the surrounding land and from above can be haphazard, taking out random buildings and leaving others untouched. Many visitors from the eighteenth and nineteenth centuries remarked on the heaps of rubble around the town.

Changes of religion, too, can alter a town. The War of Independence saw the Greeks destroying Turkish structures purely because they were Turkish. Among the first victims were the mosque minarets – so emblematic of Islam – that spiked the town's skyline in eighteenth and early nineteenth-century illustrations. In the 1820s and 1830s, they are reduced to truncated columns. After the end of the 1840s, they have gone. You can still see minaret stumps at the corners of today's Catholic church, but the large base of the Trianon's huge minaret in Syntagma Square has been cleared away.

Religious buildings as a whole, however, were not demolished. Most of the mosques/churches in Nafplio were converted and reconverted according to whichever religion was victorious at the time. After independence, these larger, well-made buildings were repurposed yet again as prisons, schools, courthouses, theatres and whatever else was needed. Religion was one thing, but basic utility and common sense was another.

The Catholic church is a good example. Its Mecca-facing footprint and its dome show it to be a mosque whose constr-uction local lore attributes to Aga Pasha's widow Fatme. She dedicated it to her husband's memory after his death. Its position on the slope of Acronafplio lends credibility to sugg-estions that its origins are earlier, possibly as a Frankish nun-nery. The Duke of Athens Nerio Acciaioli mentioned such a place in his will of 1394, in which he also bequeathed money for Nafplio's Poor Hospital. Certainly, there's an older, vaulted crypt three metres under the mosque that has been identified as a cistern for whatever structure first occupied the place.

In 1998, the English caretaker priest offered me the opport-unity to stay in the ecclesiastical buildings across the courtyard from the church. One hot afternoon, the bougain-villea blushing and still, he took me down to the crypt and opened the large stone reliquary to reveal a tumble of old and very dusty skeletons. He told me they were the remains of Capuchin monks who'd served a previous monastery on the site, but I've read elsewhere they're the bones of Frankish nuns, or the European philhellenes and Bavarian troops who died of typhus in 1833-34. The Bavarians are commemorated by the famous Bavarian Lion sculpture near Prónoia.

I held a jawless skull, yellowed and brittle with age, sus-urrating with trapped gravel, gaping as skulls do, in shock at being reduced to this. I cupped it and tried to imagine how to describe the experience in my journal: a combination of pleasure at being allowed this privileged access to a Nafplio secret, some mild disgust at handling the dead before supper, and the enormity of holding a person's naked, nameless head – someone who had walked these streets perhaps seven hundred years previously. Did a Bavarian corporal in the delirium of his typhus imagine that 160 years hence a young British man would support his dry, smooth forehead in a palm? Did some withered nun in an ecstasy of near-death faith foresee, even feel, my gaze upon her ridged hard palate? I washed my hands immediately after ascending the crypt's steep stairs.

The dark, vaulted room I stayed in at the church was part of the remains of an Ottoman bathhouse, which probably connected to the partially-ruined dome barely fifteen metres away opposite St. Spyridon church. That dome has a rickety door that was closed and chained the whole time I lived in Nafplio, but in 2022 I find the door askew and enter. There's nothing inside but an earthen floor and the domed ceiling pierced with a symmetrical decorative design that allowed steam to rise. Was this the same bathhouse, where, in 1827, European volunteers were murdered for their clothes?

In 1839, King Otto asked the local government to make the building available to Nafplio's Catholic worshippers: the soldiers stationed there and other transient European visitors. Otto himself must have attended services on occasion. Around 1840, 423 Catholic worshippers were recorded in Nafplio. Nowadays, a handful of Polish, English, Romanian and other residents attend occasional services.

I was a resident there for only two weeks. As soon as the English caretaker priest went back to the UK, the Greek administrator told me that he had to write a letter to the Pope asking permission for me to stay. I'd have to move out in the meantime. I took this as an outright lie, but I did later wonder if Pope John Paul opened a letter during breakfast in which the accommodation of a young Englishman was in question.

Nafplio's current fabric is a cross-section of its history: the ancient, the old and the under-construction. It's a town characterised by its specific architectonic and topographical absences: renovated buildings, replaced buildings, ruined buildings, abandoned buildings. There's always a hidden past, a hidden life, for each structure.

Old photos of the town are fascinating. In one picture, a neoclassical façade is pristine – newly painted and bright as new. Another photo shows the same building with broken windows, shutters aslant and black mould streaking down the walls from broken gutters. Jump forwards twenty or thirty years and it looks new again. Or it's gone and another has replaced it. It's tempting to say nothing stays the same. Few structures survive more than 500 years and remain in use without needing repairs. There are, however, buildings in Nafplio that look the same as when they were built, even if their functions have changed half a dozen times. The current archaeological museum is one of them, though steel bands now strap its bulky pillars.

Other buildings have simply gone missing. A space remains where something once stood, or a new building occupies the spot where a more historically illustrious one existed. Some of these remain in the living memories of residents, while others survive only in old photos or paintings or anecdotal histories.

During my time living in Nafplio, one aspect of the town characterised it more for me than the Venetian walls or the converted mosques – ruins were everywhere. Every street seemed to have its ruin. Syntagma Square had ruins; the building opposite the Catholic church was a ruin; the building opposite my balcony on Plapouta Street was a ruin; the building in front of Allotinó was a ruin; the buildings along the southern side of Spyridon Square were ruins and so were the houses to their rear. There was a huge ruin on Lambriniou Street alongside the Vouleftiko, and next to it a tiny yellow house with its upper storey supported on struts – a sign of its impressive age.

These buildings were almost always a brownish-grey colour. Their plaster was peeling to reveal stonework and wooden laths; their shutters were sun-bleached and warped; their doors were ajar but rustily chained; their balconies had fallen, leaving only tiered struts like pieces of driftwood. Graffiti scarred the walls, faded flyers flapped from boarded windows and electric or phone cables looped like funereal bunting beneath peeling weatherboards. I found all of this fantastically romantic – the decadence, the mystery, the history.

The priest at the Catholic church said I was paternalistic and that I was fetishizing urban decay. Just as Henry Miller had said he loved "the light and the poverty" of Greece, I apparently liked the sensation of being inside a historical stage set I didn't understand. I had no idea what any of these buildings had been. They contributed to my sense of being in some otherworldly realm where time had stopped. It wasn't decay. It wasn't anything negative. They were all prompts for dreaming.

I particularly coveted the house on the corner of the stepped road opposite St. Spyridon that led up to the Catholic church – the one with a Turkish fountain assimilated into its corner. It had been abandoned for possibly fifty or sixty years and had a garden with an apple tree. Once, the arched gateway to the garden was broken and I entered the house to see that much of the furniture was still there, opaque with dust. Filigreed sunlight came through the shutters, slicing old curtains. I wanted to live there. I dreamed of owning the place and of sitting in the garden with an iced ouzo, smugly listening to tourists on the other side of the wall speculating who owned the place.

It was almost demolished and would have been in 2018 if a last-minute buyer hadn't stepped in. They also bought the neighbouring house. I now know that it was previously a grocery store belonging to the Koulouridis brothers. It will never be mine. Indeed, all but one of those ruins I mentioned above have now been renovated or are currently in the process of being renovated – mostly as hotels or shops. The only one that remains ruined, forgotten and slowly rotting is the tiny yellow house on Lambriniou Street – apparently one of the cheaper lath and plaster constructions that may be two or three hundred years old but looks so fragile that a strong sneeze might take it down.

Nafplio has modernised rapidly in the last twenty-five years. It is prime real estate and the ruins are potential gold mines. They are also potential money pits. Many of the buildings need serious structural work – not only the floors and roofs, but also the supporting walls, whose cracks often look serious. A lot of these old buildings are not connected to sewer mains, which would require a lot of work. The old town is also subject to very strict building regulations. Old houses have to be restored as closely as possible to their original appearance, using the same materials where feasible. Modernization is allowed, but no UPVC double glazing! A building's historic listing also covers the area immediately around it, such as cobbles or fountains, which must additionally be restored according to regulations. There are even rules about what colour you can paint the buildings, what you can attach to them and what kind of signs ground-floor shops may have.

All of which explains why there are still some ruins. It could be that an individual or a family owns a building but can't afford the cost of renovation. Much easier is simply to wait for the house to fall down – something which happens faster once it has lost its roof. In other cases, ownership of a ruined building is entirely unknown or partial. You can't renovate if you can't find the owner. Nor can you act if one or more of the owners is untraceable or intractable. So the building slowly rots away decade after decade. At some stage, they become dangerous and have to be condemned by the municipality.

Some ruined sites have become part of Nafplio lore: civic embarrassments that have nothing to do with siege bombardment or religious difference. Let's start with the big one – the one that some locals call the turd. That'll be the hideously derelict Xenia Hotel.

The Xenia is the modern two-storey concrete structure atop Acronafplio, occupying the site of the fifteenth-century Castel del Toro. It would be illegal today to build on a site of such historical and archaeological significance – like building a MacDonald's on the Acropolis in Athens. However, its view down the gulf and over Arvanitia beach is unparalleled in Nafplio – probably the best hotel location in the town.

The fifty-eight room hotel opened in 1961 as part of the second phase of a state programme to encourage tourism throughout Greece. This scheme, known after 1960 as the Xenia Hotels Project, began in 1950 and the first four hotels were opened in the early fifties. One of these was the original Amphitryon hotel in Nafplio. The first hotel to be named the Xenia opened in Larissa in 1958. Subsequently this name was used for all new hotels built by the project team and most of the earlier ones were similarly renamed.

By the 1990s EOT, the Greek National Tourist Organisation, sought to privatise its hotels. The three Nafplio hotels, the Xenia, the Amphitryon and the Xenia Palace (now renamed the Nafplia Palace) were taken over by a Greek hotel group in 2000 with a plan to modernise all three. Only the latter two were upgraded and the Xenia was left closed and abandoned. It has remained in a state of dereliction ever since.

One wonders at the inability of the Greek state to make a go of a hotel in this location. Though the architecture now looks a little dated, like a 1960s Bond-villain lair, the setting is magnificent. Was it ineptitude? Apathy? Did someone unqualified get the job through nepotism or bribes? We'll never know, but the Xenia hotel came to mind in 2008 when I saw that year's official government campaign to attract international tourists.

"Greece, the true experience," was a product of the Greek Ministry of Tourism and the Greek National Tourism Organisation (EOT) in collaboration with the state-owned Olympic Airways. A series of eight posters used the tagline alongside photos that were intended to evoke the true experiences of Greece. There were a few problems, however.

The first problem was that only two of the photos used images that were recognisably of Greece (Delos and Delphi). Athens appears minutely in the background of another. Six posters feature outdoor scenes that could be anywhere in the world, including some very generic beach pictures – just sand, sea and sky. One shows a woman sitting on a beached boat with her laptop open but seemingly not turned on. The campaign was designed to promote diversity, but all of the images feature young white people. Worse still is the execution.

The image I first saw when looking through a UK magazine showed four attractive young people – two boys, two girls – amateurishly PhotoShopped onto a beach scene. When I say "beach," I mean three almost featureless horizontal stripes: sand, sea, sky. When I say "amateurish," I mean that all of the four are completely dry though capering in the sea. One of the girls appears to be running miraculously along the surface. All were obviously photographed in a studio and added to the image. The unconvincing splashes around their feet have also been added. Nor does the sea look like it matches the sky. It doesn't entirely look like the sea. A small caption says that this is "Crete Island" (is there a mainland Crete?), but no part of it looks distinctively like Crete. Google it; you'll see what I mean.

My point is: how did anyone at the EOT think that this photo and the others represented an experience of Greece? Or even that it was professional? This was a media campaign aimed at forty-two nations in thirty-seven languages. The country is crammed with breathtaking and highly distinctive beaches. Santorini? Zakynthos? Pylos? It's rife with astounding geographical landscapes. Meteora? The Vikos gorge? Crete's White Mountains? It's thick with gorgeous villages, UNESCO-listed archaeological treasures, natural beauty and diverse cultural influences. And they settled on something they could produce on a computer without leaving their office? If that's not laziness, it's incompetence.

I don't want to say that Greece as a nation is unable to sell itself. This was only one campaign and the idea of capturing the "Greek experience" is good. There were also some really great tourism marketing posters through the fifties, sixties and seventies. But the 2008 campaign gives some insight into how something with so much potential – something so easy – can be so badly mismanaged. Perhaps it was just complacency. People were going to visit anyway, right? Except, in the case of the Xenia hotel, they didn't. Other businesses in Nafplio were doing hospitality better and more successfully. (See **Tourism** for one reason why.)

So the Xenia hotel didn't work out. It happens. But that's

not the problem. The problem is that it's still here, slowly decaying for over twenty years since it last operated as an hotel. It's covered in graffiti. Its rooms, balconies and corridors are littered with rubble, broken glass, rusting metal, toilet paper and other trash. Indigents and drug addicts have crashed there periodically. For a while, an abandoned and ransacked campervan was left there. The concrete is pitted and cracked, plaster peeling in the sea-salt wind. What's going on?

Part of the problem is that any lessee of this huge white elephant has to meet strict contractual terms, for example: improving and maintaining the hotel without making significant changes to the building. The original lease agreement (now out of date) specified an investment of 515 million drachmas and also detailed periods within which any work should be completed and satisfactorily signed off. As with many legacy buildings in Nafplio, the terms were somewhat onerous.

The second, bigger, problem is enforcing the first. A deal signed in 2005 approved a programme of renovation and modernisation, but nothing had happened by 2009. Reports that the site was dangerous compelled the new owners to take interim measures in 2012, such as blocking the hotel's entrance and the open lift shafts. Young people are still able to gain access to the site without too much difficulty. The perceived illegality is probably a big part of the fun.

Another abandoned space is the Xenia outdoor disco on the road up to Acronafplio from the Arvanitia car park and opposite the Venetian Gambello traverse fortification. This neat, stone-built and paved precinct is a curious lacuna that looks as if it's waiting to welcome guests at any moment. There's a bar and railings around it, but it has lain silent and functionless for around thirty years. Some locals remember how the original dance floor was illuminated and that there was a classic mirror ball. Now, it's just another meaningless vacuity.

The Xenia hotel remains derelict at the time of writing: a large and very visible mark of shame sitting atop Acronafplio. It seems almost inconceivable that a building of this size, ugliness and absolute futility has been allowed to remain on the site for so long. But it's now privately owned. A legal battle to compel modernisation or demolition could take years and would be prohibitively expensive for Nafplio's municipality. Doing nothing is the cheapest option for everyone – the reason behind most of the town's modern ruins.

Another notorious example is the derelict pool and garden complex between the Amphitryon hotel and the paralia facing the Bourtzi. Today, it's a chaotic ruin surrounded by rusting chain-link fencing and featuring a faded, graffiti-tattooed swimming pool basin amid a swatch of scrubby, unkempt wasteland – all of this in the very heart of Nafplio's capt-ivatingly picturesque promenade. The story of how the site got into this state is more torturous than the Xenia hotel's and involves another perceived eyesore of two centuries earlier.

Before there was a pool, there was the eight-metre-high Venetian cistern built into the early eighteenth-century sea defences. These walls began to be demolished in 1866 from the S. Theresa/Moschos bastion on today's Philhellion Square but stopped at the cistern, which was still fulfilling its intended use even in 1916. Water from Aria was being channelled along the aqueduct as it had since the 1500s to be stored in the cistern's multiple vaulted chambers.

A report of water poisoning in the early twentieth century may have been the catalyst to dispose of the cistern and continue demolishing the sea defences. That process began in 1929, but in 1933 the half-demolished structure was declared an ancient monument. Old photos of the seafront show the arches of the cistern's vaults gaping emptily at the sea. It was a ruin, nevertheless, and locals considered it unsightly, so dem-olition began again in 1938. A private company bought the land for development in 1939 but demolition was interrupted by the German invasion of 1941. For the rest of the war, the cistern's arched eyes would be witness to bombings, strafing, shipwreck, floating bodies, shrapnel flying and the intentional destruction of the port area by the Germans (see **War**).

The cistern was still there in 1950, having survived twenty years of attempts to demolish it. Explosive charges finally managed to do the job that year, and in 1952 work began on the new Amphitryon hotel. The second phase of the project, beginning in 1957, included the pool and garden complex. By 1961, however, complaints were being made that the costs of both the hotel and pool were grossly over budget. Perhaps that was a warning sign. Another was that the project was originally in the hands of the EOT, the national tourism agency that was to spectacularly fail with the Xenia hotel.

The pool was finished by the early sixties and it looked great. Early publicity shots make it look luxurious, though some private photos show locals sitting in deckchairs with their coats on. The views out to the Bourtzi were magnificent and the pool seems to have been in operation until at least the early 1970s. All that remains today is the pale blue pool basin. The concrete terrace around it has either collapsed or been partially demolished.

As with the Xenia hotel, this land was leased to investors in 2000, though there is some indication that parts of the original plot had remained in private hands from the beginning. Part of the lease obliged the lessee to create a perfect reconstruction of the pool, railings and garden environment within eighteen months and then maintain it in a good condition. That didn't happen. The place is still derelict: a patch of litter-strewn waste ground behind one of the most wonderful views in the Peloponnese.

There are many ruins in Nafplio and some have their charm, lending to the general sense of history. At the same time, it's odd and depressing that so many of them are on the coast. A stone's throw from the Amphitryon pool is the abandoned site of the town's previous sea-bathing centre. The story of this facility is told in **Pleasures**, but today it is an abandoned stone and concrete site below the Five Brothers bastion. The base was constructed in 1958 with the idea that a new bathhouse would be built, but nothing had been done by the following year. The problem may have been finding someone to operate the baths.

Still, the place was up and running from the summer of 1960, even if the original designs had omitted to consider urinals or an engine-room area. Locals didn't like it, saying that it looked like a bunker and that it jarred architecturally with the Venetian bastion and sea gate immediately in front of it. Both were valid points. The baths were still in regular use during the 1970s, when the circular sea pool was added by the then mayor for children to play in. The pool remains, its concrete now black and pitted, its basin full of algae, sea urchins and probably the odd octopus.

At some point, it ceased to be a bathing facility. It was a restaurant in 1998, its terrace full of diners and its roof ventilator wafting hot calamari scents up to the overlooking cannon. Nowadays, it apparently has no building permit and its legal or rental status is uncertain. In March 2020, a 1.5m wall was added to the front of the structure to protect it from the sea which made it even uglier.

Like the Xenia hotel and the Amphitryon pool, the old bathhouse is a very visible failure. Barely a few metres along the coast is another: the so-called boat club, whose concrete rectangle in the sea is slowly rotting and whose basin is silting up. It, too, was briefly a bar and restaurant with sunbeds around the concrete rectangle – an innovative use of the space. Today it's another ruin.

One final shameful mention has to go to the abandoned three-storey structure that has overlooked Arvanitia beach for around thirty years. It is perhaps the worst and saddest of all the modern ruins in terms of its potential and location. Designed in 1969 by Kleon Krantonellis, the building operated until the early 1990s and is fondly remembered by locals who used it. It's now a concrete shell full of graffiti, litter, broken glass and twisted metal, loose cables, leaky pipes, cracked tiles, drug paraphernalia and faecal matter.

Perhaps more absurdly still, the wreck sits alongside the gorgeous coastal walk to Karathonas beach, which in 2000 was registered as part of the European Union's Natura 2000 project aimed at protecting the continent's most valuable and threatened species and habitats – a network of core breeding and resting sites for birds and other wildlife. There's a faded and partially disfigured information board next to the defunct bar/café's rotting architectural corpse.

I used to pass this skeleton often on my walks and imagine what I could do with it if I were a millionaire. A luxury abode, naturally, with large plate-glass windows for viewing the gulf and the cliffs of the peninsula, the winter seascapes, the boats coming and going. On summer evenings, I'd have a rooftop terrace and perhaps a bird feeder to attract some of those protected species to visit. Maybe I'd turn the lower floor into a bar so cool that it'd be by invitation only. So much potential. So much complacency.

There are other Nafplio buildings recorded in history and image but which no longer exist in living memory. Two of these – the houses of Nikitas "The Turkeater" Stamatelopoulos and of republican nationalist Kalliopi Papalexopoulou – are dealt with in the **Squares** chapter, but there are many other candidates.

The *palataki*, or little palace, was built to house the first governor of the nascent Greek state Ioannis Kapodistrias. There was nowhere for him to live when he arrived in 1828 and he was initially housed on Vasileos Konstantinou until a more fitting building could be constructed. Work began in 1829 and the little palace was finished the same year: a three-storey neoclassical building with a large central arch in the front leading to a courtyard. A third-floor balcony facing the square was presumably intended to address crowds. It was located at the west end of today's Three Admirals Square, where there is a palm tree and a statue of King Otto. One of the few surviving nineteenth-century paintings of the *palataki* shows it at the head of a cleared open space patrolled by three soldiers. To its left is the old Venetian city wall (around two storeys high), over which peek the roofs of the growing extra-mural town. To its right are the older houses whose out-jutting upper floors are supported on wooden struts. These would very soon be demolished and replaced by the same structures that occupy the space today. Like an Instagram influencer's photo, all other messiness (e.g. inevitable pedestrians) has been edited from the painting.

Kapodistrias's body was embalmed and laid in the *palataki* for public viewing after his assassination outside St. Spyridon in 1831. Thereafter, from 1833, it became Prince Otto's royal palace and would have hosted regal audiences with ambassadors and consuls. It probably held parties and balls for the rich and pretty. All the hopes, dreams and oppositions of early nineteenth-century Greece were concentrated for a few short years on today's vacant patch of grass, the epicentre of the nation's first capital.

Where did it go? As early as 1894, the building was declared to be in a deplorable state of abandonment and in need of urgent repair. Otto had long ago moved to Athens, gone into exile and died aged fifty-two. The early twentieth century saw the building repurposed in true Nafplio fashion as the headquarters of the Barbers and Hairdresser's Association. The scissor-wielders had to promise that they would manage and maintain the building for twenty-five years and they did. Just. It burned down on October 16 1929 after becoming the prefectural offices of Argolis and Corinthia.

Thus, the focus of Greek political and national identity during the early nineteenth century became a vacant lot. Accidents happen, of course. But it's an interesting notion that the building didn't burn down during the hundred years or so that it used candles and oil lamps for lighting, or open fires for heat and cooking. I wonder if one person was responsible. It's not about blame. Rather, it's intriguing that human error might have caused the residence of Greece's first governor and first king to burn down and be replaced by a palm tree.

Just around the corner from the *palataki*, on Plapouta Street, is the Armansperg mansion. It was originally twinned with an identical building on the other side of the street, the two presenting an impressive entrance to the town. The twin was demolished in 1953 and what remains is the hideous, single-storey concrete bunker housing a lottery vendor.

Another notable Nafplio absence is Lakka Square in the tiny Psaromahala neighbourhood that occupies Acronafplio's western slopes. It's a largely featureless car park nowadays, but it was once the site of the town's first hospital for the poor, built with a bequest from Frankish duke or archon Nerio Acciajoli in 1394 – he of the supposed nunnery on the site of the current Catholic church.

This structure survived through the centuries, no doubt kept in good architectural shape by the Venetians, to remain the town's municipal hospital into the early nineteenth century. It's not clear if the Turks used the hospital, but it was in urgent need of renovation when Ioannis Kapodistrias arrived in 1828. These were, after all, dark days for Nafplio. The War of Independence had seen thousands of Greek refugees flee Turkish destruction to the safety of Nafplio's walls. Plague, typhoid, dysentery, cholera and smallpox were rife, not to mention injuries from flying cannonballs, falling masonry, robberies and fire.

Kapodistrias's military commander Carl Wilhelm von Heideck noted in his memoirs that he, " . . . founded and built two hospitals in Nafplio, one of which was used as a civilian hospital by order of the Governor, and the other as a military hospital in Itz-Kale" – from which we can assume some renovation or extension was made to the hospital in Psaromahala. The updated building consisted of two parts: the hospital for the wounded and the hospital for the sick. You didn't want to enter with a broken wrist and leave in a coffin from the plague you'd caught there. Though the town hospital served the military, Kapodistrias saw that a new dedicated establishment would have to be constructed for soldiers on Acronafplio (see **Castles**).

With the swelling population, this hospital in Psaromahala couldn't cope with the numbers and other hospital sites were opened, probably in large houses. The original stayed open however and seemingly carried on until around 1940. There are photographs of its ruins in 1970 featuring an ornate arched doorway with relief pilasters and a semicircular pediment.

Now, there is nothing at all to suggest that a building stood on the site – or exactly where. It seems unlikely that the hospital was built squarely over the modern-day car park. Today's road was created for motor vehicles and follows the hill's natural contours, but this was just a switchback track in the 1930s and went more directly. One old and very grainy aerial photograph appears to show the hospital as a large three-storey building following the line of the Venetian walls roughly as far as the boat club. You would have passed the end of the structure before descending the sea gate stairs under the Five Brothers bastion. Part of today's car park seems to have formed a front yard for the hospital – a place for carts or vehicles to turn around and potentially for overspill in times of war or disease.

One oddity does remain. The tiny chapel of the Holy Apostles that nestles into the foliage of Acronafplio once occupied the hospital's yard. It was dedicated to St Anthony under the Venetians but became Orthodox after liberation in 1822. Thereafter, it belonged to the apostles Peter and Paul, but also to Saint Barbara, who is associated with armourers, artillery and military engineers – a fitting saint for Nafplio. This unassuming and virtually invisible chapel was used for centuries by patients and their families praying for the prolongation of life or a painless death.

A stairway shortcut from the road up to today's Lakka Square is covered in graffiti, litter, broken glass, reeking urine stains and the occasional turd (animal or human). People died here in pain, delirious, destitute, screaming, alone. The hospital was the last hope for countless anonymous people throughout 500 years of history and now it's possibly the least attractive part of the old town.

The square has an interesting appendix. Leading off from its south side is a long subterranean passage that tunnels into the base of Acronafplio. It looks like it might be a nuclear bunker from the outside, but it's a corridor to the lifts of the

Nafplia Palace (ex Xenia Palace) hotel up on the hill. You enter a dimly lit, reinforced concrete tunnel with a stone-flagged floor and a 1960's ceiling design of many faded-colour blocks. It's vaguely terrifying and often smells of disinfectant, urine or mildew depending on when you visit. Naturally, there's some graffiti on the walls. When I lived there in 1998, some local youth had thoughtfully scrawled the names of all The Prodigy's albums, including an obscure 1999 mix tape.

I used this passage as a shortcut when on my many walks about the town. It saved me retracing my steps back down past the Arvanitia car park and I could reach the sea through the Five Brothers gate. Then and now, I marvel that this is the first experience some guests have of the hotel they've booked. It looks like something out of a low-budget sixties dystopian science-fiction movie. Indeed, I was just there this morning (June 2022) and as the lift doors opened at the bottom, I stepped out to meet a group of German tourists waiting with their luggage. They looked faintly worried. I wondered if maybe they'd also walked up the piss-puddled steps from the road.

This is as good a place as any to say something about Nafplio's graffiti. Many of our modern cities have their share. It's urban lichen, accumulating over time and spreading according to levels of deprivation or civic apathy. It breeds in the interstices and the voids and in the same corners as the wind-blown trash. But not all modern cities have a millennium or more of multicultural heirlooms. Not all modern cities are gorgeously located on a rocky peninsula at the head of a gulf in the Mediterranean and surrounded by mountains. You might expect or forgive graffiti in Leeds or Liverpool, Paris or Detroit, but it looks worse in Nafplio.

Twenty-five years ago, some young philosopher had written on a wall behind the Catholic church: "Graffiti is not a crime. It's art." Presumably, this childish orthography in black spray paint was the "art" being alluded to. I don't deny that good graffiti can be interesting and require skills, but this wasn't an example of it. This was the work of a hormone-befuddled adolescent with too much spare time and too little frontal lobe development. They have little to say. They just want to posture and break some rules.

Nafplio's third century BC supporting wall has graffiti on it as does the fifteenth century gate of Castel Toro, the Sagredo gate, the Venetian sea wall below the Five Brothers bastion and the adjacent 1950s bathhouse. Perhaps the logic is: "They're ruins anyway, so . . ." Certainly, it's interesting which buildings don't have graffiti: the Vouleftiko, the Archaeological Museum, the churches. Why are they graffiti free? Perhaps they are all in very public places with almost constant movement around them. It could be that the buildings are well cared for and don't invite further decoration. We might also hope that they also retain some dimly perceived importance for the feckless daubers. As for the churches, they hold the vague threat of superstition. One doesn't deface a church, even if one thinks religion is a joke.

Malcolm Gladwell outlines the "Broken Windows" theory in his book *The Tipping Point*: that visible evidence of decay and disorder in an urban environment encourages more such behaviour. Where there are broken windows, more windows will be broken. This is evident in the Xenia hotel and the abandoned bar/café of Arvanitia. Where graffiti appears, more graffiti will breed because, you know – what's the difference? Meanwhile, a pristine and obviously valued building such as the Vouleftiko, or a building embodying deep cultural values such as a church remains untouched.

It's not an easy fix. Cleaning up graffiti is a thankless, repetitive and costly task for any municipal council, as is catching and prosecuting the people who do it. Greece has had some hard times and money is tight. On the other hand tourism is the main income for Nafplio's old town. People come to see charm and history not urban blight. Could the solution be in subtle re-education? At some crepuscular level, the pimply vandals already acknowledge ethics and values in their choices of what not to tag. It's a start. If that doesn't work, maybe amputation is worth a try.

SEA

I remember walking to the Kondogiorgos café one weekday morning and seeing a new arrival in the bay: an ugly industrial-looking platform with a crawler crane set on it. A low barge was moored alongside like a tumour. It was a dredger brought in to deepen Nafplio's perpetually silting port and it shattered the calm for the next few weeks with its labouring engine, clanking chains and splashing.

I watched its process daily. At the end of the crane's cable was a vast, toothed maw, a hinged bucket that hung, gaping, a few metres above the surface before being released to fall free, splashing dramatically and diving into the seabed mud. Then it was hoisted with a moan of diesel engine and a plume of blue-black smoke, dripping sludge. The bucket swung out over the barge leaving a trail of gushing brown and the jaws vomited a torrent of viscous slop into the waiting cargo bay.

I was watching the day when they pulled up a colossal cannon. It was a lazy morning, too early for most of the locals to be taking their coffee. An old man rode his bike along the *paralia* to catch fish off the pier. The occasional van delivered ice or bottles to the cafés. Everything started as normal: the repetitive splash, roar and hoist of the dredger. The horrible torrent. Then the crane column creaked and moaned. The cable stuttered and tautened. The man in yellow plastic galoshes on the barge's prow waved a frantic arm. *Stop! Stop!* The diesel engine went into neutral.

I'm sure there was nothing visible. The whole area around the dredger was stained grey-brown by the drifting silt. The crane operator and bargeman shouted to each other. Apparently, the plan was to jerk whatever was down there. Maybe it was a huge rock stuck in the mud. It could equally have been a bomb left over from World War Two, but that didn't seem to occur to them. The engine throbbed, the cable quivered a few times and then started to rise. Something was coming up.

It was half caught in the bucket's jaws, its mouth inside and its cascabel (the rear knob) sticking out. Evidently, the teeth had a good grip on the cannon's trunnions, the circular supports about halfway down the barrel. The thing was huge and old. Cannons hadn't been fired in anger at Nafplio since the War of Independence in the early nineteenth century. How did it end up there?

Was it a Venetian artillery piece? Turkish? Perhaps something even older. Byzantine? In 1945, the retreating Italian occupiers had apparently "taken back" the Venetian cannons of the Five Brothers bastion. Had they accidentally dropped one in the port when loading them aboard? Or was it from the wreck of the Venetian *schierazo* vessel that was scuttled in 1538 to block the port against the notorious Turkish admiral Hayreddin Barbarossa, who had just terrorised Venetian Corfu and was threatening to arrive any moment?

I realised then how many secrets were lying on the seabed around Nafplio. The port has been dredged constantly throughout history, but this cannon had never been pulled up. What else was down there? Coins? Jewels? Cargo of various kinds? How many ships had gone down in the upper part of the Argolic gulf while leaving or arriving in Nafplio? At various points in history large flotillas had left as fleeing inhabitants took all their valuables with them.

A few days later and a few metres distant, they pulled up a massive iron anchor with some chain still attached to it – another vestige of Nafplio's maritime history that had lain preserved in the mud's soft embrace for possibly five hundred years or more. Was it from the same ship as the cannon?

I also wondered where the dredged silt was going. The barge was towed down the gulf each evening and was empty the next morning. Some said that the silt was being used for land reclamation at Paralia Astros, which is prone to marine erosion. But was anyone going through all those tonnes of mud to sieve it for five thousand years of history? There was another series of dredging in 2021, when local archaeologist Christos Piteros lamented that no underwater archaeological survey of the port had been included in the scheme. It seems there are still countless treasures lying just a few metres under the calm surface – or buried in landfill down at Astros. Mycenaean imports? Fifth-century BC wine amphorae? Venetian silver? Byzantine armaments? And how many bones? Assuredly, there are hundreds of cannonballs from the centuries of sieges.

In 1998, there was very little activity at Nafplio's port. One large, rusting cargo ship was there each week carrying sand or aggregate down to Spetses. From November, a Russian cargo ship or two would come to pick up oranges. In summer, the luxury yachts would arrive – never very many but always a novelty. I and any other interested people would stroll insouciantly alongside these moored palaces to see where they'd come from and if anyone famous was onboard. There were always rumours (Tom Cruise, some Greek pop star), which turned out to be false. Had it been 1959, I might have seen Aristotle Onassis, who was in port with his ninety-nine-metre luxury superyacht Christina O. Guests on board included Winston Churchill and Maria Callas.

The modern harbour gives very little indication of how busy the port has been since its first use by sailors. Most of the present sea frontage is given over to car parking, which says a lot about how the local economy has changed. According to ancient sources, King Agamemnon set out for Aulis, staging point for the Greek expedition to Troy, with one hundred black ships. Did those multi-oared ships once sit inside Nafplio harbour when it was known as Mycenae's port? Might Odysseus, too, have dropped anchor here on his way to Aulis from Ithaca? He would certainly have passed this way.

The problem, then as now, was silt. The site of ancient Tiryns was 300 metres from the shore around 2265 BC but is now about two kilometres from the coast thanks to millennia of silting. As early as the third century BC, there is evidence that the walls of Nafplio's ancient acropolis may have run down and north into the harbour area to create a basin but also potentially to control the flow of silt. A small stretch of this polygonal wall (graffiti tagged by an imbecile) and the medieval walls above it are still visible on Konstantinopoleos Street in the Psaromahala district.

It appears that the Byzantines, too, may have attempted to control the silt. During the 1899 construction of the port's modern car park quay, a previous structure was found beneath it in the harbour's mud. The evidence suggests a five to ten metre wide mole stretching 250 metres out into the sea and made of stone blocks measuring up to half a cubic metre. A corresponding mole to the west of the harbour has also been posited where the current quay runs out towards the Bourtzi.

The Venetians were highly skilled at dredging, having done so since the middle ages in their own archipelago. In 1701, they suggested dredging a thin channel close to shore so that larger ships could enter the port. It seems this was done because the Venetians later constructed a protected harbour basin between the city walls and the Mocenigo bastion (the site of the current high school). The remains of two galleys were found buried in the mud here in 1932. Were these galleys irreparably damaged in a sea battle, or scuppered on purpose to block access? Maybe they were destroyed where they floated during an Ottoman siege. We'll never know, but it's fascinating to look at the school's south playground and imagine it full of Venetian galleys between colossal walls.

The varying depth of the port has also been one of its protective advantages, with the sea north of the Bourtzi being historically too shallow for large ships to enter. The only safe entry was between the Bourtzi and the shore, which according to various textual sources would permit only one ship at a time to pass. Multiple seventeenth-century engravings show a chain stretched taut between the islet and the shore's fortifications and, indeed, Nafplio was apparently known as Porto Cadena: Port of the Chain. There's some doubt, however, that this famous chain existed. In *The Fortifications of Nafplio*,

Allan Brooks judiciously notes that the channel between shore and Bourtzi, "reputedly could be closed by raising a chain between these two points." Reputedly, one assumes, because there is no material evidence that such a mechanism existed. All of the illustrations of the chain show it fixed to the city wall, but there's nothing to see on the remaining walls, the same Venetian walls that might have anchored such a chain. Assuming the chain could be raised and lowered from the Bourtzi side alone, a colossal capstan would have been required there. No evidence of this is forthcoming.

There is one tantalising textual clue in the survey carried out in 1687 by P.M. Coronelli, official geographer to the Republic of Venice and very likely an eyewitness aboard one of Francesco Morosini's invading fleet. This was around 270 years after the Bourtzi had been built and these Venetians had never seen it in person. A contemporary English translation of Coronelli notes that "The Bay is very spacious within, but it is stopt up at its entrance, and no Gallies can get in till they have passed through a Chanel, where they are exposed to the great Artillery."

Is the bay "stopt up" because a chain is fixed between the Bourtzi and the town walls, or because the area around the Bourtzi is so silted-up that only a narrow navigable channel exists? The phrasing of "until they have passed through" hints that access might be granted, say, by the lowering of a chain, but it's curious that the state geographer wouldn't mention either the Bourtzi or the chain in his description. The artillery he is talking about is concentrated partly in the Bourtzi.

Apart from the dubious physical evidence and ambiguous textual evidence, the practicalities of such a chain raise questions. The distance between the eastern bastion of the Bourtzi (whence pictures show the chain emerging) to the nearest town walls is about five hundred metres. Neither the wall nor the Bourtzi has moved in the meantime and all of the images are clear that the chain wasn't connected to a quay or mole. A chain of five hundred metres that was also sufficiently robust to prevent a warship from entering the port would have weighed many thousands of kilograms. To keep it taut, as shown in the engravings, would have required impressive supporting structures on each side, not to mention the intense effort of raising and holding it. Given that it weighed so much, might not a warship easily have exerted sufficient force to rip the chain from its moorings?

Chains across ports are not a fantastical concept. They have existed throughout history. There was one at Rhodes and, famously, one across the port at Constantinople. The difference is that the Constantinople chain was anchored by the first colossal Galata Tower, destroyed in the same Fourth Crusade that brought the Franks to Nafplio. Something of that size and strength would have been necessary.

Were the seventeenth-century artists making up the tale of the Bourtzi chain? Many of the historical pictures also show the islet connected to a tower on the other shore by a second taut chain, thus closing the port entirely. The tower was a nice touch, but the distance to the nearest point on the opposite shore, even with silting, would have been two or three kilometres. The weight of this chain would have been colossal and keeping it taut would have been a superhuman feat. Nor was such a chain necessary due to the port's shallowness north of the Bourtzi. Clearly, the second chain was artistic license. Was the southern one, too?

Textual sources are rife with copied mistakes. The French-English writer Abel Boyer wrote in a 1696 publication that Nafplio had a population of 60,000 – an impossibly high number that was nevertheless repeated in other publications by people who'd never been there. Had Boyer simply made an error when copying information from a 1693 writer who used the same information but sensibly kept a zero off the population? Likewise, the idea of the Bourtzi passage allowing only one ship at a time was probably untrue but was repeated by writers who hadn't actually seen the channel. We could posit that an early artist portrayed a chain that was copied by subsequent artists, who embellished the idea with a second chain.

Still, the name of Porto Cadena lingers around the history of Nafplio. It must have come from somewhere. South down the coast was the sister Venetian port of Monemvasia, then called Napoli di Malvasia. Like Nafplio, it was a well-defended position that lacked safe shipbuilding or repair facilities. As Nafplio used nearby Drepanon for this purpose, so Monemvasia used the modern inlet of Limni Ieraka, whose narrowest point is only about seventy metres wide and which was also known as Porto Cadena. A mix-up? A conflation of facts? It's another Nafplio mystery. Could there be a length of heavy chain beneath the harbour mud between the Five Brothers bastion and the Bourtzi just waiting to be discovered?

The Byzantine Empire was a maritime power. Its royal fleet mostly consisted of *dromons,* heavy ships designed for long-distance voyages and fighting. They had fifty rows of oars on each side and were heavily armed with crossbows and the famous Greek Fire, a napalm-like substance that was fired through tubes at high pressure and burned even on the sea's surface. The liquid's exact ingredients remain a matter of speculation, but it may have contained, naptha, pine resin, sulphur or nitre (saltpetre).

A variety of other ships plied the empire's possessions and included smaller versions of the *dromon,* galleys, the *chelandion* for carrying horses, and cargo ships. We can assume that a combination of these vessels would have been found in Nafplio's harbour for around two hundred years from the tenth to the twelfth centuries as the Byzantines brought materials, builders, inhabitants, soldiers and goods for trading. With each *dromon* carrying one hundred rowers, the town's population would have significantly increased each time a ship arrived in port.

Byzantine Nafplio was not a hugely precious treasure for the emperors of Constantinople. As for most other occupiers, it was primarily a safe port. The lunatic archon Leo Sgouros (see **Arrivals**) was responsible for collecting taxes in the region – something we can assume he did with no subtlety – and also for supplying ships. The latter is curious since Nafplio has never been noted for its shipbuilding. Sgouros may have deforested the region and had the ships built elsewhere in the Argolid. It's certainly the case that when the Venetians later wanted to extend the lower town on wooden piles, they had to bring their own wood.

Piratical raids from the sea had been largely eradicated by the iron hand of Theodoros Sgouros and invasion by sea was not yet established, partly due to the relatively undeveloped state of gunpowder weapons. Byzantine ships were also designed more for battles at sea. It's telling that Nafplio's invasion and siege by the Franks in the early thirteenth century apparently involved only four galleys.

The Franks had typically used their ships to make crossings and to transport goods or men on their way to a target city. Siege was their main weapon of war and land forces would be the key to taking Nafplio until the arrival of flight and the Germans in 1941. In fact, the Byzantine navy had been in decline from the eleventh century, which is why they offered the Venetians free trading rights in Nafplio in return for naval support around 1082.

The Franks and the Venetians, if not friends, were already business partners. Venice had agreed to supply ships to the Fourth Crusade but when the crusaders had been unable to pay, Doge Enrico Dandalo suggested a deal: help us invade Zadar (in modern Croatia). When the Franks later invaded Constantinople, Venice leant a maritime hand and filled its pockets. The transition of Nafplio from Frankish to Venetian ownership was therefore gradual and peaceful.

The town was important to Venice as part of its chain of Greek ports, including Corfu, Methoni, Coroni, Monemvasia, Chalkida (Euboia) and Crete on the route to its markets in the east. Ships from Venice would sail through Greek territory and onwards up through the Bosphorus or on to Egypt and Syria to pick up spices, salt and other lucrative goods. Since Venetian galleys were not built for heavy weather and their many oarsmen needed supplies at least every two weeks, it was necessary to have reliable ports of call along the trade routes.

For the next hundred and fifty years or so, the various ships of Venice would have been familiar visitors at Nafplio: the galeazze, the navi, barze, grippi, caravelle and more. They would have brought not only cargoes to and from Venice but also, like the Byzantines before them, building materials, engineers, artisans, settlers and soldiers.

It was a time of change for shipping in general. Whereas oars had been the main form of propulsion for hundreds of years, sails started to take over in the fifteenth century. You don't have to feed sails. The last naval battle with rowed warships was the Battle of Lepanto in 1571.

Marine traffic would have increased greatly from the end of the fifteenth century, when the Venetians learned that the Ottomans were building a fleet in the Black Sea. Venice acted quickly, refurbishing and adding to their fleet with forty-four light galleys, twelve heavy galleys, twenty-eight armed round-ships and four huge ships with heavy cannons and crews of three hundred or more. When the Ottoman general Hayreddin Barbarossa unsuccessfully besieged Venetian Corfu in 1537, the Doge's galleons nervously patrolled the coast for eighteen months and would have been a regular presence in Nafplio.

Silting continued to be a problem and dredging must have been done periodically. In 1647, Admiral Antonio Grimani had blockaded the Turkish fleet inside the harbour but it was silted up again in 1686 when the ships of Francesco Morosini arrived. An engraving of the time shows around eighty large sailing ships at anchor further down the gulf and crowded into Arvanitia and Karathonas bays, plus around forty smaller support vessels moored around Nea Kios at the top of the gulf. Three of the ships have come closer to the south cliffs of Acronafplio and one as far as the Bourtzi to shell the fortifications, but none has entered the silted-up harbour. Imagine the spectacle: the forest of masts and sails, ensigns flapping in the breeze – the tide of history changing again.

Each new siege and occupation involved massive movements of populations. When the Venetians arrived, the thousands of Turks living in the town were obliged to leave and seek a new life back in Asia Minor. Hundreds of vessels would have had to take the majority of the populace away to a land they'd possibly never known. They'd lived for generations in Nafplio as residents of the Ottoman Empire. Likewise, the Venetians had to leave behind their houses and established businesses when the Turks invaded. Hundreds more vessels would cross the sea back to Venice. Even if these people had been willing to live under an alien religion and see their church turned to a mosque (or vice versa), they weren't welcome. They were the enemy.

The town's existence was ever more firmly based on shipping. An Ottoman survey of Nafplio in 1715, the year it fell to them for the final time, counted 350 Venetian-built warehouses and 509 workshops or shops in the town. Goods were coming and going for centuries in significant quantities, as all of the ships sailing to the east came back via Greece. The harbour would have been populated with tall masted ships almost all the time, more so when the weather was bad and shelter was needed. The population of the town would ebb and flow with the arrival and departure of crews and troop transports. A similar effect continues today when a huge cruise ship anchors down the gulf and a thousand or more tourists flood the town for a day.

The Ottomans may not have been traders in the same league as the Venetians, but they kept up a flow of sponges, silk, oil, wax and wine through Nafplio's port. Venice was already in decline, and losing the Peloponnese had been a significant blow, so the Turks after 1715 didn't need a great amount of sea power to hold their Greek possessions.

The Ottoman Empire, too, would shortly enter its decadent stages and the hectic trade of Nafplio's Venetian years was over. Paintings and drawings of the late Ottoman period Nafplio tend to show just a handful of large ships in port. Small felucca-style coastal vessels with lateen sails predominate. Intriguingly, one watercolour painting of the late seventeenth century shows a large ship foundered and leaning on the north side of the Bourtzi. It has obviously run aground. Are vestiges of this vessel still to be found in the mud?

The port would not be full of ships again until the Greek War of Independence when the massed masts of Morosini's invasion fleet might again be matched.

It was a David and Goliath confrontation when the Greeks faced the Ottoman Empire at sea. Not only was the Turkish fleet much bigger, it was also built specifically for war, whereas the Greek fleet consisted mostly of repurposed merchant vessels. Many of these came from the Argolic islands of Hydra, Spetses and Poros, paid for in part by wealthy ship-owners such as Laskarina Bouboulina and Mandó Mavrogenous (see **Heroes**). The tiny archipelago was in daily contact with the first capital via a constant flow of fifty to seventy caiques that arrived on the wind in the morning and left in the evening when the wind reversed off the land and down the gulf. They would have crowded the water between the quay and the Bourtzi during the day's hottest hours, forming a wooden thicket of masts askew and folded sails.

The European powers were slow to come to Greece's aid, but by 1827 the assembled British, Russian and French fleets were in Navarino Bay near Pylos seeking shelter and keeping an eye on the Ottoman fleet. A polite request to move some fire ships turned into a tit for tat, then a free for all, which turned into the annihilation of the Ottoman fleet. Suddenly, the Greek seas were thick with European warships, many of which would end up in Nafplio: a formidably defended port and also the epicentre of the nascent Greek state.

It was also in 1827 that Nafplio started to receive large quantities of aid from Europe and America. The bill of lading for US ship Chancellor sailing out of New York listed the follwing cargo bound for Nafplio: 154 casks of rice, 365 barrels of Indian meal, 938 barrels of flour, seven casks of corn, 410 barrels of bread, twenty-one of salted provisions, three casks of hams, twenty-two boxes and bales of dry goods and clothing.

The Chancellor was armed against pirates and Ottoman

ships that would seek to stop supplies from reaching the be-
leaguered Greek capital. If impeded in their mission, the officers of the ship would say that they were taking supplies to
the American squadron in Smyrna. The greatest danger was
not the Turks, however. It was the Greeks waiting at the
Chancellor's destination.

The ship was greeted in Nafplio by a representative of the
US vessel Constitution, who came with a warning. A French
ship bringing aid had recently been mobbed by soldiers and
had its cargo entirely cleaned out. Another US ship, the
Trabaculo, had also been boarded by soldiers and had its
cargo stolen. Multiple vessels had faced the same fate, including one that hadn't even been bound for Nafplio but simply
put into port to escape bad weather. The soldiers were not
hungry or needy. They were selling the food for personal gain.
The captain of the Chancellor accordingly deposited a third of
his cargo in the Bourtzi for safekeeping, gave a third to the
rapacious soldiers and a third directly to the hungry poor.

Huge amounts of aid was arriving every day, as well as
fighting ships from the European navies. The port received so
many Bibles that they had to be stored in warehouses. The
Greek priests didn't know what to do with them. There were
also, inexplicably, vast quantities of musical instruments being
sent to Nafplio by philanthropic societies from across Europe
and America. One can only imagine what the naked, starving,
diseased refugees from across the Peloponnese thought when
they saw trumpets and violins flow from the cargo holds to the
warehouses.

Greece's first governor Ioannis Kapodistrias arrived in 1828
to impose order in Nafplio. An oil painting of the event shows
scores of ships beyond the Bourtzi, all of them firing cannon
salutes in celebration. The bay is white with smoke. Dozens of
smaller coastal vessels are gathered about the shore at the top
of the gulf. An even bigger seaborne event was to come.

The appointment in 1832 of prince Otto of Wittelsbach as
the first king of Greece was a consequence of the Great Powers
(Britain, France and Russia) deciding that what an indepen-

dent Greek state needed most was some teenage Bavarian aristocrat. The lad was seventeen. His appointment came with a loan of sixty million francs to help the new state develop. Suddenly, Nafplio was one of Europe's most important diplomatic centres.

Otto's arrival in Nafplio was a statement of European power. He came from Trieste on the British forty-six gun frigate Madagascar and arrived in Nafplio a few days before his official reception on 30 January 1833. The bay already contained five other British warships, three Russian, seven French, one Sicilian and probably an Austrian ship, as well as many smaller support boats and Greek vessels.

Paintings of the new king's arrival show that none of the large ships has passed the Bourtzi, suggesting that the harbour was once again heavily silted up. Still, it must have been an impressive sight with the multiple masts and ensigns stretching down the gulf. Otto was welcomed with twenty-one-gun salutes from various vessels and from the town's batteries, a reverberating thunder that would have continued on and off for days as Otto visited admiral and vice-admiral on their respective ships. White cannon smoke drifted in huge plumes, but for once in Nafplio's martial history no cannonballs were flying.

The revolutionary period and subsequent regency represented a time of increased marine traffic. Apart from the charity donations and the military presence, heavily protected ships full of gold and silver were arriving every two months from England, with predictable results (see **War**). Otto also had his own yacht for pleasure cruises and people were constantly arriving in the new capital from across the Peloponnese, from Greece in general, from the Great Powers and from America: refugees, soldiers, philhellenes, diplomats, fortune seekers, writers and travellers. The palaces and houses of the new regency needed repair, decoration and the finest furniture from Paris or Vienna. A visitor in 1840 noted that the town's population was around 10,000 and that the harbour, presumably beyond the Bourtzi, could easily float 600 ships.

Statistics from Frederic Strong's exhaustive survey of the new nation show the following shipping figures for Nafplio in 1835: 4,430 ships arrived and 4,734 ships departed. Most of those were intra-Greek voyages, with a handful going to Austria, France, Great Britain or Turkey.

Otto's stay in Nafplio was brief. Its choice as the nation's first capital had been based more on unfolding political events and on its military architecture than on its suitability. As a walled town on a peninsula, its capacity for growth was limited. There was also the persistent problem of the silting harbour that kept arrivals at bay and provoked the infamously recurring fevers or 'plague' that Nafplio was prone to. The nature of the lower town's construction, the ever-present swamp and the multiple vessels from across the Ionian and Aegean seas also meant a lively rat population. Even today, you'll see the subtle rat traps around the streets of Nafplio: beige plastic boxes with a hole in one end.

Athens was declared the new capital in September 1834 and Nafplio gradually settled into a new role as a provincial military base and large-scale penitentiary complex. The embassies and grand houses of the Great Powers moved to Athens and the ships of Europe's navies were seen less frequently in Nafplio's port. Now, the larger ships carried troops or brought cargoes of prisoners. The daily traffic of Greek caiques and other coastal vessels no doubt continued as it ever did.

Travellers arriving from the 1840s describe how ships were met with dozens of small boats rowing out to the hulls and clamouring to take passengers ashore or sell local produce, both at exorbitant prices. Meanwhile steamships started to become more prevalent than sailing ships. Small-scale fishing continued, as it ever did, for whitebait and sardines, octopus and calamari. Early photos show many small boats moored along the Akti Miaouli quay.

I remember walking along the coast to Karathonas one day in 1998 and seeing a portion of the gulf suddenly agitated by a gigantic school of fish. A small outboard-driven fishing boat was close and steered directly into the school, dragging up a Biblical quantity of fish as I watched. The silvery catch was heaped so high above the gunwale that the boat seemed in danger of going under and I followed it back to town at walking pace, where it docked at the quay in front of the Bourtzi. Word of mouth soon brought a queue of buyers that stretched down Akti Miaouli to buy these fish that seemed to be about a foot long.

The days of large ships in Nafplio's port were not over, however. Nafplio remained a significant troop base. The Greco-Turkish conflicts in Epirus at the end of the nineteenth and beginning of the twentieth century saw Nafplio's 8th Infantry sailing north and Turkish captives returning with them to be imprisoned in Palamidi. When the Messinian currant growers revolted at the purchase price of the surplus crop in the 1930s, Nafplio's troops headed down the coast to restore order.

The 1920s and 1930s also saw steamer pleasure cruisers start to appear on itineraries such as Ragusa-Venice-Nafplio-Athens. P&O stopped at Nafplio in its turbo-electric cruise ships, though the harbour was silted up again from 1919 and passengers had to enter the town by smaller tenders. It was a brief honeymoon period of early tourism that would be interrupted once again by war.

April 1941 saw the German army invading Greece and the allied forces getting out of their way. The troop withdrawal was called Operation Demon and it played out dramatically in Nafplio, which was soon flooded with soldiers and their materiel. A convoy of one hundred British army vehicles arrived early on, but it was soon realised the glut of trucks would attract the attention of German planes sallying out from Argos. They dispersed the motors as best they could with the help of Australian soldiers and took up positions outside and around the town, hiding under olive trees as they watched the Stukas bombing and machine-gunning the town, the Bourtzi and whatever else they'd seen. Huge black plumes of smoke rose over the peninsula, but the troops remained concealed.

As the time came closer for evacuation by sea, the allied troops set about destroying their equipment so that the Germans couldn't use it. Trenches were dug in Kolokotronis Park and arms were broken up within, possibly to be buried or burned thereafter. The quay was piled high with abandoned rifles and helmets. Army vehicles were pushed off the steep road to Palamidi, crashing dramatically down to the beach at Karathonas. Many of the troops then drove the short distance to Tolo's safer and more accessible sandy beach to await evacuation there.

Night time evacuation made sense. The allied troops picked their way through the fallen buildings and broken glass of Nafplio's darkened streets to the quays, from where local fishermen rowed them out in boats and caiques to the waiting troop ships. The day's catch was sometimes still in the vessels, unloaded amid all of the chaos, and reeking after sitting in the sun all day.

Thus occurred one of the tragedies of Operation Demon. On 24 April, the troopship Ulster Prince ran aground on a sandbar between the Bourtzi and the quay. Two thousand soldiers had already boarded the ship when it was attacked by German bombers. It burned all night and the next day it was bombed beyond repair or recovery. The ruined vessel was now blocking the entrance to the harbour. All other transport ships would have to anchor out in the gulf, making transfers even more hazardous.

Around 4,000 men were withdrawn from Nafplio during the next two days amid constant German bombing and strafing. Roughly 11,000 were picked up from Tolo. It's curious to look at today's peaceful beach in tourist Tolo and know that on at least two occasions in history armies swarmed across its sand. The massed vessels of the Venetian fleet under Morosini had set down troops here in 1686 on their way to take Palamidi from the rear.

But the carnage of Operation Demon hadn't ended. The Dutch transport ship Slamat was also bombed at Nafplio while filling with soldiers. It was set alight and men were machine-gunned as they tried to swim to safety. The Slamat was dam-aged but was able to move off down the gulf, aided by HMS Diamond. The Diamond returned the next day to pick up another hundred men from the sea and torpedo the ruined carcass of the Slamat, which was now a shipping hazard and a guide for German bombers. The day after, both HMS Diamond and HMS Wryneck were sunk by German dive-bombers, their crew fired upon while in the water. All three vessels sank further down the coast from Nafplio.

Operation Demon saw around 1000 men killed in Nafplio harbour and in the waters of the Argolic Gulf. The burned-out hulk of the Ulster Prince remained on its sandbank throughout the war and was still there, blackened and leaning, in 1945. According to local reports, bloated bodies were still washing up on Karathonas beach four years after the carnage.

Other vessels have sunk since and will continue to do so. In 1942, an army transport ship carrying mules and ammunition was sunk in the port of Nafplio. This may have been the large ship that sank just off the headland, its masts and funnels visible above the waterline long enough to be captured in photos. In fact, take a look at a satellite image of Nafplio and you'll see the outlines of two large submerged ships lying at right angles to each other off this headland.

The 1950s might be said to have been the start of a short and peaceful golden age for Nafplio's port, when finally it no longer needed its colossal walls and bastions for defence. In this period before the widespread use of container ships and air freight, the harbour was home to multiple iron-hulled transport vessels. The quays were stacked with crates and barrels, masted with cranes and backed by warehouses and cafés. There was a smell of seaweed and bilge water, tar and rotten onions crushed underfoot. Goods were everywhere: sacks of cement, wine from Aegina, oranges for export and timber from Athos, Romania, Odessa. Customs men strolled the shoreline, boatmen offered their rates and barefoot fishermen hauled their catch in baskets to the markets.

The cafés were full all day and most of the night, wafting

their scents of ouzo and brandy, frying whitebait and sardines. At night, the wooden boats would creak and rock, their sails folded, their oars put away, and ships' dogs would bark until dawn. With cargoes safely in their warehouses, the sailors and stevedores were free to brawl into the early hours, their shouts and the sound of splintered glass echoing into the darkened town. It was a port like any other.

Picturesque, but this kind of commerce would not survive globalisation and the economies of scale that would bring container ports. By the 1980s, Nafplio's future would be more as a tourist destination than as a port. For the first time in over 3000 years, its peninsula would not be prized for its protection, but for its accumulation of history and its decadent beauty.

But what a maritime history. Take a seat at one of the cafés on Akti Miaouli and picture the scene before you: the Bourtzi pocked with German machine-gun bullets or shelling an invasion fleet, smoke billowing; the burned-out hulk of the Ulster Prince in the foreground; Francesco Morosini's massed galleons crowding the horizon; the triumphant arrival of Prince Otto and his twenty-one-gun salutes; the splendid Turkish sultan coming with gifts for the Ottoman soldiers who'd won back the town. Imagine a hundred or more small boats and caiques moored here, waiting for the land wind to take them back down the gulf.

How many vessels are out there in the mud? How many men? What happened to that ship that foundered north of the Bourtzi? How many sailors tossed a coin over the gunwale for luck, or accidentally dropped something into the eternally shifting silt? It all looks so beautiful, so calm, but history is ceaselessly moving beneath the surface, its secrets still safe.

HEROES

If you'd asked me in 1998 to name any of Nafplio's sculptures, I would have mentioned the guy on the horse in the park, the pale guy with the weird hair (it's actually a hat) by the Tolo bus stop, and the woman in the square with nipples drawn on with a marker. I couldn't have said with certainty who any of them were, though the woman in the square was probably Bouboulina. She was the only Nafplio-related female historical figure I'd heard of. Theodoros Kolokotronis must have been one of them because his name looms over the town as large as Palamidi.

This is normal. If you aren't present when a public statue appears, you probably barely register its existence thereafter. Statues are conceptual gestures that serve no practical purpose in a town. They're typically situated only in places where they won't cause an obstruction, which implicitly means places where people can pass without noticing them. Time goes by and the person represented in the statue is either forgotten because they died more than a hundred years ago, or remembered merely as a name from schoolbooks. Increasingly, their lives or legacies are re-examined and they're found to be despicable people undeserving of a memorial.

Who stops in front of a statue (a piece of inanimate stone or bronze) to ponder the life and deeds of the person featured? Historians, maybe. But is a statue necessary to provoke that thought process? Most statues come with no more context than a name and some years inscribed on them, though at least now we can Google them. Any public statue is like the picture you put on the wall at home and, as years pass, you forget exists. You know it's there, but you never really look at it.

It doesn't help that most statues are broadly realistic representations. They may be larger than life-size, but they still show the face and body of a person we never met or knew. All statues are strangers. The majority of observers have no idea if the figure is a good likeness. Wouldn't it be better to represent notable people abstractly to evoke some sense of their contribution or significance? That would at least create some viewer interaction, some dialogue and a prompt to learn more.

Still, a town chooses to remember only certain people as part of its historical narrative. Who deserves the honour? Does size matter? If so, one person is the dominant figure in Nafplio's history, even if he wasn't born here and didn't die here.

There is no more divisive and contradictory character in Nafplio's history than Theodoros Kolokotronis, whose massive bronze likeness sits atop a horse in the park named after him. The statue was commissioned from artist Lazaros Sochos in 1889 using money raised in a national crowd-funding campaign and was made using five tons of bronze derived from Palamidi's defunct cannons. A death mask of the man himself was used for absolute veracity.

The piece didn't arrive from Paris until 1895. Even then, it was kept in storage because nobody had decided where to put it. The initial budget hadn't covered a base (a very Nafplio story, this) so a public subscription had to be held to raise more money. The townspeople were not especially happy about any of this expenditure, arguing that the swamp to the east needed to be drained, that there was an irregular water supply and that no regular marketplace existed. The statue was still in storage at the turn of the century. In fact, two identical statues had been made, the other to be erected in Athens, where it remains in the forecourt of the old parliament building on Stadiou Street.

On April 23 1901, a feast day, the statue was finally unveiled. You might imagine a few dozen local residents attending such an event, but 25,000 people flooded from across the Peloponnese and further afield to see the old warrior mounted again on his horse. King George I was there. Prime Minister Georgios Theotokis was there. A military band played and much fun was had by all. But what had Kolokotronis done to deserve this level of public interest and veneration?

He was born in the Messinian mountains and was raised on a horse in a family of *klephts* – armed bandits. Thereafter, he spent a few years serving in the Ottoman, Russian and British militaries before the War of Independence was declared. That was when he returned to the Peloponnese from Zakynthos and began to organise bands of *klephts* into something like a militia army.

His relevance to Nafplio is as something of a saviour. The Greek admiral Andreas Miaoulis had already taken the port and blockaded the Turkish supply fleet but the Turks still held Palamidi and the lower town, albeit with relatively few men and supplies. The provisional Greek government was in Argos and dithered for so long over the terms of Nafplio's surrender that Ottoman reinforcements were on the point of arriving to relieve Nafplio and attack Greek leader Dimitrios Ypsilantis in Argos. Cue: Kolokotronis.

The Old Man of the Morea (he was in his fifties) gathered a disparate band of *klephts* and they rode to the rescue. Turkish military leader Mahmoud Dramali managed to take Argos first, but had no access to water and couldn't reach his supply ships blockaded in Nafplio. He decided to head back to the safety of Corinth via the Dervenaki pass, where Kolokotronis was waiting. The Turkish army was annihilated and though he was not the only one fighting, Kolokotronis is credited with the victory.

Nafplio was taken shortly afterwards and it was famously Kolokotronis who planted the Greek flag on Acronafplio's ramparts. British visitor George Waddington was introduced to the old man shortly after the town's capitulation. He found Kolokotronis at home – a house captured from the Turks – with his *capitani* in a room whose walls were hung with pistols and rifles captured at Dervenaki. The fifteen *capitani* looked like bad sorts, were shabbily attired and filthy – most wearing the traditional red cap but others in turbans. The dirtiest and most emaciated among them was an Orthodox priest. Kolokotronis himself looked smart, possibly in uniform, and seemed not to acknowledge the soldiers moving about the space. In Waddington's estimation, Greece's current and future hero was "a robber, a butcher, a soldier, a partisan and again a robber."

The old warrior was a greater fighter than he was a politician, however, and was more accustomed to giving orders than collaborating in government. He saw Nafplio as his possession and refused to give up the strategic heights of Acronafplio. The new government would have to besiege for a month the town they had just liberated, eventually having to pay Kolokotronis to leave his eyrie. The death of his son Panos left him bereft, but he continued to be an obstacle to the executive assembly and in 1825 he was briefly jailed in Hydra for his recalcitrance. That same year, the Ottomans fought back and took the old Venetian ports of Methoni and Koroni. A powerful military personality was needed, so Kolokotronis was released from captivity to lead the Greeks in guerilla tactics against the Turks.

He became a faithful supporter of Ioannis Kapodistrias after 1827, underlining the new governor's plans with military persuasion. He supported Otto, too, when the new king arrived in 1833, but the nationalist tide was changing. The Greeks didn't want to be ruled by a Bavarian boy and have their country steered by European aristocrats.

On 7 June 1834, Kolokotronis was accused along with Dimitrios Plapoutas of conspiracy against the regency and charged with treason. The Vouleftiko was the courthouse for the trial and evidence was given for two weeks as the public watched from the crowded gallery above. Kolokotronis was brought to face charges and give testimony each day from his cell in Palamidi. Witnesses reported seeing the seventy year old as frail. He could barely walk as a result of the inhuman conditions of his prison and had been forbidden by his low-ranking Bavarian guards even to sing.

Despite his compromised condition, he spoke well and had a highly expressive face. He faced his accusers in a *fustanella*, an embroidered jacket and a red cap – the embodiment of Greekness. The verdict had seemed clear from the start: he was pronounced guilty and sentenced to death. This was almost immediately commuted by royal decree to twenty years and in fact Kolokotronis was pardoned completely the following year by a king keen to win popular support. He was named general and a councillor of the state. The old warrior died of a stroke in Athens in 1845 following a period of feasting and dancing at the royal palace and after the wedding celebrations of his son.

The government declared three days of national mourning and his coffin was borne to church in a procession that featured the entire Council of Ministers, the Council of State and many inhabitants. He was buried in Athens, but in 1930 his bones were transferred to Tripoli according to the wishes of the Arcadians. The bones lie there still in a crypt beneath his statue in Areos Square.

Kolokotronis was a commanding character among commanding characters – a man of action in the founding years of the Greek state. But why does he, of the many important people of that time, have the biggest reputation and the biggest monument in Nafplio? There were many others. Soldier Dimitrios Ypsilantis, admirals Andreas Miaouli and Konstantinos Kanaris, and politician Alexandros Mavrokordatos, for example, all played huge parts in the fight for independence.

Could it be that his personality made him a quintessentially Greek hero? Here was a man who fought in a uniform but also robbed people in mountain passes. He fought against the Turk, but also served in their army. He captured Nafplio for Greece, but Greece had to fight him and pay him to get it back. He was a patriot but was also interested in getting as much personal wealth as he could out of a battle or a siege, even if it meant torturing people and taking aid from the starving (see **War**.) Like Achilles he was a warrior of many contradictions. Like Odysseus he was a wily strategist. Family was supremely important to him. He did what he wanted, how he wanted and was imprisoned for it twice by his own government.

Kolokotronis was no angel, but he was a man, a leader who used a sword and a horse whereas others used words and diplomacy. We should remember that the people of Greece, not a government committee, gave their money for his statue. He was a popular hero.

If Kolokotronis was instrumental in freeing Nafplio, its first governor Ioannis Kapodistrias was the man most responsible for making it the town it would become. Born in Venetian-held Corfu to an aristocratic family, he was a medical doctor who went into Greek politics aged twenty-five before working in the Russian civil service. He was instrumental in helping Switzerland achieve independence and neutrality and he sparred with notorious Austrian minister Count Metternich before involving himself more deeply in the question of Greek independence. Greece would soon need a leader of its new state and Kapodistrias was a consummate politician highly experienced in the machinations of European power politics.

At the Troezen Assembly on 19 March 1827, Kapodistrias was named Governor of Greece for a seven-year term, his capital to be Nafplio. He was fifty-two. Kolokotronis was at the meeting and returned to inform the populace of this momentous news from under the plane tree in Platanos Square.

Kapodistrias arrived to celebratory cannon fire in January 1828, accompanied by the ships of England, France and Russia. People welcomed him in the streets and a eulogy for him was held at St George's church. In some ways, he was perfect for the job: a methodical, celibate, religious workaholic who woke at 5.00 a.m. and slept at 10.00 p.m. A liberal by nature, he cared passionately about making Greece a modern European state and Nafplio its modern capital. In addition to a comprehensive repair and rebuilding programme he also introduced a new hospital, a military academy, schools (the girls' school is today's library) and a properly organized quarantine system to help prevent the spread of Nafplio's infamous fevers. He built a new suburb for the many refugees and guaranteed the rights of Jewish residents long before some other European states did so.

One famous, but possibly apocryphal, story concerns his attempts to introduce potatoes to local agriculture as an aid to general nutrition. Initially, he ordered that the potatoes be handed out free to the populace, but they were suspicious of this weird tuber and it remained unpopular. Knowing his townspeople well, he arranged for a large consignment of potatoes to be unloaded conspicuously at the port under armed guard and then put into a secure warehouse as the curious townsfolk watched and gossiped. Later, the warehouse security proved sufficiently lax that many people were able to steal these apparently highly valuable vegetables and develop a taste for them.

Many of Nafplio's neoclassical buildings date from this period, the earlier houses influencing the later ones. Fountain Square (later Three Admirals Square) became the epicentre of what Kapodistrias hoped would be a sparkling new European capital and he was forward thinking enough to insure many of the town's stately buildings against fire. You can still see the rusty registration plaques (dated 1831) on some houses.

In other ways, Kapodistrias was less suited to the job. He could be distant and condescending with the other members of the government, believing many of them to be more interested in personal gain than in a strong and independent state. In turn, they suspected he was secretly influenced by Russia and working to its agenda. His biggest error however, was arresting and imprisoning the unruly leader of the southern Mani region Petrobey Mavromichaelis. This wild clan patriarch ruled over the one part of the Peloponnese that the Ottomans had never occupied and his family did not accept his incarceration with good grace. Kapodistrias allegedly added further insult by remarking that the name Mavromichaelis was unpronounceable.

On Sunday September 27 1831, Kapodistrias left home very early to attend a service at the church of St. Spyridon, the patron saint of his beloved Corfu. He had been advised at least a week previously that there was a plot to kill him and his servants asked him not to go. He ignored them all. Wearing a dark blue tunic, white trousers and a blue hat, he left the *palataki* in Fountain Square with his two bodyguards Kozonis

and Leonidas. Together, they went along Vasileos Konstantinou for a short distance before turning right on today's
Angelos Terzakis Street, then right onto Staikopoulou and left
into Spyridon Square.

Meanwhile, Petrobey Mavromichaelis's son Georgakis and
brother Konstantinos were living on Tertsetou Street just off
Plapouta (where I entered the alley to my house). They knew
Kapodistrias's routine and had decided to go and meet him.
They had done so the previous Sunday but the governor,
forewarned, had not attended church that day.

According to one account, the two assassins actually saw
him in the street on the way to the church and were surprised
when he raised his hat in greeting. They debated if they should
follow him, but instead took another route.

When the governor arrived in Spyridon Square around 6.45
a.m., he saw the two Mavromichaelis men waiting for him.
Both were dressed in their best *fustanellas* and armed with
pistols recently bought in Nafplio. They were accompanied by
two guards – Karagiannis and Georgiou – who had been assigned to keep them under observation at all times. They were
expected to attempt something reckless. Kapodistrias paused
on seeing them and took a pinch of snuff, perhaps to give
himself a necessary buzz, perhaps to feign insouciance and
mask his fear.

There are conflicting accounts of what happened next. I
take mine from Cochrane, who heard it first hand from the
priest giving the service that morning. The two Maniots sal-
uted the governor respectfully as he entered the church. If they
had intended to do it then, they momentarily lost their nerve.
Perhaps they wanted him to have his soul cleansed before they
did it. Perhaps they were afraid their guards would kill them
the instant they tried it.

When Kapodistrias emerged, they were ready. Konstantinos
Mavromichaelis was waiting beside the door with his pistol
concealed inside a fold of cloth. He withdrew it and shot
Kapodistrias in the back of the head, killing him instantly.
Meanwhile, Georgakis, who was already inside the doorway,

darted forward to stab the governor either in the right abdomen or in the heart or both depending on versions. At this point, one of the guards assigned to follow the Mavromichaeli brothers took aim at Kapodistrias's bodyguards and fired, missing. It is his bullet preserved in the church doorway under glass.

Kapodistrias's one-eyed and one-handed bodyguard Kozonis then shot Konstantinos, wounding him. A group of locals – presumably roused during the service as rumours flew about the town – rushed, enraged, upon Konstantinos and began to beat him with feet, fists and other implements. The *coup de grace* came from a nearby window (the lower part of today's Byron Hotel?) when General Fotomaras shot Konstantinos for a second time. Not content with his death, the people dragged his bloody body through Platanos Square and to the S. Theresa bastion, where they tossed the corpse into the sea.

Georgakis Mavromichaelis managed to escape and briefly took refuge in the French embassy. He was soon given up and tried by a military court, finally being shot by a firing squad atop Acronafplio.

It's a remarkable story with so many questions. Why would Kapodistrias choose a bodyguard with one hand and one eye? Why would he exit the church with his guards behind him when he knew his would-be assassins were waiting outside and when he'd already been warned they wanted to kill him? Why were the Mavromichaeli being guarded by two men who also apparently wanted to kill the governor? The whole thing was so inept, so avoidable. Perhaps Kapodistrias wanted to die. Perhaps his faith was so strong that he believed he couldn't be killed. Perhaps the sense of honour and pride on both sides was so out of control that they all had to die.

No man is indispensable, but Greece lost an important leader that day. He had already done an immense amount of work to turn Nafplio from a ruined warzone into a creditable European capital. As for Petrobey Mavromichaelis, he was later released from prison and became vice-president of the Council of State, then a senator. He also received the Grand

Cross of the Order of the Redeemer. He always publicly condemned the murder of Kapodistrias.

In February 1832, the National Assembly proposed creating three colossal bronze statues of Kapodistrias: one for Aegina, one for the Peloponnese and one for central Greece. The proposal didn't go anywhere and was raised again in 1843, this time for a statue in Three Admirals Square where Kapodistrias had lived. It didn't happen again.

Almost a hundred years later, in the centennial year of independence 1930, a statue was suggested again and funds were raised – but not enough for a statue. Additional contributions were requested from the other town councils in the Argos/Corinthia region, but only four out of twenty responded. Finally, Nafplio council paid the shortfall and the life-size statue was commissioned from sculptor Michaelis Tombrou. It was too late for the centennial celebrations, which were held at the foot of Kolokotronis's mounted majesty.

The statue was finally erected in Three Admirals Square in 1933 – more than a hundred years after Kapodistrias's death – and was almost instantly attacked. Elections were happening at the time and the political mood was running high. Parts of the pedestal were broken off and a policeman had to be paid to guard the statue through the night. This was only the start of the indignity

The statue was shortly afterwards moved to its current position in Kapodistrias Square, across the road from Three Admirals, and survived WWII intact. In 1947, a finger on the right hand was broken off by a child playing football. Something similar happened again in the 1980s and since then the statue has been the target of repeated vandalism. Four of Kapodistrias's fingers were deliberately broken off and replaced in 2017, 2018 and 2019.

It's only a piece of commemorative stone, but memories are short. Here is the image of a man who was brutally murdered as he sought to build a modern town and a modern state – a man who barely slept and who worked tirelessly for the improvement of Nafplio and the country.

Statues are representations of the past that engage in current cultural dialogue. They sometimes become targets or catalysts for political or artistic statements. For example, a different statue of Kapodistrias at the University of Athens had his face painted as The Joker in 2021 after one professor allegedly described him as a dictator. In this case, the importance of Kapodistrias in the national narrative made him a good vehicle in the debate. The vandalism of Nafplio's statue, however, appears to be the work of a standard idiot.

A lesser-known character (at least, outside Greece) is the colourfully named Nikitas "The Turkeater" Stamatelopoulos, Nikitaras to his friends. He was a nephew of Theodoros Kolokotronis and also a *klepht* from Mistra near Sparta. In his younger days, he had worked for the Ottomans as an *armatolos* – an armed bandit leader given certain privileges to maintain peace in the mountainous areas of Greece. This made him lethal with a gun and sword as well as skilled in guerrilla warfare and ambushes. The Turks would later come to regret such skills.

In 1805, hotheaded Nikitaras killed a Turk in a duel and fled to Zakynthos, where *klephts* tended to flee. His uncle was already there and they joined forces with other *capitani*, who had created the Black Fleet: pirate vessels dedicated to attacking Turkish ships. Later, he would briefly join the British Army with uncle Theodoros and together they'd learn much about military tactics. The two would then become acquainted with the *Filiki Etaireia*, a secret organisation of diaspora Greeks seeking to expel the Turks and create an independent Greece. Many of the important figures in the fight for independence were already a part of it, including Alexander Ypsilantis, brother of Dimitrios.

Once war was declared against the Turks in 1821, Nikitaras and his uncle knew what they had to do. They went over to the Peloponnese and started to fight. He was there at the liberation of Kalamata. He faced 7,000 Turks with his 200 men at Valtetsi, charging the enemy with swords when their ammunition ran out. He chased them to Tripolitsa, taunting them to come out and fight like men. At the second battle of Valetsi, he won the day and held out against a siege of 6,000 Turks at the fortified village of Doliana until reinforcements came. As soon as they did, Nikitaras and his band raced out of the village with such ferocity that the Turks fled, leaving all of their artillery on the field. "Persians! Come back and fight!" he apparently yelled.

When the Greeks finally took Tripolitsa, there was an indiscriminate massacre of virtually all of the town's Turks and Jews, along with looting and, doubtless, other atrocities. The few European philhellenes accompanying the Greek forces were appalled at the slaughter. Nikitaras, however, tried to stop other *capitani* and refused to loot or kill prisoners. He was a soldier, not a murderer.

The next big battle would make Nikitaras's name. When the Ottoman commander Dramali was forced to retreat from Argos to Corinth, Nikitaras and his uncle waited to ambush them in the Dervenakia pass. The Turks were many and carried heavy artillery with them, while the Greeks were masters of guerrilla warfare armed mostly with clubs and blades. Nikitaras led the charge and fought so ferociously that he broke four swords slashing at the enemy. It's said that by the end of the battle, he had killed so many Turks and swung his sword for so long that he couldn't open his hand from the sword's grip and needed medical attention. Trapped in a confined space and unable to use their artillery, the Ottomans allegedly lost 20,000 troops to the Greeks' fifty – possibly a victor's estimate. Again, Nikitaras did not want to loot the dead.

After the liberation of Nafplio, Nikitaras sided with Kolokotronis in all things, including the supposed conspiracy against King Otto. He was jailed with his uncle and spent the next seven years imprisoned in Nafplio. When released from the barbaric conditions in 1841, he was a broken and sickly man. He died in Piraeus in 1849.

His monument is inconspicuously situated by the side of the 1911 courthouse, behind the taxi rank on Syngrou: a nondescript obelisk with a relief scene on its base of Nikitaras battling a Turk. It was created by artist Antonios Sochos, nephew of Lazarus Sochos, the sculptor of Kapodistrias's statue. The piece was commissioned by Aspasia Potamianou according to the wishes of her husband Elias, a Nafpliot politician and unveiled in 1930 as part of the centennial celebrations.

Laskarina Bouboulina's busty bronze bust sits in a dull square on the corners of Emmanouil Sofroni and Aristotelous Onassis streets facing the port. It should not be mistaken for the more famous full-body statue of Bouboulina that stands in her home port of Spetses, which has her raising a hand to scan the horizon. If you Google the Nafplio version, you'll struggle to find many examples of it. Most visitors have no idea it exists.

I remember the place because it's where I used to turn when strolling along Bouboulinas Street for my evening *volta.* There also used to be a popular late-night bar at the back of the square where young and beautiful people would cram shoulder to shoulder amid deafening music and drink because it was too crowded to dance. It was there somebody told me that almost every twenty- or thirty-something person in Nafplio had a sexually transmitted disease because they'd all slept with each other at least once. Urban myth, I'm sure.

Bouboulina is revered principally because she personally financed arms and ships in the fight for independence, though her fight was also personal. Born in the prisons of Constantinople, she eventually found herself living on the island of Spetses in the Argolic gulf. She lost two husbands in battles with Algerian pirates and the second left her independently wealthy aged around thirty. However, the Ottomans attempted to confiscate her ships on the pretext that her second husband had fought against them in the Russian-Turkish war. She was not prepared to accept this.

Bouboulina went straight to Constantinople to speak with the Russian ambassador, a philhellene. The Ottomans were keen to arrest and imprison her, but the ambassador whisked her away to the Crimea on the Black Sea for her safety. Somehow, she managed to get an audience with the sultan's mother and convinced her to leave the Bouboulina fortune alone. It was a remarkable reversal and evidence of a strong personality

In Constantinople, Bouboulina had joined the *Filiki Etaireia* in preparation for the oncoming war. Back in Spetses, she began to stockpile weapons and built a ship, the Agamemnon, in readiness. Her funds and dedication to the cause were important in the years before the Great Powers finally gathered in support of the war and Bouboulina was among the troops who passed through the Land Gate immediately after Nafplio surrendered in 1822. It's said that she rode her horse like an Amazon rather than in the demure side saddle feminine manner. The streets were still full of smoking rubble and reeked of blood.

Why had Bouboulina come to Nafplio from Spetses? Presumably to see victory enacted, but also because that's where all the action was. The wily shipbuilder had a nose for power and money. In no time, she married her very young and beautiful daughter to Panos Kolokotronis, son of Theodoros, to create a truly powerful Greek dynasty. She also attempted to speculate in currency by setting up mints in Nafplio and Spetses. The Turkish currency had been catastrophically devalued so Bouboulina essentially began to counterfeit coins on a large scale. It didn't work because the Nafpliots were as wily as she was, examining each coin for known signs of authenticity. They also all knew what she was doing.

Englishman George Waddington met her in Nafplio in 1824 and his impressions were not complimentary. He called her "old, unmannerly, ugly, fat, shapeless and avaricious." There may be some truth in this, as she appears not to be a great beauty even in her statues and portraits. Waddington had met her just before her Nafplio house was confiscated by the national government (she had sided with the Kolokotronis in the brief civil dispute) and before she returned home to Spetses.

Her welcome was not as a heroine, however. The local

authorities initially jailed her on trumped-up charges of witch-craft and heresy. On release, she discovered that her son Georgios had eloped with a local girl. The girl's family came round to the Bouboulina house to discuss matters and the argument got out of hand. Greece's great benefactress was killed by an accidental gunshot to the head. That same year, her daughter Eleni was widowed when Panos Kolokotronis was murdered by his own government.

There are two other notable women honoured with statues in Nafplio both of them virtually unknown outside Greece. The first is Mandó Mavrogenous, who was born in Trieste to a wealthy aristocratic Greek family with *Filiki Etaireia* conn-ections. She was highly educated and was fluent in Turkish, Italian and French. Her family moved to the island of Paros in 1809 and she also lived on Mykonos and Tinos as the War of Independence approached.

Using family money, she paid for ships to repel Ottoman invasions among the islands and for bands of Greek fighters to campaign in the Peloponnese. Her men were at the siege of Tripolitsa and the battle of Dervenakia, among others. She also covered aid for wounded soldiers and their families, going as far as to sell her jewellery for the national cause. In addition to giving most of her money, she also campaigned among the politicians and fine families of Europe to highlight the Greek plight.

From 1823, she was resident in Nafplio and betrothed to Dimitrios Ypsilantis – a pairing that unnerved some politicians due to perceived links to Russia or supposed dynastic ambitions. Her own family thought she was crazy and dis-owned her for giving away so much of her money to the cause.

It was a dangerous time in Nafplio, with much chaos and violence following the initial siege (see **War**). In that same year, Mandó's house near Nafplio was broken into, robbed and burned by a group of marauding Greek militia. Left with nothing, she moved to Tripoli with Ypsilantis, who then died of illness. His monument is in Three Admirals Square, making them the only heroic couple commemorated in the town. She returned to Nafplio, living penniless, depressed and unrecognised for her colossal sacrifices. Waddington described her as "tall, thin and unattractive," though he did – like many male English visitors of the time – have a tendency to praise the beauty of Greek men in gushingly admiring tones while frowning on the women. She looks very attractive in her portraits.

The ever-honourable Ioannis Kapodistrias finally gave Mandó a salaried military rank and a house on Papanikolaou Street. A plaque marks the spot. One story is that she thanked him with the gift of an antique sword that had belonged to Constantine the Great, but where had she been keeping it if her house was robbed in 1823? Why hadn't she sold it already if it was truly so valuable? Should we believe that she was homeless and carrying an emperor's sword around? If it existed and she did give it to Kapodistrias, where is it now?

Her small, bronze bust sits half hidden under a tree in Philhellion Square, which itself is dedicated to French fighters for the Greek national cause. I wonder how many people know her story and what she gave for Greece. Certainly, I knew nothing at all before I wrote this. Let's hope somebody will pause and look at the fixed metal face and consider her sacrifices.

A larger statue than both Bouboulina's and Mandó's is found in Syntagma square. In the form of a stele, it portrays a relief carving of a woman with twin braids standing on a balcony and appearing to wave at or hail an audience. She normally has breasts and/or nipples drawn on her in marker by children (or halfwits) and often serves as a goalpost in their games. This is Kalliopi Papalexopoulou, who lived in a house on this spot before the National Bank was built in the 1930s (see **Squares**).

Born into a noble family in Patras, Kalliopi grew up in Ancona, where she studied literature and learned English, Italian and French. She moved to Nafplio in 1824 aged sixteen, already fired by the fight for independence, and married the town's mayor, Spyros. It's said that she danced with King Otto during at least one soiree, but her politics were hardening. Her father and brother had been incarcerated in Palamidi in 1831. It was a time for picking sides.

The Papalexopoulou house had a richly stocked library and quickly became a salon for military officers, politicians, artists and notable visitors of a liberal, pro-independence, republican persuasion. The 1850s proved a difficult decade, however, as Kalliopi lost first her husband, then her brother and her father. She resolved not to leave the house again but anti-monarchical feeling was growing constantly. The king had long ago moved to Athens, but the people of Nafplio didn't want to be ruled by a Bavarian or by any other king.

In 1862, the Nafplio garrison revolted against the monarchy and attempted to occupy the royal palace (the *palataki*) in a coup. Kalliopi was with them and was chased from the place by guards. Athens quickly dispatched troops to control the unrest and Kalliopi's house was targeted as a site of republican foment. She was advised to leave by the German commander General Hahn, who diplomatically suggested it was for her own safety. She famously replied that she would stay where she was. She was afraid of only one thing – rats – and she had exterminated all of them in her house. According to another version, a young soldier sent to search her house for anti-monarchists smashed down her door when she wouldn't open it. He was reprimanded and had to pay for a new door.

When King Otto was deposed the same year, Kalliopi was invited to Athens to be applauded for her stance and awarded an honorary pension of 500 drachmas. The following year, the Greek National Assembly elected Prince William of Denmark as the new king: George I.

Now in her mid-fifties, Kalliopi spent the rest of her life in the house in Syntagma Square, leaving it rarely in her familiar silk dress and velvet bodice, her hair down her back in two braids. She donated most of her pension to support the poor and gave her ground floor to shopkeepers rent-free. She died penniless in Nafplio aged one hundred. George I was still on the Greek throne.

Beside the statue of Kalliopi is a piece of architectural

sculpture featuring a Venetian lion. It is highly polished from generations of children kicking footballs at it and sitting on it, rubbing their legs over the face. It is clearly taken from some part of the fortifications and may have been placed in front of the bank to prevent a car from driving into the wall as part of an armed robbery. Such are the ironies of history. Could the original stonemason have imagined that one day, three hundred years into the future, his work would become a child's plaything rather than an expression of imperial might?

Staikos Staikopoulos is something like Nafplio's Neil Armstrong: most famous for doing one great thing. His statue by the sculptor Nikola was unveiled only in 1966 and sits on 25 Martiou, close to the Land Gate and next to the bus stop for villages including Tolo. An Arcadian by birth, he lived on Hydra for years as a leather curer before being recruited like many others into the secret society of *Filiki Etaireia*. He was ready when the revolution began in 1821 and headed directly to Argos with a personal militia to fight the Turks. His greatest triumph, however, would be in Nafplio.

It was the dark, moonless night of November 29 1822 and raining without pause. The Greeks had been laying siege to Nafplio for around a year and the Turkish officers, their supplies grievously depleted, had come down from Palamidi to meet the Greeks outside the town. Theodoros Kolokotronis had offered them the chance to leave the fortress and go free. It was time to negotiate a surrender.

Staikopoulos was encamped in nearby Aria and couldn't resist the opportunity. He and his men went up the zig-zag stairs to the top and one of them climbed over the walls to let the others in. Staikopoulos had taken Palamidi and thus opened the lower town to the Greeks (see **War** for more detail). He was made a general for this victory and was modest enough to not accept one of the many houses made vacant by the slaughter of Turks.

His next success was the siege of the lofty Acrocorinth, after which he asked Kolokotronis for a share of the spoils – not for himself, but for his loyal *palikari*. It seems Kolokotronis was not immediately forthcoming with such rewards and the two argued, though Staikopoulos sided with the old man in the subsequent civil discord when Kolokotronis refused to hand over Acronafplio to the new executive. They were both later sent to prison.

As with Kolokotronis, Staikopoulos was released when the Turks returned even stronger in 1825. He fought again at Tripolitsa and other places, finally earning the reward of land and promotion to lieutenant colonel in Otto's army. However, his mental health was poor and by 1833 he had become profoundly depressed – some said insane. He was prone to outbursts of violence and insulting the king, for which he was finally arrested and put in the prison cells below the Vouleftiko.

He was released in 1835, his health and his spirit broken by the barbaric conditions, and died the same day, penniless and aged thirty-seven. The city paid for him to have a dignified burial with full military honours, though the statue would have to wait another 131 years and would be paid for by his great-granddaughter Zacharoula. Festive events are held in his honour every year on the last Sunday of November.

Other statues in town include a bust of the writer Angelos Terzakis in Spyridon Square (temporarily removed in 2022 for resurfacing work) and a bust of the town's poet Theodoros Kostouros, who also ran a pharmacy on Vasileos Konstantinou. He sits outside the library. I don't want to suggest that these two are not heroes in their way, but writers generally don't make the big headlines. Writing a book doesn't have the same glory as slaughtering a thousand Turks.

What makes a hero? Some of the people commemorated in Nafplio made great personal sacrifices. Some excelled beyond their peers. Many of them found themselves on the wrong side of politics or the law. Almost all died badly or unjustly. We might suggest that the most morally dubious of them all was the one who came out supreme.

Theodoros Kolokotronis was a patriot, but also motivated

powerfully by self-interest. When he ordered Nikitaras to attack Greek forces at Tripolitsa, the Turkeater refused, saying
that he would gladly take on the entire Turkish army with just
his sword, but never raise arms against his compatriots. When
Kolokotronis was pardoned and released from prison, his
nephew Nikitaras remained there rotting. Did this uncle try to
appeal for clemency in the case?

Kolokotronis wanted to win and didn't worry too much
about how. He has the biggest statue and the greatest fame.
The people paid for his monument while the others were government funded or paid for by private benefactors. Such is life.

King Otto also has a statue in Three Admirals Square on the
site of his burned-down palace – a fitting metaphor, perhaps,
for a broadly unsuccessful reign. He was a strikingly handsome
and intelligent young man, tall, and very smart in his blue uniform. But he was only seventeen when he arrived and nowhere
near as politically sophisticated as his regency council. Even
when he came of age and took control, he was hesitant, neur-
otic and a ditherer. Secretly, he didn't much like the Greeks,
believing them to be self-interested and acquisitive. No matter
how improved Nafplio was, it wasn't Vienna or Paris. His decision to rename Platanos Square after his father Ludwig lasted
about five minutes (well, from 1834 to 1843) until the people
persuaded him to call it Syntagma.

Otto didn't kill Turks to free Greece. He didn't give all of his
worldly possessions. He didn't spend time in prison and go
insane for Greece. He didn't lose family members to the fight.
He wasn't assassinated. Instead, he danced quadrilles, rode his
horse, sailed his yacht, married a woman who bullied him and
finally abdicated. An interesting life – but no hero.

FANTASISTS

It was siesta time one late-summer afternoon in 1999 (the *mikro hypno*, or small sleep) and I was walking down Plapouta Street towards the bus station. It was hot and quiet. There were no locals around. Two female tourists were walking towards me and passed me in front of St George's church. A moment elapsed and I clearly heard one of the girls scoff and remark to the other, "Affectation!"

They were talking about me. I was carrying my set of *komboloi*, the so-called "worry beads," swinging them, clicking, around my palm. I'd bought them as a set of cherry-red Muslim prayer beads the previous summer in Istanbul's Grand Bazaar and turned them into a *komboloi* by removing around half of the beads to leave a palm's width of free cord and adding a *pappas* (the longer bead that both joins and separates the cord).

I'd been using this *komboloi* for over a year, initially struggling to master the relatively complex finger work. Locals had given me tutorials, amused that a non-Greek would even attempt to learn, but the trick eluded me until a two-hour wait in the bus station at Kalambaka when suddenly, unconsciously, I started to swing the beads correctly. I remember the moment as clearly as Isaac Newton probably remembered the apocryphal apple. Since that moment, the beads had barely been out of my hand. At home, in cafés, in restaurants and on buses, I always had the *komboloi*. I learned the aesthetic. I even bought a book written by the owner of Nafplio's new Komboloi Museum. This was serious stuff.

I learned that the *komboloi* was probably a variation on the Muslim prayer beads that would have been carried by many Nafplio inhabitants during the Ottoman occupations, although Orthodox monks also use knotted cords to pray and *kombos* means 'node' or 'knot'. Evidently, the non-Muslim Greeks had appropriated these beads and used them to occupy their fingers. One nineteenth-century visitor reports entering the Vouleftiko parliament building in 1825 and discovering the vice president of the new Greek government sitting cross-legged on a divan and playing with the beads while smoking a long Turkish pipe.

A genuine *komboloi* is made of specific materials. Plastic is too light and doesn't give the sharp clack required. Metal is too heavy, smells bad on the skin and offers a dull sound. The best materials are *kekribari* (fossilised amber resin) or faturan, a mixture of amber and natural resins. Both are hard enough and heavy enough, but also warm to the touch. Horn, bone and certain heavy hardwoods also make good komboloi beads. The cord meanwhile, must be strong and allow the beads to run without hindrance. Thin chain is useless and almost always breaks. Common cotton thread or rubber will soon wear through and certain kinds of manmade cord will create static friction, slowing the beads. The best option is the russet nylon used to make fishing nets: smooth, phenomenally durable and, yes, aesthetically pleasing. My *komboloi* has had the same cord for twenty-five years.

There are two main ways to use the komboloi. You can swing it around the palm, under and over the index finger in a way that's too involved to explain, or you can pinch the bead at the top of the loop (there must always be an odd number for this reason) and let the beads slowly slip one-by-one or two-by-two down the cord to make a satisfying clack.

Which is to say . . . An affectation?

I knew more about the history, aesthetics and mechanics of the *komboloi* than most Greeks. I'd actually made my own. I used it as the Greeks used it and I was respected in certain circles because I knew how it worked, what it meant. But this girl, this tourist, called it an affectation. I was upset. It upset me.

Funny thing, though: I hadn't brought my *komboloi* to Nafplio in 2022. I'd thought about it. I'd taken it out of the drawer where it had lain unused for years and swung it a few times, smiling to see that I still had the technique, imagining myself in Kondogiorgos again with my Greek coffee, marking time with the slow, sensuous drop of the faturan beads. And I became self-conscious.

I had a sudden flash of myself as I'd been back then: a wannabe Greek. I spoke Greek whenever I could – not because it was always necessary (virtually everyone spoke English in this tourist town) but because it made me feel more a part of the place. I used most of the gestures I learned from my students: the offensive splayed palm, the polyvalent circling hand, the diagonal chop (*tha fas xylo*! – "You're going to eat wood!"). I used exaggerated facial expressions and shrugs. I drank retsina though it tasted like paint thinner. It was true I wanted to be Greek. Or, at least, I didn't want to be English in Greece. I wanted to escape everything English. I wanted to escape myself and become someone else.

It turns out I was not alone in this. Nafplio has a long history of attracting fantasists and chancers, self-mythologisers, adventurers, cheats, frauds and exaggerators. Some of them didn't even come here but implied that they had.

The earliest etchings, paintings and drawings of Nafplio from the sixteenth and seventeenth centuries can be very fanciful. The artists may have created their works based on descriptions from people who (maybe) had visited rather than from personal experience. The details are wrong: the Bourtzi is in the wrong place or is excessively huge; the sea surrounds the town entirely like an island; the buildings are colossal; Acronafplio rises almost as high as Palamidi. They even invented a chain blocking the harbour (see **Sea**).

It's clear from such pictures that Nafplio was a place that most people didn't and would probably never visit: a remote Venetian trading outpost and military base – a place of hearsay and anecdote: an almost imaginary realm with its walls and castles and lofty peaks reached after days at sea. From at least the Byzantine period, Nafplio was dreamlike. Far away. Exotic.

When the Grand Tourers and early travel writers came in

the eighteenth and nineteenth centuries with their ink pens and their watercolour boxes, they produced more reliable pictures, but even they couldn't resist the knowledge that the audience back at home would be unlikely to contradict whatever was portrayed. The bastions are just a little more massive, a little more impressive. The Bourtzi doesn't sit on the water, but crouches atop a rugged column of rock like a Meteora monastery. When these artists painted views of the square, they typically chose a perspective looking west to east or south, that is: towards the Trianon former mosque, the neoclassical buildings of the south side, or the Vouleftiko. Why not the other way round? Because the image would have shown the army barracks: a utilitarian block with soldiers on duty (but nevertheless a stately early eighteenth-century Venetian structure that today is emblematic of the square.) Sketches were made of the locals in their turbans, their *fustanellas*, their fezzes and gold-embroidered waistcoats. Far away. Exotic.

One of the Grand Tourers, in the late seventeenth century, was the flamboyant young Thomas Hope, who went on to become a noted art collector and interior designer accused by his contemporaries of being conceited, tactless and effeminate in manner. He spent eight years capering through the Mediterranean, including some time in Nafplio, where he made ink sketches of the Ottoman-occupied town and noted that the bay was a swamp of noxious exhalations. On returning home, he had his portrait painted in elaborate Levantine costume with red slippers, scarlet pantaloons, Turkish pipe and turban.

In 1819, Hope published a roistering and very successful adventure novel based on his youthful experiences, well timed for the imminent War of Independence publicity. The Reverend Sydney Smith Esq. in his review of the book, *Anastasius*, noted, "It is a relief, not a disappointment to get to the end." Smith also remarked that the story, humour and characterisation were bad but that it was, on balance, "a novel which all clever people of a certain age should read." Byron allegedly wept on reading it – wept that he hadn't written it, and wept that Hope had. One of the scenes in Nafplio featured the young hero temporarily enslaved and bound face to face with another prisoner to spend a sleepless night in rapturous, close-proximity dialogue. Sample extract:

"I swore I would some day, cost what might, doff my un-couth headdress for one of those smart turbans of gilt brocade or shawl, worn with such a saucy air, over one ear, by the Pasha's Tshawooshes;– gentlemen who were seen every where lounging about as if they had nothing to do but display their handsome legs . . ."

Many of these visitors brought with them to Nafplio the impressions they had decided to have. The glory of Greece. The mystery of the Levant. The ineptitude and rapacity of the revolutionaries. It's the same today. People come to Nafplio having seen photos of the castles, the paved and bougain-villea-bedecked streets, the stately square. It's why they come and it's what they find.

One early group of young visitors were the philhellenes, those impressionable and idealistic men from across Europe and America who came to offer support in the name of Greek independence. The Americans and French were particularly driven by the concept itself in the early 1820s, while the other Europeans wanted to fight for the past glory of Greece. Around 360 arrived in Greece from 1820 to 1822, the best of them with something useful to offer and the worst of them looking to receive some of the money loaned by the great powers to aid the revolution. Byron, perhaps the most illustrious philhellene of all, and not averse to a bit of self-mythologizing himself, disparaged them as "adventurers."

Petrobey Mavromichaelis had called to the international community for arms, money and counsel at the start of the War of Independence. He hadn't asked for fighters, and most of the merchants, students, butchers and tailors who started to arrive by ship from 1821 had little or no fighting experience. Those who did were not accustomed to the mountainous guerrilla war waged by independent Greek militias who fought for and were furiously loyal to charismatic clan leaders. Nor were they typically able to bring their skills to the new government, which operated on a system of old allegiances, suspicion and factional infighting.

There was little for the philhellenes to do. They were often to be found in Nafplio's cafés, raucously drinking in the square or earnestly discussing the politics of the day, perhaps secretly feeling like heroes. Maybe they twirled *komboloi* and affected elements of the local attire. Often, they ran out of money and had to beg for alms in the streets where the jaded residents would stone them away. Some were slaughtered in battles they were ill-prepared for. Many more died of disease and the fevers that affected Nafplio for centuries. A few, in desperation, were even persuaded to join the Turks, who treated them better than the Greeks they'd come to "save."

One American philhellene was killed while directing cannon on the battlements of the lower town during 1827's civil disturbance. A cannonball fired by the Greeks under Theodoros Grivas in Palamidi struck him, but he did not die immediately. London's *Medical Times* of that year reported dispassionately how the cannonball took off the man's hand, the hip it had been resting on and the top part of his thigh, releasing his intestines into the open without rupturing them but causing a "trifling haemorrhage." He was transferred to the eighty-four gun warship HMS Asia, notable in the Battle of Navarino, and was found to have no pain whatsoever, conversing with all normality about his experiences before dying suddenly three hours after being hit. Unnamed in the article, the soldier was Lieutenant William Townsend Washington, nephew of George Washington.

More than one naïve group of philhellenes was murdered in a Nafplio bathhouse in 1822. It seemed that a method had been developed to invite them into the sauna-bath, where they were obliged to undress. This way, they could be killed without staining the clothes that would later be sold. Another group of French and German philhellenes were robbed of their clothes at gunpoint by the same Greek soldiers they'd come to help. They were left naked in Nafplio's streets. One romantic young Englishman who had abandoned his studies at Cambridge to aid the Greek cause was found starving and half dead in Nafplio's streets, while in 1827 a less fortunate French phil-hellene shot his own head off while attempting to clean an unfamiliar rifle. This was Paul-Marie Bonaparte, a nephew of the emperor Napoleon.

It seems inevitable that there would also be some un-pleasant characters among the philhellenes. One such was Thomas Fenton of Scotland, who "had proved himself totally divested of every principle or feeling of a gentleman" acc-ording to contemporary visitor James Emerson Tennent. He was so appalling that the new government actually asked him to leave Nafplio. As well as his general bad behaviour, it seems he had also offered himself as a paid assassin. He was ult-imately stabbed to death or shot (depending on the version) after attempting to kill the Englishman Edward John Trelawny.

These youths came with good intentions wrapped in dreams of adventure and glory, as did I at their age. Most con-tributed nothing. That's not to say, however, that all phil-hellenes were useless. Byron famously expended a fortune and his life on the cause (give or take an inept personal doctor). A lesser-known good guy was Dr Samuel Gridley Howe, an American physician who came to Nafplio in 1824 to treat the wounded and sick for no pay. He slept on the ground in his clothes and when finally obliged to return home, he raised $60,000 there to provide clothes and food for the Greek rebels. Perhaps even more impressive, was that for all of his altruism Howe was unimpressed with the locals, describing Nafplio as "a den of thieves" in a letter to fellow American charity worker, J.P. Miller, and referring to "the avarice of the chiefs, the rapacity of the soldiers and the cunning trickery of the people in this place" (see also **War**).

A monument to the French philhellenes was built in 1903 and can be found today in Philhellinon Square, across the road from the port car park and opposite café Napoli di Romania.

Another somewhat less impressive memorial exists inside the *frangoklisia*, the current Catholic church. You'll see it on your way out.

Heinrich Schliemann is considered by some to be the father of modern archaeology. Others have called him a fraud and a cultural vandal, largely due to his method of digging a massive trench right through an archaeological site to see what he could find. The truth is that he found *a lot*.

Schliemann excavated the so-called Treasure of Priam, a fantastic haul of gold and jewellery from the site of Hisarlik, now thought to have been ancient Troy. He also found heaps of gold and artefacts at Mycenae and Tiryns in the Argolid, just a stone's throw from Nafplio. In fact, Schliemann seemed to find treasure wherever he dug, which was either amazing luck, brilliant scholarship . . . or something else.

I read a book about the German digger when I was living in Nafplio in 1998 and he came across as a brilliant self-mythologiser. Here was a self-made millionaire who spoke around fifteen languages both ancient and modern, and who didn't let anyone forget about it. He had his own language-learning system and said he could learn one in six weeks. He'd read Homer to local children or gathered shepherds in ancient Greek, presumably more for the spectacle of it than for the understanding. His memoirs were full of exaggeration or out-right lies about things he'd done and people he'd met, such as claiming to have witnessed the great San Francisco fire of 1851 when he hadn't been there (he based his account on con-temporary newspaper reports).

Schliemann appealed to me greatly. He was an adventurer, a scholar, a maker of news, a discoverer of secrets that had lain millennia in the earth. So what if he was a bit of a liar and a conman? He was colourful. I knew that fiction required different interpretations of the truth. Schliemann made his own reality, as did I.

I didn't know it at the time, but Schliemann had been a temporary Nafplio resident on various occasions. In 1884, while excavating Tiryns, he stayed at the Hotel des Etrangers in Syntagma Square and followed a strict daily routine. He'd wake up at 3.45 a.m., take four grains of quinine to protect against the fever and then pay a boatman to row him to the open sea, presumably beyond the Bourtzi. There, Schliemann would swim for five to ten minutes before climbing back into the boat along the oar, a technique he had mastered. Later, he drank a coffee (black, no sugar) at the Agamemnon café in the port and rode out to Tiryns, arriving before dawn and sending back the horse so that his co-archaeologist Dörpfeld could use it. The millionaire was careful to note the cost of both the boatman and the coffee in his diary.

What route did Schliemann take from his hotel to the dock? I imagine it would have been the most direct, exiting the square by the north corner of the Venetian barracks (now the museum). There would have been soldiers on guard in their sentry boxes, perhaps observing him with mild suspicion. The military bugler would wake the rest of the hotel residents around dawn. Then Schliemann would have cut down the side of the Panagia church and along Farmakopoulon Street to the corner of the dock where the little boats still go out to the Bourtzi. It's a route I've taken countless times.

It's interesting that he took his morning coffee at the Agamemnon café (apart from the fact that nowhere else was open so early). Around eight years earlier, he had made world headlines when he'd uncovered astounding treasures at Mycenae. One of these was the so-called Mask of Agamemnon, a solid gold burial mask that was purported to have covered the face of the mythical king. How did Schliemann feel as he sat with his coffee, watching the swaying lanterns of ships in the port, knowing that he of all the men on earth, only he during three thousand years of historical endeavour, had resurrected a Homeric hero – literally pulled a legend from the muddy earth and shown it to be true? Proud, one assumes. There were, however, a few problems with the find.

The first is that four golden masks were excavated from Mycenae and three of them featured bloated, bald, distorted, almost cartoonish faces – shoddy art, even if hammered from sheets of gold. But the so-called Mask of Agamemnon is virtually perfect. It is deeply impressive: the face of a wise and stately man, kinglike, almost lifelike. It has features the others don't have, notably a moustache, cutout ear flaps, a classical straight nose and a distinctive 'closed eye' effect.

The mask was apparently discovered after the excavation had officially closed, something that had also happened with Priam's Treasure at Troy. According to some, Schliemann had been away from Mycenae in the few days prior, potentially visiting a relative of his wife, a goldsmith, in Athens. The implications are clear: with the dig coming to a close and no spectacular finds to burnish his reputation, Schliemann had a fake mask made and 'salted' the site to find it later. Critics of this theory have observed that Schliemann was observed daily on this dig by the Greek archaeologist Panagiotis Stamatakis and that the press, too, were there in the final days. However, we've also seen that Schliemann was an exceptionally early riser, arriving on site long before anyone else.

It's curious that the Mask of Agamemnon has the features it does. The Classical nose is from a much later period of Greek art. The craftsmanship is very precise. Most damningly, it's the only mask to have a moustache and such a pronounced beard. It looks oddly like the statesmanlike and regal figures of Schliemann's Germany: Otto von Bismarck or the kings Wilhelm I and II. One might even say that it looks like a craftsman's response to a shopping list of kinglike, heroic features.

It's a bold claim that Schliemann faked the mask outright, but it wasn't the first time he'd been accused of salting his digs. He'd also allegedly had copies of genuine finds made on other sites and handed them to the Turkish authorities as real, keeping the originals and smuggling them away. There were further rumours of gathering multiple finds from a site and 'refinding' them all together for a bigger impact. As for the ancient inscriptions he claimed to have found in his garden in Athens, there was definite proof that he'd bought them.

Some of the details in this case have been challenged. Was

Schliemann really away just before the find? It's not clear. The discovery was only so late in the dig perhaps because rain had prevented work previously. Another intriguing possibility is that the Mask Of Agamemnon is a "repurposed" genuine find: Schliemann took an existing mask from Mycenae and had it made more regal, more Agamemnon-like.

It all comes down to the suspiciously unique moustache. Reports of the find in the *Argolis* newspaper of 1876 are clear on one thing: "[The mask] has an engraved beard four to five inches long, but no moustache." However, the earliest photograph of the mask, five weeks after the discovery, shows a moustache. What had happened? The fact that the moustache is also upturned in a most nineteenth century manner is also peculiar. Schliemann's own take on the mask in his 1880 book, *Mycenae*, is fascinating. Doth the lady protest too much?

"In a perfect state of preservation, on the other hand, is the massive golden mask of the body at the south end of the tomb (No. 474). Its features are altogether Hellenic and I call particular attention to the long thin nose, running in a direct line with the forehead, which is but small. The eyes, which are shut, are large, and well represented by the eyelids; very characteristic is also the large mouth with its well-proportioned lips. The beard also is well represented, and particularly the moustaches, whose extremities are turned upwards to a point, in the form of crescents. This circumstance seems to leave no doubt that the ancient Mycenaeans used oil or a sort of pomatum in dressing their hair. Both masks are of repoussé work, and certainly nobody will for a moment doubt that they were intended to represent portraits of the deceased, whose faces they have covered for ages [...] We are amazed at the skill of the ancient Mycenaean goldsmiths, who could model the portraits of men in massive gold plate, and consequently do as much as any modern goldsmith would be able to perform."

As it turns out, the dating of the mask suggests that it's a few hundred years away from the Trojan War and so can't have belonged to a king who fought in it. A test of the gold might show whether the mask was a copy fabricated for Schliemann by a modern goldsmith – but only if the gold isn't genuinely from the tomb and reworked. The National Museum in Athens has declined to test the mask, and who can blame them? It's a magnificent and inspiring find and a great testament to Heinrich Schliemann.

Did Schliemann sit in the Agamemnon café, looking out at the Bourtzi, knowing that only he would ever know the truth about that handsome ancient face? Did he worry about being found out? I don't think so. His mission was to prove that the myths were true. He didn't go to Troy to discover the site's history; he went to find Priam. He didn't go to Mycenae to see what lay in the earth; he went to find Agamemnon. And find them he did. The world applauded and accepted because the world wanted to believe in the truth of myth. Ambiguity pleases nobody and facts are tiresome things.

Another curious footnote. At the time Schliemann was in town supervising the dig at Tiryns, Nafplio was in the process of having its Venetian walls periodically demolished. Huge bastions remained. Did he stroll the town in the evenings, after dinner maybe, looking at ragged gaps in huge protective walls? Did he wonder at the vanishing history even as he sought to excavate the history of another, millennia-older civilisation? Archaeologists discover what has passed: fallen and buried remnants whose events can only be dimly guessed at. Schliemann was in a town whose history was being wiped before his eyes. Was he interested? Or was there no glory in that story?

One man above all others was responsible for me ending up in Nafplio aged twenty-five. He was also briefly here in 1939. I discovered Henry Miller on the day after I handed in my BA dissertation during the final weeks of university. I was in the library looking for something to read that I wouldn't have to write an essay about and I found a plain brown, cloth-bound hardback of *Tropic of Cancer*. I'd heard of it – nothing more. It turned out to be the most galvanising book I'd read in my life so far, virtually erasing everything I'd studied and setting the literature meter back to zero.

Miller was a man who was desperate to be a great writer, modelling his early efforts on Dostoyevsky. The problem was that he couldn't write a novel. He couldn't do structure. His response was a kind of genius: he decided to reject literature altogether, to reject story and structure and plot. He'd write whatever he liked and not change a word. He'd make himself a writer through sheer force of will. In the first pages of *Tropic of Cancer*, I read, "A year ago, six months ago, I thought that I was an artist. I no longer think about it. I *am*."

That's all you had to do! Decide you were an artist. Write whatever you wanted and stick out your chin at snivelling naysayers who didn't think it was art. Miller went to 1930s Paris in his forties, lived like a bum and made himself a writer, albeit of a very odd book. *Tropic of Cancer* is toxically masculine and misogynistic. It has no story. It often rambles. Sometimes, it's just plain bad. But it believes in itself, by God. It's earnest and brave and it does not give a shit. This was the spirit of a true artist. Miller wrote himself into a new identity and existence.

George Orwell praised the book as something genuinely new in his essay 'Inside the Whale', while also presciently predicting that Miller had nothing else to offer except more of the same. Miller was my god as a twenty-something would-be writer. I wanted his literary fire and self belief. I wanted my work to be art even if I hadn't really written anything yet. More than anything, I wanted to create a myth around myself that might become a reality.

Forced out of Paris by the oncoming war, Miller came first to Greece to visit his friend Lawrence Durrell. They arrived in Nafplio by ship from Corfu in January 1939. Winter in Nafplio can be cloudy and rainy, but January is a special month thanks to the *alkionides meres*, the halcyon days, during which the weather suddenly improves for a fortnight or so and typical winter days transform into sunny ones with temperatures in the twenties centigrade. According to folk tradition, this is the period when the kingfisher, the mythical *alcyone*, nests by the sea and protects its eggs amid a balmy breeze provided by Mother Nature. How like Miller to arrive in Nafplio during a mythical burst of light.

He was disparaging about Nafplio itself, which reminded him of a provincial French town: "dismal and deserted" at night, peripheral and officious. He wrote nothing about its streets and its decadent Venetian glory, though he must have sat in the cafés of the square and looked out at the Bourtzi – the view that everyone takes away with them. Rather, he noted the garrison, a fortress, a palace, a cathedral and the mosque converted into a cinema.

But then Miller had a very eccentric concept of Greece before he arrived. He'd read a lot of Durrell's fanciful letters about the country, in which "the dream and the reality, the historical and mythological were so artfully blended." In Paris, he had also listened to a drunken girl called Betty Ryan rhapsodising about "a world of light such as I had never dreamed of and never hoped to see."

Miller told people that he most loved the "light and the poverty" of Greece. He claimed to feel most in tune with the illiterate peasants and goatherds (with whom he couldn't converse). He identified most strongly with a gatekeeper serving a life sentence in Palamidi; a man dressed in tatters, whose greatest ambition was to raise a little corn on a ragged swatch of land within the fortress. Miller's Nafplio, like Schliemann's, like Hope's, like mine and the philhellenes, was a fantasy, a delusion. He admitted to knowing nothing about Greek history. He hadn't read Homer at that stage. His approach was to observe and create his own interpretations.

Walking the ruins of Mycenae, largely ignorant of the millennia of history and myth, Miller fabricated his own versions based on idiosyncratic impressions: the colossal stones, the stately burial chambers, the impossible skein of time. He wrote his own histories, which were naturally more authoritative than anything in books. He was a demiurge – a creator of worlds. Facts and reality were irrelevant. Reading his most celebrated, his favourite and most finished book *The Colossus of Maroussi,* one often wonders, "Is this the same Greece?" Miller saw what he wanted to see based on the poetic unreality of his original conceptions. He was, at that stage, transforming his literary identity from satyr to transcendentalist. Greece was his trigger and his model: purity, simplicity, poverty and profundity lost in the obscurity of myth. Nafplio didn't fit his script. Nafplio was too real for Miller.

I hadn't understood (or had blinded myself to) Miller's failings in 1998. I glossed over his negative comments about Nafplio and set out to be him, creating my own creative topography as he had in Paris and making myself a hero. I didn't write anything except letters, using a manual Olivetti typewriter with an English keyboard I'd bought from a delighted Greek shop owner – a most writerly of writing instruments. The novels would come, but I started with letters as Miller had in Paris. The aim was to gain experience. I had so little to write about. All I knew was literature: Miller's poisoned well. Or as Kurt Vonnegut observed: "I think it can be tremendously refreshing if a writer has something on his mind other than the history of literature so far. Literature should not disappear up its own asshole, so to speak."

Nafplio gave me plenty of experiences and anecdotes to fuel my self mythology. I filled a thick journal with them. I also met other fantasists, other people on a similar path. There were backpackers, itinerant fruit pickers, an alcoholic Buddhist, a French paraglider, a Lebanese masseuse, a Serbian poet and a fugitive male escort. The most memorable was a millionaire who reluctantly invited me to supper on his yacht one evening when I was living at the Catholic church.

I'll call him Jean le Pew, a French-Canadian with a fortune hazily connected to vineyards. He arrived as the sun was setting and just as the English caretaker priest and I were sitting on the balcony of the church's recently refurbished accommodation. The light was purple-violet. Swifts were jagging above the courtyard. The priest, already well on the way to inebriation, looked over the edge and said, "The guy from Karathonas! He's come!"

The priest used to walk along the coastal walk to Karathonas beach each morning (a fact attested to by his virulently sunburned, almost radioactively scarlet face) and swim out to the tiny islet before returning to open the first bottle. The previous day, he'd been breaststroking by a large motor cruiser when the owner looked down from the gunwale and exclaimed, "That man has the eyes of a priest!" Introductions were made and the boat owner promised to visit the church later.

Le Pew and his wife were around seventy. He was white-haired, florid faced, portly and dressed in a marine style (white polo, navy shorts, deck shoes). His wife was elegant and be-jewelled, albeit with dentures that clicked and sucked when she spoke. She was the voice for the pair, referring to her husband only in the third person.

"Jean le Pew would like to read from scripture," she announced, looking up from under the purple bougainvillea.

The priest and I descended – he somewhat unevenly – to the church. He was reluctant to do a service for only two people. Nor was he in the right frame of mind, having been drinking since three. Jean le Pew had brought his own small leather-bound bible and the priest suggested a verse or two, but le Pew had his own ideas.

I took a seat a few rows back and Mrs Le Pew sat at the front. The priest, hastily and sweatily attired in cassock, stood to one side and we were all treated to Jean le Pew's performance. He stood with one leg out in front, his Bible arm raised like a Demosthenic rhetor, and proclaimed the verses in a sonorous, emphatic voice as if the church were at full capacity. On the front row, Mrs le Pew simpered and stifled gasps of admiration, her dentures sucking like a storm drain as I tried to catch the priest's eye in a classic *WTF?* moment. He kept his composure. He was trying hard to stay upright.

When le Pew's voice echoed into silence amid the old mosque's dome, Mrs le Pew clapped, her bangles and rings tinkling. I was already writing it up in my mind.

"Jen le Pew would like to invite you to the ship for supper," twittered Mrs le Pew, looking at the priest and not at me.

"That's very kind," said the priest. "But I was planning to dine with Matt tonight. Is he invited, too?"

They looked hatefully at me, a random youth. I didn't look like a priest. Not even like a novice. They clearly wanted to say no, but their desire to have a genuine priest blessing their gangplank was overwhelming. So we all went down to the port, the priest leaning on my shoulder down the marble steps, and we boarded a colossal white motor yacht that had a crew of three Italians, including the personal chef.

Few experiences have been as surreal and dreamlike as sitting on the rear deck of that yacht while being served supper by men in white uniforms. Common tourists, plebs, walked the quay and looked at us, wondering how we'd made our millions. Palamidi was an illuminated mantis on its dark mass above. The lights of the old town twinkled. And the priest became drunker and drunker. When offered water by a concerned Mrs le Pew, he exclaimed, "Water? I never drink water, madam! Fish make love in it!" I remember distinctly that nobody laughed.

After dessert (a lemon sorbet, I believe) we were hesitantly, with glances at the leaning priest, offered a nightcap. A whisky perhaps? Why not! I saw that Jean le Pew had two bottles in his minibar: J&B and a single malt that may have been Glenmorangie. He poured us meagre measures of the cheap blend.

It was the kind of evening I'd imagined, dreamed about, before arriving in Nafplio. Life as fiction. I as the hero in startling and barely credible narratives. There I was, temporarily housed in an old Turkish hammam, part of the town's Catholic church, knocking about with an alcoholic priest and dining with delusional millionaires on yachts. This wasn't fantasy; this was real.

On the way back to the church, the priest – now largely

without the power of coherent speech – sustained himself mostly upright by gripping onto the back of my trousers. It must have looked like I was taking a mumbling half-wit for a walk. At the foot of the marble stairs, he got his foot wedged in a pothole, fell and went rolling in the street, one shoe off and swearing like a scaffolder. People in the neighbouring restaurant observed the scene with some humour and my epic evening turned to comedy.

The next day, we discovered that Jean le Pew had left the drachma equivalent of €500 in the collection box.

WAR

Nafplio has spent just a handful of its c. 3000 inhabited years actively engaged in war, but most of that time in preparation or expectation of war. Its founding geography is defensive. It's difficult to imagine, while sipping a frappé in the square or ambling the blossom-strewn streets, the horrors of war in these same spaces. Burning buildings. Disease. Despair. Famine. Massacre, torture and depredation. Let's bring some of that alive.

The town has been attacked multiple times: by Argos, the Heruli, the Goths, the Avars, the Slavs, Theodore I Palaiologos, the Franks, the Turks, Albanian mercenaries, the Venetians, the Germans and by Greeks themselves. These are the ones we know about. Who knows what trouble the Mycenaeans faced? The third-century BC walls were presumably erected to keep somebody out. Someone else may have left the town in ruins for Pausanias to find in the second century AD.

Each attack would have had similar effects on the town: indiscriminate slaughter, plunder, prisoners, destruction of property, displacement and often enslavement. Bodies would have lain in the streets, rotting and causing disease. Piles of rubble may have remained for years afterwards, the previously interred buried beneath. The sea would have bobbed with bloated corpses. The town would have reeked of putrefaction.

Those earlier conflicts are largely lost in history. We know that the Frankish siege of Acronafplio in 1212 ended in a relatively civilized negotiated surrender. A treaty between the warring parties agreed that the acropolis would be divided between conquerors and conquered, with two castles co-existing. It was the last time anyone would share.

The first Ottoman attacks began when the Morea was raided by Bayezid I in the late fourteenth century. Then Murad

II's forces invaded the Morea twice in the first half of the fif-teenth century sacking and destroying settlements but eventually withdrawing. After Mehmet II seized Constantin-ople in 1453 he, too, turned his attention to the Morea, inv-ading in 1458. By 1461, he had conquered the entire peninsula save for the Venetian colonies themselves. War with the Ven-etians followed in 1463. It dragged on until 1479 but Nafplio remained safe within its walls, now seriously improved.

War with the Turks broke out again in 1499 and Bayezid II attacked Nafplio in 1500. The attack was repelled and Bayezid turned south taking Methoni, Navarino and Koroni that same year, leaving only Nafplio and Monemvasia in Venetian hands. Venice took the diplomatic initiative and signed a peace treaty with the Turks in 1503, renewed in 1513 and 1521.

Sultan Suleiman I, the Magnificent, would not be placated, however, and he declared war again in 1537. In September, his general, Kashim Pasha, laid siege to Nafplio for fourteen months, bombarding the lower town from the heights of Palamidi. Despite more than a year of cannonballs raining down on the town with random death, destroyed buildings and water supplies running low, Nafplio held out. Kashim's forces retired to Argos leaving a garrison on Palamidi. Remark-ably, the Venetians still had the resources to quickly expel the Turks from the heights above the town.

It was the Venetian defeat at the naval battle of Preveza in 1538 that forced the Republic to seek peace terms with the Turks. Nafplio was lost not by siege but by the treaty of 1540 that ceded both Nafplio and Monemvasia to the sultan.

The Venetians and Ottomans had very little in common, least of all their religions. There was no question of the inhabitants staying. A huge exodus followed the end of the siege, with dozens of ships taking people back to a place they may never have seen. The Venetians had been in Nafplio for over 150 years. Generations had grown up there, running their businesses, building houses, making a life. Many of them would have been wealthy and successful from the flourishing international trade they served.

Typically, such people remain nameless, but one Venetian Nafpliot family has risen through the murk of history to be briefly visible. The Nassins, father Niccolo and son Zorzi, fled the old town leaving assets worth 3,672 ducats (around £385,560 today) – probably a house and a warehouse with goods left inside it. In recognition of their loss, the Venetian state gave the Nassins the position of prior at the Lazaretto Nuovo in the Venetian lagoon for the lifetime of father and son. Their ill fortune was not over, however. They lost more family in the next round of plague.

Peace under the Turks lasted around two lifetimes: 146 years. Then Francesco Morosini came from Venice in 1686 as Captain-General of a massive fleet. He brought a secret weapon: his German-Swedish field marshal Otto Wilhelm Königsmarck, who came from a long line of military men and was considered one of the best in the business, which is why the Venetian Republic hired him.

The masterstroke of this reconquest was to stop at the beach of Tolo before reaching Nafplio and drop off a land force that would march to the rear of the hill of Palamidi, largely unseen, advance to the edge of the cliffs overlooking the town and bombard it as the Turks had done in 1537. At this date, the vast fortress complex had not been constructed and there were few Turkish soldiers stationed there. Moreover, they had become complacent during years of relative peace.

Acronafplio and the town were well defended thanks to the last Venetian occupation, but they were fortified primarily against a land or sea approach. Königsmarck bombed Nafplio from above, probably with a combination of standard cannon balls and hollow shot filled with gunpowder. Buildings collapsed and fire raged without pause for fourteen days, lighting up the night and reflecting across the sea to Argos.

Contemporary engravings show a siege on multiple fronts. The Venetian fleet shelled the town from the south while land batteries to the north fired upon the sea defences and the Bourtzi. Morosini's encamped army was also massed in front of the land walls for a direct attack on the main gates.

Francesco Morosini had served for twenty-three years in the service of Venice, culminating in his command at Candia where in 1669 he been forced to come to terms with the Turks. The loss of Crete after the twenty-one-year siege led to his trial in Venice and although acquitted he spent the next fifteen years in effective retirement until his recall as Captain-General of the invasion fleet.

A flamboyant sort, he always wore red and reputedly never went anywhere without his pet cat Nini, who accompanied his master even into battle. The year after the Nafplio siege, Morosini was fighting in Athens and was the one responsible for firing purposely on the Parthenon (then an Ottoman powder magazine). He blew the roof off. Afterwards, he tried to prise off some of the west pediment sculptures but made a mess of it. They fell and smashed to pieces. When the Turks re-took the Acropolis, they saw that someone had tried to remove the sculptures and perceived that maybe they were valuable to the infidel. Thus the Parthenon sculptures began to be sold off.

Morosini was the Republic's last great hero and his reward was to be made Doge in 1688. He died in Nafplio in January 1694 having returned to resume fighting the Turks at the age of seventy-five.

During the siege, the Turks sent reinforcements from Argos and Corinth but these were defeated by superior numbers and skills. Another engraving from the same time shows the Turks gamely fighting back, most of the town's batteries pluming with cannon smoke. The Bourtzi, however, has Venetians swarming up its sides from smaller boats. They would have slaughtered the Turkish soldiers present and turned the guns on the Five Brothers battery just opposite.

Two weeks of fire and ceaseless bombardment caused huge damage to the town. Hundreds died, many of them civilians. Again, these people remain anonymous. Their personal tragedies, their agony and their loss is totally unrecorded. We think of war as dates and battles and outcomes, but its greatest cost is always human. Not a single street in Nafplio is without its own small horror.

One small incident does echo through the noise of artillery and the roar of conflagration. Three soldiers were tasked with cutting off the water supply to the town by stopping the aqueduct where it passed close to the Land Gate. They did so, knowing the extreme risk, and all three were killed. Four more were wounded trying to help. Three lives lost in an inconsequential act on the grand canvas of history.

Morosini organised a triumphal entry into Nafplio through the Land Gate and the officers received their prizes. Königsmarck received a gold basin filled with 6000 ducats (around £630,000 nowadays) for his good work, though he was dead of plague just two years later off the coast of Methoni. Around 7000 of the remaining Turkish residents and the entire surviving garrison were shipped off to the Ottoman-held island of Tenedos.

The town had to be substantially rebuilt, particularly the first-period Venetian fortifications that Morosini had just destroyed. Before that, someone would have had to remove the bodies from the streets and the battlements. Were they burned in a trench outside the walls, or taken down the gulf by ship and dropped into the deep water? Someone had to clear away the rubble and dig out the rotting corpses. Maybe someone was pulled from the ruins alive to discover that their Turkish town was now a Venetian one. The mosque was going to be a church. Everyone they had ever known was dead or exiled.

So it goes. It all started again in 1715 with Ali Pasha, who stormed the Peloponnese with a fleet and land army of up to 100,000 men. Complacent within its lofty walls, Venetian Nafplio had only around 1,700 soldiers, only a few of whom were stationed in Palamidi. When the Turks approached from the rear (as Königsmarck had in 1686) and exploded a mine, the Venetian troops in this "impregnable" fortress mistook the blast for a much bigger attack than it was and fled to the lower town. The ones remaining in the fortress were taken prisoner and shipped off to the dungeons of Istanbul, presumably to rot. Thus began the bombardment from above. The whole siege lasted merely eight or nine days.

History records that the Turks massacred the population and the garrison, while the more important citizens were taken prisoner for ransom. This may be an occidental exaggeration of the Islamic force's brutality. A nineteenth-century engraving shows Venetians flooding Nafplio's quays to escape in multiple vessels. They had known in advance that the Ottoman forces were coming from Corinth and up the Argolic gulf. They had eight further days to get some possessions together and flee. It's therefore possible that not many people remained to be massacred.

Then the whole process started again: churches converted back to mosques, new taxation system, new people brought in from Turkish dominions. There would be 106 years of peace before the War of Greek Independence.

We have more information about the Greek War of Independence in Nafplio than any of the other wars. Perhaps that's why it can look like the most traumatic for the town and its people. Much of the violence was between the self-interested Greek factions themselves.

There's a certain dark irony that it started the same way as in previous centuries. Nobody had learned anything. The towering Palamidi had been the key to Nafplio's protection since 1540 and three times it had been used to attack the lower town. The Venetians recognised this in 1686 and turned it into a phenomenally strong castle complex during the early eighteenth century, but its Achilles heel remained the same. Though precipitously inaccessible on three sides, its fourth is just a stroll. It's where the current road approaches the main gate and where most attacks have been made. In 1715, the Venetian troops simply ran away. So much for impregnability.

In 1822, Turkish-held Nafplio – its minarets and mosque domes visible over the city walls – had been under blockade by Greek forces for over a year. No food or water was going in, except rain and any birds unfortunate enough to land there. Sixty to seventy people were dying daily of starvation and fever. On November 29, Staikos Staikopoulos entered Palamidi with his own band of troops, physically climbing the walls and dropping down the other side to open the door. After some inevitable slaughter, they then used its cannons to shell the town and the fortifications of Acronafplio. The rocks by the sea were crowded with hundreds of people sheltering from the cannonballs. Some swam out to the Bourtzi, which was still in Turkish hands, for safety.

The small Venetian church of S. Girardo existed in the bastion of the same name and Staikopoulos's men found that the Turks had been using it as a storeroom. The day after entering the castle was the feast day of St Andrew and so they cleaned out the space to hold a service, thereafter dedicating the church to that saint and renaming the fort in his honour. Since then, a service has been held every year to remember Nafplio's liberation.

Barely three days after the bombardment started, the exhausted Turks surrendered Acronafplio and the lower town. This was littered with rotting corpses and heaped with rubble. The few survivors had resorted to eating horses, camels and their own dead. The stench was unbearable. Greek commander in chief Theodoros Kolokotronis raised the flag of freedom on the ramparts of Acronafplio.

According to one source, Kolokotronis ordered that all Turkish furniture, utensils and valuables be gathered and stored in the Trianon mosque for later distribution as spoils of war. Another version has he and his men storming into the precincts of Acronafplio before any negotiations could occur and plundering everything they could, killing all Turks who stood in their way and torturing the bey mercilessly to discover where his "treasure" was hidden. Meanwhile, the Bourtzi was bloodily stormed by Greek, French and German troops to eradicate the Turkish soldiers (and sheltering citizens) there.

Amid all of the chaos of these initial days, plague broke out again. Contemporary sources suggested this was caused by Greek soldiers plundering the clothes and possessions of dead Turks, which harboured traces of whatever illness habitually struck the town. More likely it was caused by the unsanitary living conditions and tainted water supply. Ioannis Kapo-distrias's private secretary later described this particular outbreak in his memoirs.

According to Fotios Chrysanthopoulos, the usually fatal disease had many strange symptoms. Extreme fever caused many to go out to the sea in search of coolness, day or night, and drown. Their families were forced to nail up the doors to keep them inside. Other delirious sufferers stripped naked and threw themselves out of windows or from the town's fort-ifications. If they didn't die, they either had to return via the Land Gate naked and injured, or simply lie broken where they'd fallen because nobody would come close to them for fear of contagion. It was worse for the philhellenes, just arrived, because they had no family and often didn't speak the language. At its peak of infection, the plague caused the victim to go insane and hallucinate. Some imitated priests and blessed their own families at home. The few who survived were permanently robbed of one or more senses: sight, hear-ing, even memory. It was probably typhoid or cholera.

Disease was bad enough, but being Turkish was worse. When the tide of independence turned and the Greeks started to rise against the Ottomans, massacres occurred on both sides. The infamous Chios Massacre of April-May 1822 saw Turkish troops slaughter around 52,000 men, women and children on the island as a summary lesson to the Greeks. It had the opposite effect of convincing Europe to unite behind Greece and it also made the Greeks even thirstier for revenge.

According to one estimate, there were around 50,000 Turks living in the Peloponnese in March 1821, but a fraction of that just a few months later. The villages were littered with corpses. According to William St Clair, "Upwards of 20,000 Turkish men, women and children were murdered by their Greek neighbours in a few weeks of slaughter. They were killed deliberately, without qualm and scruple . . . Turkish families living in single farms or small isolated communities were summarily put to death, and their homes burned down over their corpses."

Multiple sources, including St Clair, recount the story of Greek rebels who captured the crew of a Turkish vessel and roasted fifty-seven of them alive on the beach at Hydra amid much merriment. There were also massacres of Turks in Navarino, Monemvasia, Tripolitsa, Dervenaki near Nafplio and in Corinth. In the latter case, the Turks made a deal with their besiegers that they would give up the town if they were granted leave to return to Asia Minor in neutral vessels. This agreed, they moved towards the sea but were soon attacked by a gauntlet of screaming and spitting Greek women. One starving and exhausted Turkish couple handed their baby to a Greek soldier, who cut off its head – an encounter witnessed and recorded in his diary by a German officer who tried to prevent the killing.

By late December 1822, refugees from around the Peloponnese were flooding into Nafplio for safety. A visitor described the very frequent occurrence of finding children dead in the street. They had starved to death. Women were scavenging in trash and drains for food.

Hatred for the Turks had not abated. A Greek Orthodox priest accused of helping the Turks had his hands purposefully scalded with boiling water by an angry mob. He was then buried up to his neck with syrup daubed on his face to attract flies and died after six days. A Jewish man trying to escape was captured, stripped and had his intestines pulled out before being paraded around the town and hanged. Perhaps he'd been mistaken for a Turk. Or perhaps an independent Greece was being conceived as a monocultural place. A massacre was surely coming. The normal procedure was to kill all the men and divide the women and children as (sex) slaves, often to be killed later if they proved recalcitrant or too expensive to maintain.

We should remember that many of the same troops who had committed the massacres at Tripolitsa and Dervenakia were now in Nafplio. Perhaps a single incident was the catalyst – an angry soldier, a "disrespectful" Turk – but finally the mood grew sufficiently homicidal. The Greeks made a festive pyramid of severed heads and the slaughter might have continued until every Turk was dead, but the arrival in port of the British warship Cambrian and the intervention of its Commodore Hamilton saved many Muslim and Jewish residents. A visitor to the town at this time was shocked to see the bodies of two Turks dumped outside the city walls to putrefy. Better to contaminate the air everyone breathed than bury a Muslim.

And the frenzied ransacking went on unabated. Anarchy is one effect of war. All morality vanishes once you start frenziedly killing without consequence. There are no rules. There are no ethics – and never more so than after a siege. Military commanders throughout history have known that it's best to let the men "blow off steam" before regrouping. The Greek soldiers took the most for themselves and European officers were given just two or three Turkish girls for their pleasure. Some of these girls were taken to Athens and sold to the consuls, who typically saw them returned safely to Turkey.

Nafplio had swollen to perhaps the greatest population in its history so far. The enclosed old town contained around 10,000 people, with another 10,000 camping outside the walls in tents or sleeping rough. The port was thick with Greek and international vessels. Soldiers were billeted eighteen to twenty to a house. The Greeks had formed themselves into private militias that stalked the streets in their gold-embroidered red jackets, their silver-bedecked guns and their pleated white *fustanellas* that looked like kilts to foreign observers. But the Greeks weren't here to fight. Nafplio had been taken. They were here to get paid.

There were rumours that the Great Powers were about to send money to aid the fight for independence – loans rather than gifts, but money all the same. And since Nafplio was the focus of the fight for independence, the money would arrive here. Clan chiefs and their loyal *palikaria* swarmed to the town in anticipation of the riches they were due. Observers wondered if independence was their true motivation. There were still plenty of Turkish soldiers to fight in other parts of Greece.

The historian Steven Runciman has since written that the main driver of the war for the Greeks was religious – not independence, but the extermination of Muslims and Jews.

The town was becoming a psychological powder keg. Hundreds of armed men, their bloodlust not yet sated, had been "promised" payment and no payment was forthcoming. With the land around the town ravaged by war, there wasn't enough produce to feed even the troops. The militia sallied out to raid local villages already destroyed by the Turks. Clan chiefs started to fight other clan chiefs for the spoils. One group briefly took control of Palamidi until they were paid in full. Some Greek soldiers even started to rob and murder locals or the European volunteers for their clothes. They didn't need the clothes, but they could sell them. They were here to get paid. Disease continued to spread among the weak, the hungry, the refugees and the beggars. Bodies were putrefying in the streets and floating in the harbour. Bodies stank invisibly below the blackened rubble. Bodies piled up in the hospital at Psaromahala and people lay dying on the ground to the sound of musket shots and shouts.

Civil war broke out in 1824. Theodoros Kolokotronis had taken Nafplio and was not especially predisposed to cooperate with the new national government based at Epidaurus. He didn't mind if the government wanted to use Nafplio as a base, but he wanted to retain control of Acronafplio for himself. They could use his town if they liked. Invited into the new assembly as a placatory gesture, Kolokotronis turned out to be not a "team player" and was reluctant to let go of his castle. In March, his son Panos refused to give up Acronafplio and the new government was obliged to besiege the same town the Greeks had besieged just two years before. It would be two weeks before they could come to an agreement.

From the mid 1820s, the first gold and silver began to arrive from Great Britain by ship and would continue to arrive every couple of months. More revolutionary militia leaders were flowing into town. The Reverend Sheridan Wilson was there and observed that "the sight of beautiful English gold threw the poor penniless natives into extacies." It would be fair – an understatement even – to say that the money didn't reach those who needed it most. According to one source, Kolokotronis immediately received 50,000 piastres as a payoff to release his claim on Acronafplio. The politicians then generously rewarded themselves for their own services. All personal debts were paid off, whether they existed or not. "Corruption is the wrong word to describe the chaos," says St Clair. "It was more a kind of financial anarchy."

Military leaders claimed pay and rations for hundreds of soldiers who didn't exist. Meanwhile, the militia spent their money on exotic Albanian arms, decorative equine accessories, splendid jackets and silver-tooled swords. The shops and markets were full of such stuff, but not enough food. Meanwhile, just across the bay, Argos was being looted and burned by the Ottoman pasha's troops. The flames could be seen reflecting off the sea all through the night. Thirty minutes down the coast, more Ottoman troops were camped at Myloi.

When European visitors arrived in Nafplio later in 1825, they found virtually no English coin in circulation. It had all vanished – hoarded by the poor who had managed to receive it and put into the hands of private bankers by the rich and influential who had taken the larger share. Treasure fever had gripped the entire town. One bemused visitor in 1825 observed the population frenziedly digging up Platanos Square, believing it to conceal buried Turkish riches. And still things were about to get worse.

The war was by no means over. The failed Battle of Phaleron near Piraeus saw around 2,000 Greeks soldiers killed, leaving only Nafplio and the southern Mani region in independent hands by 1827. Many of the Greek troops fleeing Phaleron came to Nafplio and decided to take it for themselves. Theodoros Grivas occupied Palamidi, while Acronafplio went to Giannakis Stratos and Nasos Fotomaras. The town wasn't big enough for the two camps, so they set about fighting and shelling each other from the two forts. It wasn't organised enough to be called civil war. It was simply chaos.

The two factions looted what was left of Nafplio and destroyed large areas just to spite each other. One camp
purposefully burned the huge olive grove of over 30,000 trees,
that the Venetians had planted and which stretched from the
foot of Palamidi to Aria. They sold the roots and remaining
branches for firewood. Shepherds were robbed of their flocks
and villagers of the meagre produce that hadn't already been
stolen by the militias.

At this stage in the war, as the town shelled itself for profit,
around 8,000 people were on the point of starvation. Nafplio
was still full of refugees whose houses and farms had been
destroyed by Turks or marauding clan militias. They clam-
oured at every arriving ship for charity and waited outside
warehouses for food or clothing. Many were crushed to death
in the scrums. However, it was Grivas – the tyrant of Palamidi –
who took the aid. His soldiers would enter the ships before
they could unload and steal the cargo at gunpoint. If the
distribution had already begun, they would beat the poor away
with rifle butts and commandeer the supplies.

Kolokotronis was still in the lower town and assisting in the
battle against Grivas, but he too saw an opportunity. As one
American vessel began to give barrels of flour to the poor, the
charity representative received a handwritten note from the
old warrior: "Stop distributing my flour!" The charity man took
the note to Kolokotronis's house and found the family dining
contentedly. A stand-up argument followed, during which
Kolokotronis explained that the flour was meant for Greece
and *he* was Greece. Ergo, it was his flour. Nafplio briefly
became known to locals and Europeans as a *listarcheio*, the
rule of the thieves.

Up in his fortress eyrie, Grivas was becoming ever more
psychotic. His personal torturer Dimitrios Hatsiskos was using
a range of medieval techniques to find where people might be
hiding their treasure. The most notorious of these was to make
a hole through the floor and compel the victim to lie naked
with his genitals in the hole, a stone tied around them and
dangling into the next room. Once the genitals had swelled

horribly, the stone was released but the victim could not remove the swollen organs from the hole. In some cases, the wood around the hole might be sawn out so the victim could walk around carrying the piece of wood, their purple-black penis and testes bulbously wobbling through the hole. All in the name of independence.

At one point, the Ottoman commander of the area offered to pay Grivas ten million *grosci* to hand over Palamidi to the Turks. Grivas saw an opportunity, but the price was too low. He also wanted to be made commander of the entire Peloponnese, or, if not, to be allowed to safely depart to any other country. Ibrahim was too slow to come back with an answer and Grivas decided to fight on, a patriot after all.

Grivas was prised from Palamidi only when Ioannis Kapodistrias arrived as the first governor in 1828. After seven years of siege and civil strife, the town he entered could hardly have been less promising as the nation's new capital. Piles of rubble lay everywhere, the corpses beneath it reeking. The sewers were blocked with debris and bodies. The aqueduct carrying the town's only source of clean water was damaged. The unpaved streets that hadn't been destroyed were still barricaded against attacks from militia or Grivas's soldiers. Shabby wooden huts had been built everywhere inside the walls to house refugees and these were a focus of disease and vermin. The shops were destroyed or had no provisions. The army was disbanded, but the town was full of jittery soldiers. The navy was scattered, the judicial and educational systems non-existent. All of Nafplio's fortifications and barracks were badly damaged. Such were the effects of war. Everything had to be fixed again.

Kapodistrias began a huge programme of building, cleaning and repair. Nafplio acquired new neoclassical structures that would hopefully make it look like a national capital. The displaced and the refugees, meanwhile, were moved to the suburb of Prónoia just a short walk from the Land Gate.

As for Theodoros Grivas, he continued to be colourful for the next forty years, fighting for the Greeks, condemned by the

Greeks, pardoned, condemned again, made Inspector General of the Army and even an MP. He was unpredictable to the end, dying aged sixty-five in Messolonghi after a lifetime of battle. So much for karma.

The fighting was over but Nafplio remained a military base on a war footing. Following Kapodistrias's assassination in 1831, King Otto invested further in updating and maintaining barracks and fortifications, including parts of the land defences damaged in the 1820s. The Land Gate received a new drawbridge, the old one having seen the bodies of many thousands traverse it: invaders, traders, refugees, fugitives, the persecuted and the dead. A sum of 10,000-12,000 drachmas was allocated each year to renovate and maintain the fortifications.

The town was now defended by a battalion of infantry, a division of light infantry and the artillery of 260 men based in the barracks of Platanos Square. An additional division of gendarmerie was in place to keep the peace, while the garrison of the Royal Phalanx was something like a royal bodyguard. Uniforms were everywhere, but Nafplio would not experience another war for a hundred years.

The Greeks knew that World War Two would come to Nafplio. Their 8th infantry had already been fighting the Italians in Albania. Preparations for the inevitable aerial attack included an air-raid siren on the courthouse roof and subterranean shelters, such as the basement of the National Bank and inside the walls of the Grimani bastion. Trenches were also dug at the Five Brothers bastion and in Syntagma and Three Admirals squares. The aerial attack was short and effective, frustrating the allied troops' evacuation plan, Operation Demon. Many Nafplio families fled to the safety of Karathonas beach, where they could observe the German Stukas out of Argos bombing allied troop ships. On April 28 1941, the first motorised German troops entered the town, flying the swastika from Palamidi's heights and capturing around 2000 allied troops who had not escaped by sea.

A further 1,300 English soldiers were marched over from Tolo to join the others under armed guard in the high school yard. Any Greek civilian who tried to aid or communicate with the prisoners faced immediate and violent reprisals. All of these captives would soon be transferred by train or by forced march to a dedicated POW camp in Corinth.

The German commander told all Greeks to return to work and to hand in any weapons. A traffic ban was imposed from 6.00 p.m. to 7.00 a.m. and the inhabitants were forbidden to gather in groups of more than two people. Anyone found sheltering allied troops would be shot. Private vehicles were seized where required and the railway station was commandeered. The Germans additionally forced the whole male population to construct fortifications along the coast, though many escaped this task by fleeing to the mountains.

Some of the first German soldiers in town were there for R&R and spent their time in Nafplio cleaning out the shops for souvenirs to send home. They were billeted in hotels such as The Grande Bretagne and in many private homes. Around thirty German pilots from the airport at Argos stayed at the recently opened luxury hotel in the Bourtzi.

From June 1941, Hitler gave the Italians charge of most of Greece and they took control of policing and the prisons of Palamidi and Acronafplio. The carabinieri had their office and detention centre in the Viga in Syntagma Square, though the archaeological museum was the offices of the German investigative office – possibly the Gestapo seeking spies, gathering intelligence and keeping an eye on the Italians.

History records the Italian occupation as a hard one. There was widespread famine and a tuberculosis outbreak in 1941-42. Around 180 people died from starvation, disease and executions during the entire occupation. Local recollections provide more colour, with memories of Italian soldiers sharing their food or chocolate with neighbourhood children. The officers in general were gentlemen and greeted the townsfolk in the street. The carabinieri, meanwhile, would sing on their patrols, adding a bizarre charm to this military occupation.

Christmas 1941 saw a hard winter with snowfall in Nafplio. People with farms had chickens, but the shops were virtually empty. Cabbages (kraut) hung on hooks in the butchers' shops. Most people who had meat on the festive table had obtained it on the black market. The Koulouridis grocery in Spyridon Square (see **Squares**) distributed sugar, flour and honey to needy families. A soup kitchen by the sea in front of the customs house served *fasolada* (without oil), chickpeas, lentils and bread. The churches were full of people.

By 1944, the war was going badly for the Germans, who had turned against their previous allies the Italians and bombed Argos as part of the backlash. There was barbed wire along the *paralia* and warships in port. As part of their plans to withdraw, the Germans rigged the port and various factories with explosives to destroy them. Apparently, Greek workers intrigued to ensure that the charges would be enough only to damage rather than destroy.

On the morning of September 14 1944, the German command instructed all residents of the old town to leave and to head for Prónoia. No reason was given. Some loitered instead in Kolokotronis Park in case they needed to rush back. The blasting started at noon and saw huge black plumes rising over the town. Many structures were damaged by flying shrapnel, but the port was not completely destroyed. By 2.00 p.m., the last of the Germans had left. Nafplio was free again. Bells rang and Greek flags unfurled on balconies. Four years of occupation by Germans, Italians and Bulgarians was over.

Postscript 2015: Ludwig Zacaro and Nina Lahge, a German couple on holiday in Nafplio, walk into the town hall and hand over a cheque for €875. They have calculated that this is the World War II reparations bill per person that Germany owes Greece. Since Zacaro is retired and their funds are limited, they have opted to pay only for Lahge. They tell Mayor Dimitris Kotsouros that they chose Nafplio because it was the first capital of Greece. Kotsouros bemusedly takes the payment and forwards it to a charity.

There are very few traces of Nafplio's centuries of war. The rubble was cleared many times, the houses rebuilt, the walls patched up, the bodies buried. Walking around the town today, you'd barely guess at the magnitude of death and destruction it has faced – the fire, the explosions, the famine, the plague. You occasionally see cannons or their projectiles used decoratively, but where are the stellated shrapnel holes? Where are the bullet-pocked walls? It's probably not a very good message to announce to tourists that a hundred people were publicly beheaded on such and such a site. That might spoil the vibe.

I was standing atop the Five Brothers bastion one late-summer day in 1998 when my foot scuffed over an object. There's a circular area to the right that must have been a machine-gun emplacement in WWII and the object under my shoe was a used high-calibre brass shell casing. It was only mildly tarnished. Had decades of footfall erosion brought it to light at that exact moment for me to pick up and examine?

German? Italian? British? I had no idea. I lost it very quickly thereafter, but I'm sure it's still in Nafplio somewhere. It's all in Nafplio – somewhere.

PUNISHMENT

"By day, all red tape, lawyers and judges everywhere, with all the despair and futility that follows in train of these bloodsucking parasites. The fortress and prison dominate the town. Warrior, jailer, priest – the eternal trinity which symbolizes our fear of life."

So Henry Miller summarised Nafplio in 1939. It was a perspective I couldn't understand or accept in 1998, but I was seeing a different Nafplio. In 1939, there was a large three-storey prison dominating Acronafplio and more cells hidden behind Palamidi's massive walls. Thousands of prisoners were incarcerated in the town, sent here from across the country and sundry war zones. Nafplio had transformed in fewer than a hundred years from Greece's bright and modern capital to its militarised penal colony. On a windless day, residents of the lower town could sometimes hear the massed prisoners of Acronafplio rattling their metal cups against the bars, singing or shouting. How did Nafplio come to this?

The Venetians and Turks no doubt had prisons of some sort, if only for punishment and torture. Both empires, however, were sufficiently thrifty to recognise that keeping people locked up for decades also meant feeding them and guarding them – an unnecessary cost. After their respective sieges, each empire simply moved prisoners to other places: the Turks to Istanbul and the Venetians back to Asia Minor. Either that or they executed hundreds after the siege. Prisoners weren't good business in the colonies.

Nafplio's state prisons began just a year into Kapodistrias's governorship (1829), with cells organised on the Vouleftiko's ground floor. Shortly afterwards, the Miltiades bastion of Palamidi became the prison where Theodoros Kolokotronis and co-conspirator Dimitrios Plapoutas were held before and after their trial for high treason in 1834. The conditions were notoriously barbaric.

An eyewitness account of 1835 reported that Palamidi's prisoners were kept in virtual sewers amid their own excrement. Things hadn't improved materially by the 1840s, when a newspaper described the prisons as having a hideous stench and conditions not fit for beasts. Prisoners were chained naked in the dark.

It's not clear why this period of incarceration was so inhumane. The Miltiades and Andreas forts had not been designed as prisons and perhaps the new government was using whatever spaces were available (subterranean stores, cisterns) and making hasty structural modifications where necessary. Moreover, the concept of a stinking dungeon as a place for punishment may have carried over from the Middle Ages, which weren't as distant in the past as the date suggested. Brutal public punishments such as breaking criminals on a wheel had ended only recently in Bavaria (1813) and as late as 1841 in Prussia.

Kapodistrias stated officially in 1830 that prisoners should serve a purpose and be subject to compulsory labour. Those serving criminal sentences were expected to work in agriculture, shipyards, road repair, mining and whatever else was necessary for national regeneration. These men were also used to demolish the town's walls, particularly the eastern land defences. Prisoners sentenced to up to two years would work inside the prison.

There was also a workhouse staffed specifically by military delinquents at Palamidi. These men made woollen and cotton cloth for army supplies, paying the costs of their own incarceration while simultaneously exerting "a salutary moral and physical influence on the criminals" according to Frederic Strong in 1842. It was essentially slave labour organised by the new Greek state at a time when most prisons in the country were privately owned. Only Nafplio, Athens and Chalcis were government-run prisons. This small textile factory was demolished in 1950.

Palamidi was notionally a controlled military zone, but some nineteenth-century travellers were taken inside on tours – not only of the impressive fortifications but also of the infamous Miltiades prisons. Jane Loftus was there in 1860 and observed twenty-five brigands sentenced to death, plus some political prisoners. She praised the views but offered no opinion on the surreal nature of making a spectacle of condemned men as part of her trip. Nor did she see where the men slept.

Michaelis Mitsakis visited Miltiades in 1897 and was shocked by the conditions: "What holes and what abysses and what confusion and what agony! ... You think you see the entrails of a colossal monster ... over a hundred creatures devoured, their eyes twitching restlessly within its infinitesimal stomach pouches. So it is possible for people to live – ten, twenty, thirty years!" He described how the prisoners lived in subterranean holes: "where no light has ever entered, where you descend by wandering stairs into three or four successive pits, one deeper than the other, one more gloomy than the other, one more sinister than the other, where the light of the lamps is automatically extinguished by the humidity."

An English magazine of 1890 offered more details, noting how the prisoners were crowded in open yards and observed from above by guards on platforms. Visitors could lower coins into the yards to pay for small handicrafts created by the prisoners from bone, wood or wire. They used these coins to gamble or to buy fruit and tobacco. The article added that two yards existed: one for convicts serving fewer than twenty years and another for those facing the death sentence. There was no uniform and nor was there any work programme or routine. The prisoners were expected to simply wait out their decades within the walls.

Andreas Karkavitsas visited the prisons of forts Andreas and Miltiades, the Vouleftiko and the Bourtzi in 1892, talking to guards, prisoners and the executioners. "Christ, I'm afraid!" he wrote, fearful that even a month in such places would make people forget their religion. Fort Andreas, as a place for prisoners with lighter sentences, had slightly better conditions. The Bourtzi at this time probably contained only the executioners, who were themselves prisoners. Figures from 1888 list 123 prisoners in Miltiades, 173 in the Vouleftiko and 221 in Acronafplio.

Early photographs show that all of this penal infrastructure was still in place at the start of the twentieth century. Grainy images show the dividing walls within Miltiades' courtyard and the higher platforms patrolled by guards. It appears that the prisoners below are using long rods to pass their handicrafts to visitors standing at a gallery. In another picture, shabby corrugated roofing appears to provide some shelter from rain or sun.

Palamidi's prisons closed in 1923, having never really been suitable. The Vouleftiko prison, meanwhile, closed in 1900. It had been a pre-trial detention centre since 1862 and an especially unpleasant site with a damp, sunless yard and overcrowding that led to disease.

A purpose-built prison was organised near Tiryns two years later using a house built for Kapodistrias but rendered surplus by his assassination. Nafplio's age-old issue of marshy land initially caused malaria among prisoners and guards, but manpower was not an issue and better drainage soon solved the problem. The incarcerated men then worked in different disciplines, including furniture making, carpentry, blacksmithing, shoemaking and basketry. Encouraged to think commercially, they also took commissions for furniture and shoes from private individuals. An agricultural prison remains on the same site today. It has been called the most-escaped-from rural prison in Greece, with around twenty escapees between 2012 and 2016 (primarily thieves and drug dealers). I recall hearing one tale of a prisoner who managed to escape in a helicopter that his accomplices landed on the prison property, which is both too ludicrous to be credible but also sufficiently absurd to be true.

Nafplio's twentieth-century reputation as a penal colony was due more to Acronafplio's prison than Palamidi's, which had been a convenient but not purpose-built solution. The new three-storey prison on Acronafplio dominated the town. It is now the site of the Nafplia Palace hotel and it offered its prisoners some of the best views experienced by any convict ever. It was intended for those with sentences of three years or more and made extra secure from 1885 when Nafplio's 8th infantry was stationed on the hill. There was also a womens' prison from 1895 – a house in which the guards were older women. Its inmates included women and girls convicted of infanticide, theft, bigamy, concubinage and matricide.

Large numbers of Turkish prisoners arrived from the Thirty Days War in Epirus during 1897 and a further 900 in 1912 during the First Balkan War, but Acronafplio's prisons acquired their greatest notoriety when they became the holding pens for political prisoners. These were primarily communists who may have committed no actual crime other than to disagree with the government. Initially, they were placed within the general prison population, but they immediately began to proselytise and spread revolt. From that point, they were kept in a separate wing.

The first political prisoners arrived in Nafplio after the failed Venizelist coup in 1935, but many more would follow. The Compulsory Law 375 of 1936 stated that anyone could be sentenced by a military court, even to death, solely for his or her political beliefs. This qualified as espionage against the state. Many of the condemned communists were fighting for workers' rights, while others were against fascism in Spain and Germany. They sometimes found themselves sent to Acronafplio for four to five years even without trial.

The government was so virulently anti-communist that in 1937 prison guards loyal to Ioannis Metaxas opened fire with machine guns at prisoners locked in their cells, killing a teacher called Pavlos Stavridis. Conditions would worsen during the occupation years of WWII, when many of the communists locked up without trial and without having committed any crime were executed by the Germans or Italians. Others died of hunger or disease. The Italians additionally turned the military hospital into a prison to create more cells and in 1943 imprisoned one hundred of Nafplio's citizens. During the occupation as a whole, 239 of the 625 prisoners in Acronafplio were executed.

The fluctuating allegiances of the war meant that in 1941 Italian soldiers from the Albanian front were treated at Acronafplio's military hospital before being imprisoned, only then to be released and become guards. The prison's buildings were also damaged earlier that year by the Luftwaffe's bombardment of the town.

Many of Acronafplio's communists were released at the end of the war and a few of them stayed in the town. I remember one old man who used to walk along Akti Miaouli angrily haranguing the coffee drinkers. He was short but robust and walked with a rolling limp. Not understanding what he said, I believed he was an unfortunate madman simply railing at the world, at foreigners, at tourism – whatever. He never asked for money. Somebody told me he was a communist who had been imprisoned in Acronafplio for years, brutalised, tortured, racked with disease and simply turned out onto the street at some stage. Nobody took him seriously.

But it was business as usual after the war. From 1946, there were 700 prisoners registered in Acronafplio's cells. The figure was 900 in 1947. In 1948, eleven prisoners were executed within a brief period and other prisoners went on hunger strike in protest at executions in general. Some of these men were shot to death in their cells without trial.

How many people in the lower town knew what was happening? If they could hear tin cups rattling, they could surely hear machine-gun fire. Official execution dates must have been known to the victims' families, though at this stage such punishments were no longer public spectacles. Throughout the 1940s and 1950s, Nafplio must have been a darker place with a thousand men incarcerated atop the peninsula. Henry Miller's assessment, which at first looks like hyperbole, becomes much closer to reality when we understand what he saw. Here was the power of the state in architectonic form: the prisons, the bars, the walls, the scarlet-draped guillotine and the firing-squad wall. The word "Acronauplia" was painted in huge letters on the side of the hill facing the town – not a site of historical interest and source of charming views but a state threat.

It wouldn't be ethics that rescued the hill from this dark reputation. Tourism proved to be a greater force. In 1960, Acronafplio was designated a tourist site even though all of the prisons were still active. Only in 1963 did the convict population begin to move to other prisons and only by 1966 were all of Nafplio's prisons closed. They were gone by 1970 and a new age began for Nafplio.

One of the things that most people know about Nafplio is that the executioner lived in the Bourtzi. This is correct but highly simplified. The true story of Nafplio's executioners is difficult to reconstruct from the many, often contradictory sources and versions but here's my attempt.

There must have been executioners in Nafplio under the Venetians and the Turks. We know that the Venetian Republic favoured brutal public punishment or executions for crimes such as homicide, theft and blasphemy. The Venetians were also highly advanced in spy networks and paid informers. The Turks, meanwhile, preferred public hanging, decapitation and drowning depending on the crime.

Execution has been an expression and a tool of executive power in civilisations throughout history. Eradicating the worst criminals was traditionally cheaper than warehousing them at the state's cost, though ethically more questionable. For much of its history, Nafplio was a defensive site amid a landscape and seascape of constant threat. There were pirates in the Argolic gulf, *klephts* roaming the hills and mercenaries or agents of other empires attempting to gain entry. Such people inside the walls were far more dangerous than outside.

The Greek War of Independence created a new modern state that would require codified laws. Only with Kapodistrias's arrival in 1828 could this begin in earnest. It seems there were only three executions under his governorship: one in 1828 and two in 1830. One of these sentences was for a sailor who murdered the passengers on his ship and took control of the vessel – the kind of thing that wasn't generally encouraged. His punishment was to be shot in the head by soldiers in Kalamata. A further execution came shortly after Kapodistrias's death when his remaining assassin, Giorgakis Mavromichaelis, was sentenced to death and shot in October 1831 by a twelve-man firing squad in front of a large crowd on Acronafplio.

The arrival of King Otto and his regency council in 1833 changed everything. The Bavarians had followed the French in seeking less brutal and macabre forms of execution, though it remained the preferred punishment for the many robberies and murders occurring in Greece following the anarchy of the 1820s. A new law specified beheading as the method of choice. It was quick and considered more merciful than smashing somebody to death with iron bars and leaving the barely-living body impaled or dangling from a gibbet.

The official executioner arrived in 1833 from Marseille – the port from which most Europeans arrived in Nafplio. He was a Frenchman who came with his two assistants: a Bulgarian and an Italian. They also brought a second-hand French guillotine with them – a gift from Otto's father Ludwig. It's tempting to suggest that this same guillotine was one of those used in the revolutionary Reign of Terror just forty years previously, when 17,000 people were publicly executed across France. Clearly, the French needed to build a lot of guillotines.

The first official execution by guillotine seems to have been a pirate called Giorgios Mitromargaritos in 1833. He had been sentenced to death and had been awaiting an executioner in a Palamidi prison cell. The condemned man attended mass at the church of St. Andreas on Palamidi and was beheaded in Prónoia with an audience. A different account suggests the execution took place privately within the fortress, but this was contrary to the original idea of the guillotine being a public spectacle. There is a later photo of the machine being set up outside the Land Gate in anticipation of an audience. Within a day or two of this first Ottonian execution, the guillotine was transported to Messolonghi to behead nine robbers. This turned bad when the robbers attacked their executioners and had to be restrained by guards.

The executioner and his assistant were already trained in the use of the machine but neither they nor the new Greek state had reckoned on the national spirit. No matter how heinous the crime or the criminal, the crowds would attack the executioner with stones, punches, kicks and verbal abuse. Wasn't he also a murderer? Worse, he was a murderer paid for his work. The executioner received about the same salary as a university professor (300 drachmas) plus another hundred for each kill. Clearly, this was reprehensible. Indeed, press reports of early executions often focused on the honour and fortitude of the victim. In 1834, a convict executed for triple murder was praised for his bravery during the trial and his execution.

The procedure at this time was to take the guillotine to the place where the crime had been committed and execute the perpetrator in public there. In 1836, the machine was shipped to Athens to execute two murderers, but the executioner was attacked and killed at Piraeus, having barely disembarked. He must have been recognised from previous executions. The assistant presumably decided he would not participate further.

Now there was a problem. Someone new had quickly to be found to operate the blade. One man volunteered (or was compelled) at the last minute, but mounting the scaffold sent him into a panic attack. Maybe it was the throng of baying Athenians who wanted to kill him. Maybe it was the enormity of having to drop the blade but he passed out (or pretended to) and could not be roused. Meanwhile, the crowd jeered and laughed. An urgent message had to be sent to the king for a temporary reprieve since nobody wanted to kill the murderers. One version states that the two had their sentences commuted to life in prison, while another says they were taken to Aegina and shot in the back of the head by Bavarian troops. The latter is more likely.

With good reason, the original guillotine operators opted to resign. Subsequent ones were attacked or killed. Replacements were becoming increasingly hard to find. In 1836, the *Times* of London picked up a story from the Bavarian press about the issue, remarking that "the [Greek] government will probably be obliged to employ a man with a mask, who may not be known to the public, to carry out executions." The part about remaining unknown is what brings us finally to the Bourtzi.

Hasan Arnaut is said by some to be Nafplio's first official executioner, but it's more likely he was one of the early ones about whom we have more detail. He was an Albanian who had already been condemned to death and his assistant was an Algerian. The two had to be trained to use the equipment by whoever remained as the outgoing executioner and their first job was in Argos: three robbers. Shortly after, they were in the small hilltop village of Karitaina to kill four more robbers. It seems likely that some of these robbers were *klephts* who had been part of militias during the revolutionary chaos of the 1820s and returned to the thieving life in the 1830s.

The executioner remained an unpopular figure and Arnaut was more hated than most. A Muslim, he had smirkingly sworn allegiance to the king on a Bible and made some panto-mime attempt at the sign of the cross. Accordingly, he and his assistant lived at the Bourtzi, where nobody could see or attack them. They were escorted to and from their island to execution locations by an armed guard for their safety.

It was a dangerous job before, during and after the work. One story is that Arnaut and his assistant retired following the customary eight years of service, during which time they had paid off their crimes. Their bodies were found in front of a Nafplio café the next day, beaten to death by locals or relatives of an executed man. Their earnings remained untouched in their pockets and no lawyer would act as executor for it. The bodies were thrown into the sea rather than buried. Another pair of executioners were allegedly attacked and burned by locals before they could even start work.

After such events, nobody volunteered to do the job during the next forty years. Typically, a prisoner condemned to death would have his sentence commuted to life imprisonment and be made executioner. In this sense, the executioners remained prisoners and the Bourtzi was their prison as much as their home. We know the names of some of these men: Poriotis Sofras, Kritikos Amiradakis, Argitis Bekiaris, Ioannis Zisis and Kyriakos Sotiropoulos. Bekiaris was from Argos and had a reputation for being inept. It's said that his extremely poor mother would not accept any of her son's blood money. After his sentence was completed, he retired from the job but went on to commit another murder on an amateur basis, becoming a prisoner again.

Despite (or perhaps due to) the unpopularity of the guillotine operators, a large audience usually attended the executions, of which there were around twenty-five a year during the nineteenth century. The machine would normally be set up during the night and covered with a scarlet cloth. Dawn was the moment of death and the crowd would hush as the victim took his position over the block, his neck locked into a metal collar so that he could smell the bag his head was about to enter. The blade was already raised and merely had to be released. It was all dark theatre.

The metal fell, the strapped body jerked and the head fell into a sack that was "bone-stiff with blood" according to one who'd seen the machine in action. There was no dramatic spray towards the viewing public because the flat side of the blade was pressed against the stump. Rather the blood would hiss and sputter on the inside, unseen and dribbling into the bag that was never cleaned. When the pressure had eased, the steel would rise with rattles and creaks and the public would see just two vertical lines on the blade where the neck arteries had been severed on the way down. The executioner would then wash his hands and the machine as the crowd came alive to pelt him with stones and abuse.

Did the victim feel anything? It is unlikely given the severed spinal cord. Did they see or hear anything in the seconds following rapid decapitation? A French doctor called Gabriel Beaurieux did an experiment in 1905 to find out, using the head of a guillotined criminal called Henri Languille. The doctor quickly plucked the head out of the zinc bucket and saw that the lips and eyes were fluttering erratically. He spoke to the head, which opened its eyes and focused on the doctor's, meeting his gaze, before seeming to slip into unconsciousness. Beaurieux then shouted the criminal's name and again Languille opened his eyes to focus on the doctor before slipping away for good.

Given the difficulty of finding and keeping executioners, a new law of 1846 permitted execution by firing squad. The absurdity would reach a new level in 1848 when the executioner killed his assistant one night in the Bourtzi and himself had to be executed (once they could find a replacement). It's not clear what happened between the two. A simple argument? A card game gone bad? A lovers' quarrel? An accusation of theft? Did the ceaseless splash of waves send them insane? What kind of atmosphere existed in that island fortress occupied by two professional killers? Was it haunted by the phantoms of men dismembered in the heat and the thunder of artillery bombardments?

Imagine the scene that night as you sip your coffee on the *paralia*. The crazed executioner, his face spattered with blood, his eyes wild, looks out through the arched windows towards the lights of shore and imagines the crowds that will attend his death. Did he consider dashing his head against the walls to escape that shameful spectacle? Did he wait sleeplessly for dawn and discovery, the body of his assistant cooling there beside him on the stone-flagged floor?

Something had to be done. Palamidi was chosen as the exclusive site of executions in 1890 to prevent the necessity of the executioners travelling and perhaps to limit the growing opposition to state execution as an outdated and inhuman

measure. It didn't really work. In 1896, a public outcry followed the execution of fifteen convicted robbers one after the
other in Palamidi. The event made headlines worldwide, but
the people of Nafplio were especially scandalised that their
town, the nation's first capital and supposedly a model of
European modernity, had become known as an international
focus of punishment and death. One local newspaper remarked that "it is utter disrespect and denial of the sacred and holy
of the national struggle to turn Palamidi into a slaughter-
house."

Some of the most famous Nafplio executions were those of
notorious assassins. In 1905, a man called Antonio Kostas
Gerakaris stabbed Prime Minister Theodoros Diligiannis to
death in protest at a new gambling law and was sentenced to
die in Nafplio. He was held in solitary confinement until the
day of his execution at the Miltiades bastion in Palamidi. He
prayed at the tiny church of St. Andreas for an hour before
asking if he could spend his final night drinking alcohol and
talking to a friend. The guards agreed, locking his friend up
with him until the next day. They apparently spoke all night – a
conversation unrecorded but presumably loaded with immense significance. What do you say when you know your life
will end the next day? Regret? Repentance? Remembrance?

In the morning, he asked for coffee and the prison priest
took his confession. At 5.00 a.m. he was led to the *Alonaki*, the
"little threshing floor" – a small area around 200 metres beyond the fort's walls that would still have been stained with the
blood of previous executions if no rain had fallen. The
guillotine was waiting. When asked by his prosecutor if he had
anything to say, he remarked that they were punishing him
justifiably.

The executioners remained in the Bourtzi for their own
safety and continued to drop the blade until 1913, when the
guillotine was retired and death by firing squad became the
only form of execution. One of their final jobs was the
execution in 1911 of the two men who had unsuccessfully
attempted to kill George I of Greece while he was on Syngrou

Street in Nafplio. Some sources record that the executioners remained in the Bourtzi until 1935, after which the fort was renovated by the German architect Wulf Schaefer, though this seems unlikely unless we're talking about the twelve members of the military firing squad.

It's difficult to reconcile the Nafplio experienced by summer visitors with the Nafplio still in the memories of some older residents: the looming prison block of Acronafplio, the secret executions on the notorious *Alonaki*, the terminus for so many political prisoners and assassins. In some ways, it was the same Nafplio that had existed for hundreds of years previously: an expression of military strength and state power.

The town might have continued like this for decades more, but a force more powerful was about to arrive. It had been approaching for a century or so, but the trickle was about to become a flood powerful enough to wash away entire structures. Tourism was about to arrive in Nafplio.

TOURISM

People were visiting Nafplio from the beginning, though they usually had a job or a mission. Stonemasons, architects, soldiers, bronze foundrymen – most of them spent time here temporarily. Very few of these, however, were travellers in the sense that they had gone to Nafplio just to have a look, just for the experience.

Travelling has been a dangerous activity for much of human history. Crossing land borders and travelling by sea put travellers at risk of robbery, piracy, murder and suspicion of espionage. Anyone choosing to travel usually had a good reason for doing so. Some were gathering information for a client or for a book. Some were on a religious pilgrimage. Some were itinerant traders. The bravest among them were travelling for the sheer hell of it.

It makes sense that Nafplio became an increasingly attractive destination for travellers as it developed. The natural setting alone is beautiful, but it became more impressive still when the castles and walled town came into being. This human activity made a pair of hills and a silted harbour into something scenic, something comparable to, but more picturesque than other similar walled towns. Monemvasia, for example, is a very attractive fortified town on the coast to the south of Nafplio, but the relation between its gigantic rock and the lower town lacks Nafplio's aesthetic impact from the sea or from the land – though Monemvasia, known as the Gibralter of Greece, is gorgeous inside the walls.

Early travellers would typically have been either wealthy or well connected or both. It was relatively difficult to get passage on a ship (land travel in Greece being via mule track until the nineteenth century) and spend time in a place unless a person had independent means and/or contacts at the destination. It also helped to speak a little of the local language, which limited opportunities to the highly educated.

The first traveller we know much about was the Turk known as Evliya Çelebi (Dervis Mehmed Zillî), who visited Nafplio in 1667. He was an explorer and writer who passed through Syria, Palestine, Russia, Albania, Circassia, Egypt, Sudan and much of Europe, including Austria, Croatia, Germany and, of course, Greece. From him, we have valuable descriptions of Nafplio during the first Ottoman occupation (see **Presence**).

The importance of such descriptions is that the explorer or traveller brings curiosity to their experience and wants to record it for others. They understand that their readers expect to know what a place is like. What do the people wear? What's different? How does it feel to be there? Moreover, a traveller such as Çelebi saw so much that he could bring wider perspectives to his observation, comparing and contrasting. He doesn't necessarily know what could be relevant to his readership so he gives us a little of everything. Does it matter that there were 200 houses on Acronafplio at the time? Maybe not to his contemporaries, but his account is now one of the very few that tells us about the Ottoman town.

The next travellers were the young gentlemen on their Grand Tour: wealthy, educated, idealistic and in search of adventure. Thomas Hope was in Nafplio in the late eighteenth century making his ink drawings and watercolours while admiring the exotic dress of the townsfolk. Lord Byron came a little later and no doubt influenced many more with early poems such as *Childe Harold's Pilgrimage, The Giaour, The Bride of Abydos* and *The Corsair.*

These men were ostensibly augmenting their education by visiting the sites and the culture they'd studied in university libraries, but really they were enjoying the exhilaration of travel. Wearing local clothes, they crossed mountain passes on horseback and risked robbery by *klephts.* They went armed with sabre and pistol and stood alone in the ruins of mythological places that had once been text but now were real. Nafplio to these visitors was a fantastically exotic place with its Ottoman janissaries, its pashas, its camels, its slaves, minarets and harems.

The concept of the Grand Tour contributed substantially to the foundations of what would become tourism across much of Europe. These young men had to stay somewhere when they arrived. Initially the accommodation may have been in the house of a friend or a contact, but increasing numbers of travellers, especially in Nafplio amid its archipelago of ancient sites, meant the eventual appearance of inns. These had probably existed in Nafplio for years due to the amount of international trade, but the Grand Tourers were looking for something else: a home from home, or at least some representation of what they expected accommodation to look like in a place like this. They were a clientele with certain needs: places to sleep, places to eat, places to rent horses or local guides – all of which represented a rudimentary visitor infrastructure.

Nafplio remained relatively unknown until the first decades of the nineteenth century. It was an Ottoman-controlled backwater whose Venetian fortifications were impressive but rotting into decadent glory. A town full of functionaries serving a dying empire. Its present was already its past. The War of Independence changed all that.

We can consider the philhellenes as travellers. Yes, they came from across Europe to help the Greeks reclaim their country, but they also came for the pure adventure of it. Like the Spanish Civil War for Hemingway and Orwell, or the Second World War for Mailer, Vonnegut, Heller and the rest, the drama of war was often a source of inspiration. Nafplio had been accustomed to foreigners for a while and now there were even more in the restaurants, cafés and bars.

There are no mentions of Nafplio hotels in traveller accounts before the nineteenth century. An inn was a place for itinerant travellers – a stop on the road while trading or treading the pilgrim trail or simply covering more ground than could be traversed in a day. A hotel, on the other hand, was a destination in itself, used by someone who wanted to stay in a place rather than pass through it.

It's not clear when the first Nafplio hotels opened. There is mention of a Hotel London in 1834, a house offering just eight rooms to guests. The Afthonia hotel was also allegedly in business by 1840. It's possible these were just converted inns and too small to accommodate the number of visitors.

Cochrane says in 1830 that there were two hotels where the guest could enjoy the comforts equal to any hotel in civilised Europe. He was delighted to be offered an English breakfast of tea and bread for one drachma. Friedrich Tietz mentions a lodging house run by two Viennese sisters among the coffee shops of Syntagma Square in 1833. It was apparently a good place to eat Austrian food and also "furnishes an important chapter in the *chronique scandaleuse* of Napoli" according to Tietz. Is he suggesting that the place was also a brothel? He slept on board the vessel that had brought him until someone offered him a vacant room in a gloomy house in a dirty street that he called his "wretched asylum." His bed was the same straw used by the horses on the ground floor and he was plagued all night by vermin.

Prince Hermann von Pückler-Muskau had more luck in 1836, perhaps because he had chosen one of the first hotels. Like many of the richest and most prestigious visitors, he noted the price of everything: "At the Hotel d'Europe, I paid for two gentlemen's rooms and two servants' rooms 28 francs a day, and for the very modest luncheon I paid 6 francs per person, excluding wine."

Frenchman Théodore Moncel must have missed the Hotel d'Europe in 1843. He stayed in a traveller's inn that did not entirely meet his standards. His notes read: "Large rooms bare, with no other furniture than an ugly little iron bed and a half-made chair, in front of a table coarsely hewn, conveniences in the kitchen, a steep wooden staircase, rather badly placed – this was the finest inn in Nafplion."

British traveller George Weston arrived in Nafplio around 1844 amid circumstances that showed travel could still be hazardous. He noted: "Found a very tidy inn in the Hôtel de la Grèce. On our arrival, alarmed by a report, which turned out but too true, that a band of thirteen brigands had escaped from prison here and taken to the mountains, where they had been playing all sorts of pranks; stopped altogether 107 persons – one they robbed, a relation of the master of the hotel, of four thousand drachmas; they also took off ten horses, laden with merchandise, going to Tripolitsa."

Certainly, 1840 marks a kind of watershed in the number of travellers to Nafplio. The upheavals of the 1820s had passed and King Otto's brief time in the town had civilised it according to the standards of the European visitor. For the next sixty years, the rudimentary infrastructure would grow to include more interpreters, restaurants, shops, means of transport (carriages, horses, railways, steamers) and entertainment. A dragoman was typically employed to escort visitors around the town and to various sites. Ships arriving in port would be met by fleets of bumboats selling fruit, crafts or passages to shore.

Towards the end of the century, Nafplio began to appear in travel guides such as *Gaze's Tourist Gazette, Cook's Excursionist* and *Appleton's European Guide Book for English-speaking Travellers* (in which Nafplio "is pretty but has no monuments of interest.") and the famous Baedeker guides. In all of these publications, the pre-eminent hotel is the Hotel des Etrangers in Syntagma Square, where Heinrich Schliemann stayed.

The Etrangers seems to have opened in the early 1880s and was famed for its cleanliness, comfort and ground floor restaurant, the Olympia. Englishwoman Isabel Armstrong stayed there in the early 1890s and remarked on the oddity of breakfasts served on tables in the corridors. She took her dinner at the Mykines. The Hotel des Etrangers may still have been in operation in the early 1930s, though the building was later demolished and replaced (see **Squares**). At some point in its later history, the hotel name was translated and its sign painted in Greek: *Xenodoxeion Ton Xenon.*

It was a period of many hotels. Today's Alpha Bank was the

Amymoni hotel with a bakery on its ground floor. There was the Mykines hotel opposite the Trianon. In 1844, John Murray called the Aris hotel the best but frowned on the Hotel d'Abondance, which was dirty, full of vermin and expensive. There was also a hotel Byron near Syntagma Square (the same one as today?) whose clientele was entirely Greek. The Agamemnon near the harbour, meanwhile, was judged expensive and bad.

In 1939, Henry Miller and Lawrence Durrell stayed at an unnamed Nafplio hotel that Miller described as "crazy." The lobby had etchings of ancient Greek sites, but also paintings of native Orinoco Indians. The dining room was "plastered" with letters from satisfied guests extravagantly praising the hotel. Anti-intellectual, Miller observed that the "silliest" of them were written by professors of celebrated universities. The rooms were freezing because they were the only two guests and the owner didn't want to turn the heat on.

It's fun to speculate about which hotel it might have been. Miller doesn't say whether it was in the square, which had at least three hotels. The Hotel Des Etrangers may have attracted Miller with its French name and the ground floor restaurant could have been the dining room he referred to. The Europa, if still in operation, seems to have been a luxury establishment, as was the newly opened Bourtzi hotel, and neither of the two writers was wealthy at this point. Miller would surely have mentioned if he'd stayed on an island. The Mykines, too, had a restaurant. It was on the top floor under the roof beams, but Miller doesn't mention which floor the dining room was on.

The Agamemnon was known to be expensive, but the two writers might have selected this one knowing that they were going to visit the Mycenaean sites. The earthiness of the port locale would have appealed to Miller, and perhaps the maritime clientele had brought those paintings of Orinoco Indians. Another candidate was the Hotel Grande Bretagne, one of the first hotels visible on docking in Nafplio and another with a French name. It was a large establishment with a ground-floor restaurant and was just the sort of place that might have had fawning letters from guests. But Orinoco Indians? It's another Nafplio mystery.

Why did these people come to Nafplio? Many of the guide-books named it as a good base to visit Tiryns, Epidaurus and Mycenae, which were the real attractions. Nafplio just had the hotels, the train station and the horses. Its castles, fountains, mosques and churches appear not to have interested these nineteenth-century visitors much. Isabel Armstrong referred dismissively to the town's fortifications as "a jumble of Venetian and Turkish work," while for Miller the town offered "a few crazy monuments." Ancient history was seemingly the only history that had any interest or significance.

However, the power of the guidebook was as strong then as it is now. Some restaurants and bars in today's Nafplio are inexplicably packed with foreign visitors when the locals know they're not the best. The Internet tells people which are the top ten tavernas or things to do and that's where they go; that's what they do. They don't know any better. In the 1880s and 1890s, the guidebooks struggled for things to suggest to Naf-plio visitors, but one thing kept appearing. The Baedeker guide for 1898 elaborates:

> "Those who wish to inspect the interior of the fortress apply for a pass (*adeia*) at the commandant's quarters (*frourareion*) in the town, either personally or through the landlord of their hotel. The visitor is accompanied by an officer or soldier. When the prisoners, all of whom have been convicted of serious offences, are at exercise in the yard, they are allowed to offer to visitors, across the barricade, carved articles of various kinds at low prices."

Why? Why would the cultural tourist – drawn to the Argolid for its wealth of myth and history – voluntarily ascend to Palamidi to gaze down into the stinking pit full of prisoners and pay for badly-made knick-knacks carved with filthy hands from wood or bone? Even Miller and Durrell did it. Why? Because it was the thing to do in Nafplio. The guidebook said so.

It seems absurd, but I had a similar experience – let's call it an epiphany – in Cairo. My guidebook told me to visit one of the old neighbourhoods because it was colourful and authentic. I found myself walking down an unsurfaced street covered in rotting food, puddled with mule urine and lined with rickety makeshift houses. I believe a large animal was lying dead in the gutter (possibly a donkey). The locals watched me walking through their poverty in my sun hat, my camera gripped sweatily to my chest. Their faces should have been contemptuous but it looked more like mystification. Why had I travelled from another country to look at his slum? Was I mocking them? I was asking myself the same question. Why was I even in Cairo when I'd never had any particular interest in the country? Because the guidebook . . .

Guidebooks have a lot to answer for. Sure, we're not obliged to use them, but it can be stressful arriving in an unknown town without any idea or resources. Where do you stay? Where do you eat? What are the best things to see and do? What if you miss the best bits? The danger, the reality, is that we find ourselves in an old church or looking at a statue or visiting a certain shop and numbly consuming the experience even as a small voice, a tiny squeak at the back of our rational minds tries to tell us, "Wait – when did you ever give two shits about any of this stuff? Why do you need a photograph of this statue of a person you know nothing about? You've spent forty-five minutes standing in line to see a church ceiling you've never previously had any interest in or knowledge of just because it's here and the guide says . . ."

It appears the French were among the first to appreciate Nafplio as a destination in itself and value it intrinsically. Early twentieth-century French-language postcards show Syntagma Square or the Bourtzi or Palamidi as sites in their own right. A French chocolate company even featured a view of the paralia on one of its bars. The Hotel Grande Bretagne was one of the establishments of this era, opening around 1920 and active to around 1970. It was noted for its modern plumbing and its ground floor restaurant. It was a shell when I lived in Nafplio in the late 1990s, but has since opened again as a very swish boutique hotel. The Greek government, too, was starting to organise at this time, creating its first national tourist infra-structure in the early 1900s. The Bureau for Foreigners and Tourism Expositions came in 1914, badly timed for a world war, and in 1929 the Greek National Tourism Organisation (EOT) was born and was re-founded in 1950.

When does travel become tourism? The early twentieth cent-ury was something of a golden age of travel. People arrived in Greece by steamer or diesel-driven cruise ships and travelled with guides (human and written). They consulted bulky rail and ferry timetable books and went to outfitters to be given the correct attire for a Mediterranean summer or a tour of the Holy Land. Such travel was beyond the means of the average working person. Indeed, many of these early travellers privat-ely published accounts of their trip for friends and family at a time when the only working-class voices in print appeared in the Crime section of the newspaper.

As noted in **Punishment**, 1960 marked the moment when Acronafplio was designated a site for tourist development – a plan rather than a reality at that stage. The process had already begun with the Amphitryon hotel in 1952 and Greece in general welcomed 200,000 foreign tourists in 1955, a five-fold increase over the previous five years. The Xenia hotel arrived on Acronafplio in 1961 and more of the hill was taken up in 1979 by the Xenia Palace hotel, later renamed and reconfig-ured as the Nafplia Palace. The Bourtzi hotel, however, had peaked too early and was already closed by the 1970s.

Cheaper and more available airfare was one of the main catalysts for the increased visitor numbers. Charter flights from the UK began in 1950 and grew rapidly due to a *de facto* relaxation of international air transport regulations. Charter flights in turn led to the affordable package holiday. These holidays combined flight, transfers and accommodation into a single price that millions would pay in the late '50s and 1960s to spend a week or two in the sun.

It should be clear that Nafplio was never one of these package destinations, with its tiny, pebbly town beach and Karathonas a facility-free wilderness a few kilometres distant from available accommodation. Nearby Tolo, however, developed very quickly as a package destination and remains one (though less so than its hectic 1980s and 1990s heyday). Nafplio's popularity was due to another phenomenon.

The late 1960s and the 1970s saw the development of independent or "hippie" travel in which individuals would fly to a place and explore using local transport, hitching, or driving cross-continent in camper vans or on motorbikes to see a country in a more "authentic" manner. These mostly young people were looking for experiences and possibly transcendence of some kind, whether religious, philosophical or narcotic. They knew about the history and the ancient sites, but they were also seeking the "hidden gems" and the "secrets" that the mass-tourism masses would never see.

If that last paragraph seems to contain numerous "scare quotes," it's because the language of travel has now become so clichéd and infected by marketing speak. The origins lie in the 1970s when the differentiation started to be made between travel and tourism. "Real travel" was exploring alone or in a couple and "discovering" places that few other travellers had seen or knew about. Nafplio was such a place with its rich palimpsest of history, its castles, its neoclassical façades and its medieval back streets. It was "hidden" outside Athens and away from the large sandy beaches.

The debate continues over travel versus tourism. I remember travelling through Egypt with an eclectic group of Aussies, Kiwis and Scandis. We in our traditional feluccas or our broken-down local mini-buses scorned the large Nile cruise boats and air-conditioned coaches with their dumb tourist passengers. We were seeing the "real" Egypt. But we all went to the same places and all stood in the same crowds fending off beggars. The "tourists" just did it in comfort.

Now Instagram continues the debate, seeking the perfect image of the Eiffel Tower or the Tongariro Crossing or the Taj

Mahal – "perfect" meaning that there are no other people in the shot. You were the only person there. You discovered it. Your perfect photo is identical to ten thousand other photos taken from the same spot, but you have successfully replicated the meme, the cliché. Does the photo prove anything? Travel today can be as superficial as following the dialogue, the script that you absorbed before you left and repeating it thereafter as your own. Cynical? It's more difficult than ever to travel with a mind free of expectation.

The 1970s and 1980s were also the age of the guidebook. We've already seen that nineteenth-century travellers were using their Cook's guides or their Baedekers, but these were principally sources of hard information: where to stay, where to hire horses, ferry timetables and the rest. They were typically emotionless and impersonal. The new generation of guides was more focused on experience. *Lonely Planet* started in 1973 with a literally homemade guide to budget Asian travel but expanded to other countries in the 1980s. The first *Rough Guide* (to Greece) came out in 1981 – a later version of which I was carrying when I arrived in Nafplio. *Europe: a Manual for Hitchhikers* was published in 1980. Slightly earlier, but of the same genre, were the *Blue Guides* with their detailed historical notes. Their guide to Greece came out in 1967, stating that it had been, "compiled for the independent educated traveller wanting to avoid the monotony of international uniformity."

All of these guides included Nafplio in their itineraries and the town found itself in a pincer movement of both travel and tourism: the tourists arriving on excursions from beery Tolo, the travellers arriving by bus from Athens or as part of a circular Peloponnesian route that would also take in Monemvasia, Areopoli, Koroni, Methoni, Olympia and the villages of Arcadia such as Andritsaina and Dimitsana.

The 1970s Greek travel narrative tended to paint the country as a quaint, largely agricultural nation that had been historically retarded by the Ottoman occupation. One 1967 London *Times* travel feature about Nafplio old town observed that its streets and environs were alive with the sound of donkeys, sheep, goats, horses, chickens and pigs – as if it were a medieval village rather than a neoclassical town of around 8,000-10,000 people.

Greece joining the EU in 1981 was another powerful influence on growing tourism, as was the release that same year of the Bond film *For Your Eyes Only,* which used locations in Corfu and Meteora. I remember watching the film as a child and immediately craving a visit to Meteora's otherworldly landscape. I'd spend the snowy Christmas of 1998 there, sharing a honeyed herb tea with a blind monk and later suffering a sleepless night of dual food poisoning in Kalambaka. My Nafplio flatmate had diarrhoea and I was vomiting, occasionally both at the same time. Unforgettable.

The initial effect on Nafplio was an increase in accommodation. The EOT – which had access to larger plots of land and larger pots of money – had invested early in big hotels such the Xenia and the Amphitryon, but perhaps this had been their mistake. Large hotels were part of a mass tourist infrastructure and normally found alongside golden swathes of beach. Visitors to Nafplio did not typically identify themselves as tourists. They were coming to experience a town with a rich historical and cultural heritage. It was more fitting and "authentic" to stay in a converted Venetian house or neoclassical mansion in the back alleys.

Again, Nafplio's distinct geography dictated its development. There was almost no more room on the peninsula to build new structures. Regulations made it complicated to demolish or rebuild. Abandoned or inherited houses could become boutique hotels or rental rooms and they did in ever-greater numbers during the 1980s. The town was changing.

By 1990, visitor numbers to Greece hit nine million for the first time. It was a decade influenced by the *Shirley Valentine* film and Louis de Bernières' *Captain Corelli's Mandolin.* True, not all of them were coming to Nafplio, but a certain kind of traveller could not avoid the town. Any trip to the Peloponnese would have to include it because the southern mainland is not Greece's principal beach terrain. Yes, there are great beaches, but the Peloponnese is more about Mycenae, Corinth, Olympia, Sparta and other historical sites. Figures are hard to find and unreliable, but some official numbers from 2006 show around 3,500 visitors arriving in Nafplio almost every month throughout the year. Only December-March shows a dip, but there are still visitors. The annual figure was around 73,000.

With the increase in hotel beds, retail and food were obliged to catch up. Where once Staikopoulou might have contained a couple of restaurants, now the whole street is lined with them. Where once Syntagma Square and the seafront contained most of the bars and cafes, now almost every street and corner has a place. It becomes exponential. More choice brings more people. There's more reason to return, especially for the year-round Athenian visitors.

Visitors want souvenirs. In the late 1990s, many of Nafplio's shops were selling what we might politely term tat: branded tea towels and key rings, reproduction classical vases, faded postcards on leaning carousels, *komboloi* and costume jewellery that would break or give you dermatitis thirty seconds after your plane took off. I recall that even my habitual hairdresser in a tiny two seat place down the side of the town hall had a display of dusty sunglasses for sale, their lenses opaque, their arms bent. I believe he never sold a single pair.

What do people want to buy? I guess some people did buy replica Greek vases or plates and take them home as evidence that they'd been in Greece, not knowing or caring whether the design was red-figure or black-figure, Attic or Mycenaean. It was a "Greek Vase" that you could put on a shelf as some vague nod to culture. "We have a Greek Vase in our house." In my childhood home, we had a white-plaster bust of Beethoven on top of the TV, though none of his compositions had ever sounded in the house and nobody in the family played music. I knew it was Beethoven only because it said so on the base. As for the Nafplio-branded tea towel, I can't imagine a worse souvenir: a daily reminder of bougainvillea-bedecked streets, anise-infused ice and Argolic gulf sunsets as you go about your habit-anaesthetised domestic drudgery.

Nafplio's retail profile has changed during the 2000s. Nowadays, you're more likely to find artisanal honey or olive oil, local aloe vera products, fine cigars and whiskies, designer jewellery and interesting clothing that doesn't have "Nafplio" printed on it. The town has become something like a brand in itself. Its neoclassical style, national significance and multicultural history have cohered into something Greek but distinct. Nafplio looks newer, remade.

The hotels, too, are a little more *chi-chi* and boutique than they used to be, designed as much for the Athenian weekender as for the European summer visitor. It's worth noting that the year-round Greek tourism is one of the reasons why quality stays high in the town. National tourists are not going to accept poor-quality tourist food. They need reasons to come back a few times a year.

There is now more accommodation than ever before. As of 2022, Nafplio's old town has at least one hundred hotels and pensions within its roughly twenty hectare area and approximately the same number of café/bars and restaurants. There is barely a street without a tourist business on it.

As well as more hotels, shops and restaurants, the tourist boom has also created another interesting phenomenon: the *kamakia.* A *kamaki* is a harpoon or a spear typically used in fishing, but it is also a young male who preys on foreign tourists. Just as in the natural world, predators gather where there is an abundance of prey and the 1970s marked a trickle that would become a flood of prey.

The *kamaki* is traditionally a young man who frequents the bars, clubs, beaches and other sites where female tourists are going to be. His aim is simple: to sleep with as many as he can throughout the summer. It is not particularly difficult work because many of the women who come on holiday are hoping to have just such an experience and are often drunk enough to require very little persuasion.

I knew *kamakia* during my time in Greece and observed them at work, amazed at the ease and astounding rapidity of their success. I was sitting in a bar one night when a trio of Norwegian girls came in. They had got off the bus from Athens barely two hours previously. Within minutes, shots had been sent to them by one of the resident *kamakia*, who then approached his chosen girl and invited her upstairs (where a room was prepared for such eventualities). Blushing, she accepted. She returned barely fifteen minutes later, her face a little redder, her hair a little less brushed, clutching a single rose from her suitor and laughing at the applause from her friends. The Norwegian group then moved on to the next bar and the process continued.

Another time, I was with one of the town's champion *kamakia* during a lazy summer afternoon. He was waiting for the bus to arrive from the airport to cast his eye over the new arrivals – the "fresh fish" as they said. There was one tall woman with a backless sundress that caught his interest. "I would like to run my fingers over her back," he told me, mimicking the action with his hand. "I will do it tonight." And he did.

Later in the season, his girlfriend came over from Athens with a few of her friends and they all went out to dinner together. I asked him the next day, "Doesn't your girlfriend have any idea that you're sleeping with dozens of other women?" He replied: "She doesn't even know that I've slept with all of her friends."

It would be easy to moralise about this. Certainly, the *kamakia* are faithful to nobody. They also seem to consider it a numbers game or even a joke. I remember one June in which a particularly ugly English girl was one of the package tourists. The *kamakia* called her "The Monster" and yet all of them had sex with her anyway because she made herself available. I recall one waiter who would take tourists to a room above the bar at the end of his shift. One day, his Greek girlfriend came to pick him up, a girl of outstanding beauty and poise. Why was he spending most of his evenings taking raucous, sloppy drunks up to his room? Because he was a *kamaki*. Because he could and because they wanted him to.

Putting aside the faithfulness issue, this is all consensual.

The visiting tourists are looking for a holiday fling with an exotic local. The whole scenario is an aphrodisiac: days spent in a bikini on the beach, the romantic sunset, the hot wind, alcohol and the piercing gaze of a handsome local man. Where's the harm? A sexually transmitted disease, perhaps. A subsequent break-up when the regular partner finds out.

There is some irony in the whole transaction, however. Part of the reason why the *kamakia* exist is because they have far less success with Greek women. Greece is still a conservative and patriarchal country, especially in the smaller towns and villages. It's not good for a girl's reputation if she's thought to be "easy," so Greek men sometimes consider their country-women hard to get or "high maintenance" particularly when compared to a girl who'll say yes after a single shot and a well worn chat-up line. She said yes before she got on the plane.

This said, there's also a complex set of codes around sex between the Greeks – or at least there was back in 1998. I once asked one of the *kamakia* how I could improve my chances with the local girls. After he had finished weeping with laughter at the idea – "Don't you know? We think all Englishmen are gay or paedophiles!" – he explained to me that the key was to conduct the relationship in secret. You couldn't just go up and chat to a girl in the town because everyone was watching: her friends, her extended family. It was necessary to take her to a different place so that she could pretend she wasn't with anyone and thus maintain her social purity.

I saw this with some of my older female students. It might be said that sixteen-year-old Maria, say, had a boyfriend. Nobody knew his name, his age, where he lived or what he did, not even her friends. At least, they weren't saying. It was all rumour. I remember once being surprised to discover that the waiter in my local café was the boyfriend of a student. Not only was he much older than her, but I'd never once seen them together even though she lived on my street.

There's also a question of respect. I was once with a group of female language teachers, one of whom was Greek. We were in a bar and a *kamaki* drifted over to make his play. My existence was irrelevant – British masculinity is a pathetically diluted, a veritable homeopathic solution to the *kamakia*. He started to hit on the Greek girl, who spoke to him solely in English. Only when his lines reached maximum cheesiness /offensiveness did she slip into Greek. He was genuinely mortified and apologised, saying he would never have spoken to her like that if he'd known she was Greek. She deserved respect. The foreign girls were just body count.

For many guys, the *kamakia* phase is a youthful right of passage. For others, it never ends. There are bar owners in their fifties, married and with children, who continue to take advantage of the opportunities presented to them throughout the summer. There is, perhaps, something a little more pathetic in this. Young men might be forgiven their immaturity and raging hormones, but the Viagra-popping, hair-dying, gut-sucking old lothario tends to look embarrassing as he aims to pass the five hundred mark.

The Nafplio I lived in was one of familiar ruins, streets of abandoned buildings, family businesses and smilingly poor customer service – still largely a marginalised historic vestige. But it's senseless to talk about Nafplio as ever being unspoilt. It has spent its entire history being spoiled and remade – from Byzantine to Frank, Frank to Venetian to Turkish and back again. Its changes take generations and sometimes last longer than lifetimes. This is merely the current version.

However, some people are worried about Nafplio's future. Is it losing its character? So many of its residents have left to make way for tourist infrastructure. So many houses have become hotels. Is its future something like Barcelona's gothic quarter, where no Spaniards live – where nobody lives except the ceaseless tides of visitors? Is Nafplio becoming a parody of itself, the neoclassical façades made up like models, the streets paved with gleaming marble and every ruin renovated? Will it stop being a town and instead become a stage set, a living museum, a mere spectacle? A performance of a version of history? A dead centre amid the modern town?

None of these things is inevitable. Nafplio can steer its fate if it wishes, though some of the stories in this book suggest we shouldn't be too confident about that. I'm an optimist. I'd say this is the best version yet of Nafplio. It retains much of its Venetian and Turkish heritage. It has mostly buried its horrors in the history books. It has embraced its special and unique beauty. Everything is still there in its fabric, in its stories.

There's a Nafplio for each visitor and each time. No matter how the town changes, it will always be 1998-99 for me. That's the Nafplio I carry in my mind. I can walk the modern streets, but I see the mildewed ruins and the vanished supermarkets. I can look at the views from Palamidi and Acronafplio and see myself in them before I lost my hair and my romanticism.

Or did I lose the romanticism? What is this book if not a paean, a hymn, a dream of Nafplio that has never left me?

TOUR

Nafplio is best explored on foot and without any particular route or destination. Almost every street has its curiosity: its ruin, its fountain, its historic house or ancient fragment. Some are partially concealed and others hidden in plain sight. You just need to know what you're looking at. Having travelled through the town's history, let's take a final stroll through the past and present to see some of the small details that are representative of the place as a whole.

We start facing the reconstructed Land Gate at the start of 25 Martiou. The white statue of Staikos Staikopoulou is behind us. To our left are the original walls of the Grimani bastion, their lower courses rusticated to help deflect cannonballs and a sentry box still occupying the upper corner. You can access this sentry box by approaching via the garden of the derelict Xenia hotel on Acronafplio. The tower above is the bastion of the Castel del Toro, which used to be the end of the fortified upper town until the Grimani bastion was built over it. There's also a rectangular relief sculpture of the lion of St Mark, the symbol of the Venetian Republic.

You can follow the line of the old town walls between the Grimani bastion and the Land Gate. These would have continued to the right, at the same height as the gate, through today's courthouse to Kapodistrias Square, where the Dolfin bastion was situated. In front and below us, we can see what remains of the moat, which would have been much wider and connected to the sea when the coast was along today's Sidiras Merarchias Street. We're not going to enter through the Land Gate, though. Instead, we go left towards the bastion and cut alongside the café/restaurant to ascend the dirt path close to the Venetian walls (take the road if you have doubts or mobility issues). This gives us the chance to be close to the masonry that enclosed the town for hundreds of years. You'll see another, larger, lion of St Mark just before you reach the road built in 1935. Previously, this passage between Acronafplio and Palamidi was a deep trench cut through the rock by the Venetians and ending at the top corner of the Grimani bastion. You can see the masonry edge jutting out on the right as you reach the junction to the Arvanitia car park.

This was previously the end of the town with nothing beyond it but a slope to the beach. The opening you can see in the corner of the wall is a passage that leads through the inside of the walls in both directions, up and down. Above us and to the left (but out of sight) is the end of the caponier: the covered artillery corridor that faced the land approach. These two structures must have been connected in some way, perhaps an elevated bridge, to provide safe passage for gunners moving between batteries.

From here, we could go up to Acronafplio, but see the **Castles** chapter for a route up there. Rather, we'll head along the right side of the Arvanitia car park down to the corner where the pine trees begin. The path is blocked by a fence prohibiting entry, but you can go around it by descending briefly to the left. A path shows where everyone else has done this. NOTE: choosing to continue on this part of the tour is entirely at your own discretion and risk.

The coast path takes you through a corridor of resinous pines and soon the sea opens to your left. Steps go down to the rocks in a couple of places if you want to swim. On this south side of the Peninsula, you could forget that the town exists at all. There's only sky and sea and distant coast to your left, and rocky cliffs populated with prickly pear to your right. Don't forget to turn around occasionally to look back at Palamidi rising massively above the town. It will soon be out of sight.

You'll next pass through the "Despot's Cave" archway, where winter waves burst over the rocks and flood the path. The route now curls round to the right towards the light beacon on the point. Stand here and look across the coast at the village of Myloi. About eight hundred metres directly in front of your feet are two large shipwrecks lying on the seabed.

A little further on is a ramp leading up and to the right. This is the entrance to the "secret" Orthodox cave chapel of Panagitsa, which is all but invisible from the path. It was known as Santa Maria di Grotte when built during the first Venetian occupation (1388-1540) and later became a school where the Greek language was kept alive in the Ottoman periods. Today, there's a more modern exterior structure (c. 1850) but the grotto cave is highly atmospheric with its candles and icons. The views down the gulf are also stupendous.

Continuing, we circumvent the other barrier and pass the abandoned boat club on the left. Ahead is the tower of Santa Maria built into Acronafplio's walls. Its stonework differs from what we've seen so far and it may originally have been Frankish, though the Venetians made improvements to it after 1401. It looks like there are traces of third century BC polygonal wall below it. Look carefully and you'll see a walled-up gate in the corner between the boat club buildings and the tower. This probably led to Santa Maria di Grotte. It's above the level of the current path and would have had a staircase leading down to a bridge over a small sea inlet. Such entrances were necessary when the harbour was silted up. On the other side of this tower, we see a keyhole gun port low in the masonry to cover the length of the wall. The port is probably a Venetian addition and is carved from a single large block. It is "upside-down" because the vertical slot is for sighting the weapon. There's another arched gun port to the left of this keyhole and higher up the tower is a larger opening for cannon.

We now go towards the Five Brothers bastion, passing another arched gun port on the right, to arrive at the Gate of the Ovens by the eucalyptus tree. The derelict structure of the old town bathhouse is on our left. Tietz called this a sluice gate and it may have been used to wash out the city. It was also previously an area of slaughterhouses, which would have needed cleaning regularly. It was on these very steps that Tietz encountered his first resident of Nafplio, a sixteen-year-old beggar boy lounging in the sun and dressed in rags. Let's go up.

We ascend at an angle over slippery cobbles that have been trodden by centuries of visitors, refugees, fugitives and invaders to emerge beside the car park at the foot of Psaromahala. In front of us in a curious little house that Tietz identified as the residence of Carl Wilhelm von Heideck, one of the regency council charged with managing the country while the new king was still only seventeen. Previously, Heideck had been Kapodistrias's Commander of Nafplio, controlling military and civil construction in the town, on Acronafplio and on Palamidi. An easel was visible in the window, reminding Tietz that Heideck was an enthusiastic and skilled artist. It is his work that you see on the cover of the book, quite possibly painted from this very spot.

Tietz also notes the palm tree in the garden. Today, there is just a tall stump with a sign affixed in Greek. It says "The phoenix, according to legend, was planted by the first governor of Greece I. Kapodistrias 1828-31." The tree is of the species persimmon, also known as a phoenix, though it remains questionable whether the workaholic Kapodistrias would have taken time out to frivolously plant a tree for no particular reason. The palm was damaged by a piece of flying shrapnel during the German bombardment in 1941 of a ship made in Northern Ireland. The wound proved fatal sixty-seven years later when a powerful storm of December 2008, ripped the top off the tree, breaking it exactly in the place where the shrapnel had weakened it. Such are the random vortices of history, an iron plate from Northern Ireland is hit by a bomb made in Nazi Germany and eventually decapitates a palm planted by the governor of a new state in Greece the century before. Imagination couldn't envisage these events.

The house was traditionally known as Amymoni and Heideck was not its only illustrious resident. He later returned to Munich and a subsequent tenant was poet Theodoros Kostouros, whose father ran a pharmacy on Vasileos Konstantinou. Kostouras went to school in Nafplio and trained as a pharmacist in Athens before returning home to take up the family business. He would stroll around Nafplio writing poetry, prose, satire, chronicles and plays. He died in 1986 while still a Nafplio resident. Today, the house is an upmarket rental property.

We now go up the road to the right, named Kostourou after the poet, and avoid the stepped shortcut on the left that is full of rubbish and graffiti. This initial part of the hill was once covered by the town's medieval hospital. Arriving in Lakka Square car park, we see the Venetian chapel of the Holy Apostles on our right, its wall covered in ugly graffiti, and continue quickly across the car park, past the bunker-like portal to the Nafplia Palace's entrance tunnel towards the colourful houses.

The faded mustard-hued house on the right of Zygomala street (number two) looks like it may once have been a small shop and indeed it was. Now apparently abandoned, it was owned by the Giannopoulos family and operated as a small grocery from the 1960s. You can still see some dusty objects through the cracked and dirty windows.

Number one in the same street may be one of the oldest houses in the neighbourhood, with its ancient wooden balcony, peeling paint and green door. The tiny abode was apparently a tavern run by a local fisherman famed for his talent with the *bouzouki* and singing *rebetika* songs. He died in 1957 and it seems the house has been empty since, silently rotting when once it was full of music and conversation.

Continue along this street and you'll see old houses converted into tourist accommodation. It's a great place to stay: close to the centre of the old town with no vehicles and hardly any people passing. A little further and you see on your right a ruined plot that reveals a few thousand years of Acronafplio foundations dating back to before Christ. There's currently no sign or indication of how old the masonry is.

The road bifurcates hereafter: up towards the Sagredo gate then on along the very top of the town to the Castel del Toro gate, or down onto Konstantinopoleos Street (not to be confused with Vasileos Konstantinou, which was named for a Greek king rather than for the Roman emperor Constantine).

We choose the latter and continue straight towards the tiny white church that seems to block the end of the street.

On our right is a very grand and well maintained three storey building. This was built by the Venetians and probably served as their governor's residence. However, it is more famous as the palace of Aga Pasha during the second Ottoman occupation. When the Greeks retook Nafplio in 1822, it became the seat of the Executive for a few years during the 1820s.

If the church of St. Sophia seems wedged awkwardly between streets and houses, it's because this structure is the oldest surviving building in the old town. Everything else has grown around it. The Byzantines built it around the eleventh or twelfth century and during the second Turkish occupation it was the only church where locals were permitted to worship in their faith. Walk up the steps beside it on the right to see a Byzantine window and the rear, whose stonework appears much older. The façade and interior were restored by General Nasos Fotomaras in 1825 and it is regularly renovated, but the rear aspect retains all of its Byzantine character.

From here, we continue to the stepped street and go left down the red marble steps of Kokkinou Street, crossing Kapodistriou, and continuing down to Staikopoulou – a street of restaurants and shops. We turn right and walk along to the Komboloi Museum, where I spent many an hour chatting to the Serbian man who made and sold the merchandise. If you're curious about the history and aesthetic of the *komboloi*, pop in to look at the beads made of amber, faturan, bone, wood and coral. The small museum is upstairs with examples of *komboloi* for the last hundred years or so. (There are also many other *komboloi* shops in the town, but this was the first.)

Just in front of the shop, you can cut up the arrow alley to St. Spyridon Square to look at the bullet hole left by the Kapodistrias assassination, the Turkish fountains and the ruined Ottoman bathhouse. We're going to continue straight for a few metres to the corner that curves left onto Terzakis Street. We are now following the same route taken by Ioannis Kapodistrias on the morning he was assassinated.

Turn right at the jewellery shop on the corner. Now we are on the *megalo dromo* of Vasileos Konstantinou with its combination of Venetian and neoclassical houses. Look up and you'll see that many of the Venetian houses (with bare stonework) had a third floor added in the nineteenth century. Three Admirals Square soon opens up to our left with the statue of King Otto and the palm trees where his palace used to be. The square was lined with trees in the early twentieth century and that pattern remains today. Keep a lookout on the right for the old pharmacy and the town hall that was built as a school.

Let's stop briefly at the main road (Syngrou). In front and to the left is the white statue of Kapodistrias alone in his square, watching the traffic go by and wondering why he has no fingers on his right hand. Palamidi rears up to the right. We're going to turn right and pass in front of the neoclassical and Venetian façades (including the bus station) to the next corner with Plapouta Street. The enormous Venetian building here is the mansion of Count Josef Ludwig von Armansburg. All that remains is to cross the street and pass through the Land Gate to where we started.

Between 1706 and 1894, everybody who entered or left the town came this way. The gate may be a modern reconstruction, but it's in the same place and we are walking in the footsteps of almost everyone mentioned in this book between those dates: Theodoros Kolokotronis, Ioannis Kapodistrias, Staikos Staikopoulou, Francesco Morosini, King Otto, Carl Wilhelm von Heideck, Empress Elisabeth of Austria (and queen of Hungary), Field Marshal Otto Wilhelm Königsmarck, Sultan Ahmed III, Laskarina Bouboulina, Aga Pasha, Lord Byron, Thomas Hope and all of the European authors who wrote about the place.

Those are just the names we know. Thousands more anonymous soldiers also passed this way and tens of thousands of Turkish, Venetian, Albanian, international and Greek citizens: traders, farmers, fishermen, artisans, writers, sculptors and total nobodies. This is true of any town but in Nafplio we can pinpoint the main entrance. We know that this strangely lonely, freestanding gate in a patch of scrubby nothingness was once the portal to different worlds, different languages, different empires. The time-withered and weather-worn lion atop the gate is original and saw it all.

I'm sure that locals complained when money was spent to reconstruct the Land Gate, but it's an inspirational relic of the past. Yes, the Castel del Toro tower has seen more, and the church of St. Sophia yet more, but there's something powerfully symbolic about a gate that so many people passed through, entering or leaving on the way to make history. It's a rectangular void into which numberless people have vanished. We'll never know their names or what they did, what they thought, how they died. All we know is that they passed this way during a moment of their lives.

More evidence of Nafplio's history remains than in other Greek towns, even those towns that have very similar histories of ancient, Venetian and Turkish inhabitants. Those other towns weren't Greece's first modern capital. They didn't welcome the first king of Greece and the nation's first governor. It's easy to look at Nafplio today and dismiss it as charming and pretty. It becomes so much more fascinating when you walk its streets and imagine them as they were. At various times, they were dark, stinking, littered with bodies, burning, disease-riddled and desperate. At other times, they were shining, hopeful, modern and a model for European values.

Nafplio has long been an international town – a town for travellers and traders. It continues as such, and will keep changing as it always has.

CHRONOLOGY

14C BC	'Nuplija' mentioned in Egyptian temple of Amenhotep III
12C	Mycenaean tombs in Prónoia
9C-8C	Geometric period tombs
800	Part of the Kalaureian amphictyonic league
7C	Allied with Sparta
3C BC	First known fortifications on Acronafplio
2C AD	Town ruined and abandoned
267	Attacked by Goths
399	Attacked by Avars
589	Attacked by Slavs
746	Earthquake
9C	Byzantium takes an interest
1082	Byzantium grants Venice free trading rights in Nafplio
1180-1208	Sgouros family archons of Nafplio
1204	Frankish crusader Boniface besieges Nafplio
1212	Franks take Nafplio, which becomes the fiefdom of Otto de la Roche
c. 1300	Franks build frescoed east gate in Acronafplio
1388	Sold to Venice
c. 1394	Hospital for the poor built
1470	Bourtzi constructed
1482	Castel del Toro completed
1540	Ceded to the Turks
1647	Turkish fleet in port
1686	Reconquered by the Venetians
1688	Outbreak of 'plague'
1715	Taken back by the Turks
1791	Outbreak of 'plague'

Chronology

1810	Lord Byron in Nafplio
1821	Greek War of Independence begins
1822	Greeks enter Nafplio
1822-23	Sixty to seventy people dying each day of fever
1825	Civil war
1827	Civil anarchy when Grivas takes Palamidi
1828	Arrival of Ioannis Kapodistrias, first governor
1831	Kapodistrias assassinated outside St. Spyridon church
1833	Arrival of Bavarian Prince Otto of Wittelsbach and his executioner
1834	Capital (and Otto) moved to Athens
1865-95	Majority of Venetian lower-town walls demolished
1884	Heinrich Schliemann stays in Syntagma Square
1885	Train station opens
1900	Vouleftiko closed as a prison
1928	Earthquake
1929	Palataki (Otto's palace and Kapodistrias's house) burns down
1939	Henry Miller and Lawrence Durrell visit; Bourtzi hotel opens
1941	Operation Demon and sinking of Ulster Prince
1941-42	Widespread famine and TB epidemic
1945	Germans blow up the port area
1952	Hotel Amphitryon built
1961	Hotel Xenia built
1969	Arvanitia beach created. Old train station closes
1980	(Current) remodelling of Syntagma Square
1985	Coastal walk paved
1999	Land Gate reconstruction erected
2010	Rock fall closes coastal walk
2014	Another rock fall on coastal walk

BIBLIOGRAPHY

Armstrong, Isabel, *Two Roving Englishwomen in Greece*, London (1893).

Boyer, Abel, *A Geographical and Historical Description of those Parts of Europe which are the Seat Of War*, London, (1696).

Brooks, Allan, *The Fortifications of Nafplio*, Aetos Press, (2019).

Buchon, Jean-Alexander, *La Grece continentale et la Moree 1840-1841*, Paris, (1843).

Cochrane, George, *Wanderings in Greece Vol. I*, London (1837).

Coronelli, P.M., *An Historical and Geographical Account of the Morea, Negropont, and the Maritime Places, as Far as Thessalonica* (trans. R.W. Gent.), London (1667).

Du Moncel, Théodore Achille Louis, *Excursion par terre d'Athènes à Nauplie*, Paris, (1845).

Gell, William, *The Itinerary of Greece*, London (1810).

Gell, William, *The Itinerary of the Morea*, London (1817)

Hope, Thomas, *Anastasius; or Memoirs of a Greek*, Harper (1831).

Kouria, Aphrodite, *The Nauplion of the Foreign Travellers*, Emporiki Bank of Greece, (2007).

Leake, William, *An Historical Outline of the Greek revolution*, John Murray (1826).

Leake, William, *Travels in the Morea*, John Murray (1830).

Levinge, Godfrey, *The Traveller in the East*, self-published, (1839).

Loftus, Jane, *Mafeesh, Or, Nothing New*, London (1870).

Miller, W. , *The Latins in the Levant*, New York (1908).

Pecchio, Giovanni, Tennent, James, and Humphries, W.H., *A Picture of Greece in 1825*, Collins (1826).

St Clair, William, *That Greece might still be Free*, OUP (1972).

Tietz, Friedrich, *St. Petersburgh, Constantinople, and Napoli Di Romania*, New York (1836).

Bibliography

Trant, Thomas Abercromby, *Narrative of a Journey Through Greece in 1830,* London, (1830).

Strong, Frederic, *Greece as a Kingdom,* London (1842).

Waddington, George, *A Visit to Greece in 1823 and 1824,* John Murray, (1825).

Weston, George Frederick, *Journal of a Tour in Europe and the East, 1844-1846,* London, (1894).

For historical photos of Nafplio:

https://nafpliooldphotos.gr/index.php/
https://www.facebook.com/groups/545440435537591/media

INDEX

Index

CPSIA information can be obtained
at www.ICGtesting.com
Printed in the USA
BVHW051024031222
653296BV00011B/83

9 780957 584631